Viscount Bury

Exodus of the western nations

Viscount Bury

Exodus of the western nations

ISBN/EAN: 9783744650830

Printed in Europe, USA, Canada, Australia, Japan

Cover: Foto ©ninafisch / pixelio.de

More available books at **www.hansebooks.com**

EXODUS

OF

THE WESTERN NATIONS.

BY VISCOUNT BURY, M.P.

IN TWO VOLUMES.
VOL. I.

LONDON:
RICHARD BENTLEY, NEW BURLINGTON STREET,
𝔓ublisher in ©rdinary to 𝔥er 𝔐ajesty.
1865.

PREFACE.

It is right to state at the outset the grounds upon which the writer of these pages ventures to address the public; and to define the object and scope of his work.

During the latter part of the administration of the Earl of Elgin, as Governor-General of Canada, and in the early years of that of Sir Edmund Head, the writer was in Canada, where he held the combined offices of Civil Secretary and Superintendent-General of Indian affairs. A Governor-General is compelled by his position, as the representative of a constitutional sovereign, to surround himself chiefly by those who form his Cabinet for the time; it therefore becomes the duty of the Secretary—the only Englishman except his chief in the civil employment of the Crown—to associate with public men of all parties, and maintain intimate relations with politicians of all shades of opinion : the writer had thus an opportunity of watching closely the working of our colonial system in the most important of our provinces. Since then, circumstances have made him acquainted with most of the leading public men in our other North American colonies, and with many in both the Northern and Southern States of America.

For some years past it has been evident, that the relations between England and her dependencies are on anything but a permanent basis. Authorities differ widely as to the course which ought to be pursued ; nor can any just conclusion be arrived at without understanding the manner in which our colonial system was gradually formed. The object aimed at in these pages is, to give an account of the successive changes which took place in the spirit of our policy ; and, by comparing the system thus built up, with the course pursued by other nations, to appreciate at their just value maxims which now guide the English Colonial Office.

The conclusions arrived at appear to be the logical result of an inquiry conducted with every desire to be impartial : indeed, far from supporting a preconceived theory, they differ entirely from the opinions which the writer entertained when he began his task three years ago. One thing he desires to state clearly : he cordially concurs in the doctrine laid down by Sir George Cornewall Lewis, that no separation can with justice take place between a nation and her colonies, except by mutual consent and agreement.

LONDON,
April 13, 1865.

CONTENTS TO VOLUME I.

CHAPTER I.

Statement of the Subject—History of Europe and America to be studied conjointly—Our Colonial System 1

CHAPTER II.

THE FIFTEENTH CENTURY.

State of America before it was known to Europe—Causes which led to the Discovery of America—Rise and Development of Knowledge, Arts, and Science in Europe 29

CHAPTER III.

DISCOVERY OF AMERICA TO TREATY OF NUREMBURG.

[1492—1530.]

The Discovery—Spanish Conquest—Views and Proceedings of England, France, and Spain—Rise of Diplomacy—State of Europe —The Reformation 54

CHAPTER IV.

FROM THE TREATY OF NUREMBURG TO THE ACCESSION OF ELIZABETH.

[1530—1558.]

Spanish, French, and English Adventurers—The Reformation in England 78

VOL. I. *b*

CHAPTER V.

WARS OF RELIGION.

[1588—1570.]

Religious Quarrels complicated with Politics—Champions of the Catholics and of the Protestants—The Dutch—French Civil Wars 110

CHAPTER VI.

THE HOLY LEAGUE.

[1570—1603.]

Formation of the Holy League—Reaction in Europe against the Reformation—English Maritime Adventurers—Downfall of the League—French Discovery 152

CHAPTER VII.

EUROPEAN MANNERS IN THE SEVENTEENTH CENTURY.

[1603—1648.]

State of Manners in France—In England—History of John Smith—Social Condition of Holland 191

CHAPTER VIII.

FRENCH SETTLEMENT OF ACADIA.

[1604—1648.]

Henry IV. sends De Monts to Acadia—Compagnie des Cent Associés 237

CHAPTER IX.

EARLY DAYS OF VIRGINIA.

[1606—1625.]

The Puritans—Northern and Southern Companies of Virginia . . 248

CONTENTS.

CHAPTER X.

THE SPANISH MONARCHY.

[1620—1625.]

Historical Sketch of the rise of Spanish Power—Its Decline—Proposed Marriage between the Prince of Wales and the Infanta of Spain—His Marriage with Henrietta of France 266

CHAPTER XI.

THE PURITANS.

[1620—1648.]

Puritan Agreement with the Southern Company of Virginia—Their Settlement of New Plymouth 286

CHAPTER XII.

DUTCH SETTLEMENTS AT MANHATTAN AND IN BRAZIL.—NEW SWEDEN.

[1614—1648.]

Hudson's Voyage—Assemby of XIX.—Swedish Emigration—Cession of the Dutch Settlement 293

CHAPTER XIII.

MANNERS AND MODE OF LIFE IN THE COLONIES AT THE TIME OF CROMWELL.

[1625—1660.]

Quarrels between Charles I. and the Parliament—Virginian Legislature recognized—Charles quarrels with the Scotch—Cromwell—Execution of Charles—The Commonwealth—Social Condition of Virginia—Of New Plymouth—Of the French Colonies . . 323

CHAPTER XIV.

REFUGEES.

[1690—1698.]

Maryland—The English Church—European Rulers—Emigration of Covenanters, of Cavaliers, of Rebels, of Huguenots—The French on the Mississippi 361

CONTENTS.

CHAPTER XV.

POLITICS IN THE ENGLISH COLONIES UNDER WILLIAM III.

[1685—1702.]

Views of James II.—He confiscates Colonial Charters—Accession of William and Mary—Political Temper of Carolina, of Virginia, of Maryland, of Pennsylvania, of New York—Their position with regard to the French and Indians 387

CHAPTER XVI.

PARTITION TREATY.

HOW BULL THE CLOTHIER, FROG THE DRAPER, AND BABOON THE BARBER, DIVIDED LORD STRUTT'S ESTATE.

[1689—1702.]

The Partition Treaty—Pamphleteers of the reign of Queen Anne—Grand Alliance—Death of William III 414

CHAPTER XVII.

SPANISH COLONIES.

[1713.]

Council of the Indies—Character of Spanish Settlement—Mode of life among the Creole nobles—The Indians—The American Church—A Spanish Mission—Inquisition—Revenue . . . 439

APPENDIX 483

EXODUS

OF

THE WESTERN NATIONS.

CHAPTER I.

Statement of the Subject—History of Europe and America to be studied conjointly—Our Colonial System.

THE Spaniards conquered the countries round the Mexican Gulf, and founded there a military colony. Within a few years the warlike Caribs of the islands and the soft natives of the mainland had submitted to their sway. One adventurer conquered Mexico; a second seized Florida; a third overran Peru. Before the middle of the seventeenth century, Spanish nobles ruled with more than viceregal pomp in Central America, in Caraccas, in New Granada, in Chili. Spanish missionaries laboured in Paraguay. Spanish colonists dwelt on every spur of the Sierra Nevada, and the Andes. Spanish cities on the South Sea and the Atlantic were adorned with stately cathedrals and monasteries. Great warehouses in every seaport

CHAPTER I.

1519

1532

town were crammed with specie and precious stones from Spanish mines. From the sources of the Colorado and the Rio Bravo del Norte, to the Straits of Magellan, the Spanish tongue was spoken. From a thousand fortresses on either ocean waved the gold and crimson standard of Spain.

This vast territory was governed with a rigour which no other nation attempted to exercise. The Spaniards admitted no foreigner into their colonies on pain of death. Their commercial policy has been aptly described as a monument of systematic tyranny. The Creoles fared as badly as the native races. All power was in the hands of an oligarchy composed exclusively of Castilians, who wielded it with such cruelty that the whole race of American Spaniards in a few generations had arrived at the last stage of degeneracy. The haughty courage of their race died out. The descendants of the 'Conquistadores' forgot the use of arms.

1604 The French established on the St. Lawrence a state on the model of their own. Seigneurs, armed with all the authority of feudal law, levied " droits d'aubaine " and " droits de moulinage " upon the inhabitants of Canadian hamlets with the same unsparing rigour as at home. The settler emigrated at the desire of his feudal lord; the locality of his home was determined, not by his own choice, but by the exigencies of military service. The nucleus of every village was a stockade. Every seigneury was conceded with a view to its strategic position. The settler's minutest action was superintended by his superiors: he was drawn for military service by an unsparing conscription. His temper, gay and volatile, submitted easily to this galling yoke. The peasant was content to remain a serf: his seigneur was born a member of a governing caste into which he had no chance of admission.

CHAPTER I.

A few poor emigrants left England for the temperate latitudes of America. They suffered much from neglect and hunger; many died; some took to piracy; but the remnant established a foothold in the wilderness. Vacancies in their ranks were filled by fugitives from religious persecution, from political persecution, from justice. Gradually they drove back the Indians: they made farms and homesteads. As their numbers increased, they convoked assemblies and made laws for their own guidance. Occasionally, some great English gentleman or court favourite would obtain from his royal master the grant of an immense district, to which he transported a few families who became the founders of a new colony. Any one was thought good enough for the plantations: when honest husbandmen were not to be had, persons of loose life, discarded serving-men, and the sweepings of the hulks were accepted. But the patentee usually got tired of his bargain, and sold his interest, or withdrew, leaving his people to grow up unassisted. The settlers sprang from a race which had struggled too fiercely for liberty at home to relax their hold of it in America: they grew more self-reliant, more independent, every

1606

year. Their fierce temper brought them often into collision with the mother-country. When a sect was persecuted, its members took refuge in the plantations: thus there was a constant relay of combative men fresh from successive scenes of strife. When Protestants had the ascendant, Catholics were persecuted and fled: when Catholics were in power, Protestant victims crowded to the sanctuary. As time went on, their ranks were recruited from many nations and many creeds. They absorbed Dutch, Swedes, and Germans; Roman Catholic fugitives, Puritan fugitives, Calvinist fugitives; loyal men, traitors; men flying for conscience' sake; the scum of the gaols and bagnios; men emigrating to avoid the pressure of want; men kidnapped in the streets of Bristol and Glasgow, and sold for slaves. But the two main branches of the emigrants still preserved their distinguishing characteristics. The men of Maine retained the republican temper of the Puritans, the colonies of Virginia and Carolina preserved to the last their loyalty to the crown. Though they by no means forgot their mutual animosity, these fierce exiles were ready, at any attempt at interference, to make common cause; they became the freest people on earth: they were brave, self-reliant, turbulent, impatient of authority.

The policy of England towards them was to let their internal affairs alone, and to make as much money as possible out of their trade. They were absolutely unused to control: trifles at which the

French or Spanish emigrant would have smiled, grievances which would have seemed to the colonists of another nation no grievances at all, roused the Anglo-Saxon to madness, and were eagerly seized on as a pretext for revolt.

Neither England, France, nor Spain now retain one foot of their original possessions; yet few things are more striking than the certainty with which each of these nations has branded its own impress on the people it has ceased to govern. There is a radical difference between one sign-manual and another, but in each case the mark is indelible. In old nations the formation of national character must be sought for in far-off causes. The geographical position, the mildness or severity of climate, the degree of fertility of the soil, the growth of manners, the development of laws, the accidents of conquest or of defeat, the occurrence of plagues or famine, physical causes repeated through many generations, have moulded history, and gradually but surely governed the result. But these influences require ages to work. The nationalities of America are vigorous, but they are young: three centuries and a half is the life of the oldest of them. Race has more to do with their peculiarities than any other cause. The Mexican or Peruvian is emphatically Spanish. The English Canadian, or the United States man, Anglo-Saxon ; and certainly no one ever watched a Canadian habitan take off his hat to a friend without seeing that he was a Frenchman.

The formation of national character cannot, therefore, be traced in the history of America. To understand the emigrant we must study the mother-land; watch it as it emerges from barbarism, note its conduct amidst the rude shocks of the fifteenth and sixteenth centuries. We must observe the growth of the haughty and intolerant spirit of Spain; the persevering independence of the fishermen and burghers of Holland; the island pride and pluck of the English; the religious wars of the French; their obstinate adherence to feudalism, and the national light heart that breaks out undepressed through all.

Spain lost her colonies; but the marks of her old tyranny still remain. The people were kept in tutelage so severe and so minute, that they have been, to all appearance, unfitted for freedom. Since the downfall of her power, the Mexicans, the Peruvians, the Venezuelans, and others that once were under her command, have been a prey to one objectless revolution after another. Mexico, having tried all forms of government in turn, has now become an empire. France has lost her colonies. But her laws still linger in the tribunals which she founded; her language and her religion still dwell on the lips and in the hearts of her descendants. England lost the territories she originally possessed; the great Republic is a house divided against itself; the sons of the Plymouth Puritans and of the Quaker founders of Pennsylvania are fighting as fiercely, as their fathers fought of old, with the descendants of the ruffling blades and roisterers of Smith, Baltimore, and Berkeley. After the lapse of two hundred years, the Roundheads of New England are again foot to foot and hand to hand with the Cavaliers of the old dominion.

More fortunate than either France or Spain, Great Britain has had an opportunity of trying a new system on a new field. The Atlantic, the Pacific, the prairies of the Saskatchewan, the great lakes and the Polar sea, are the boundaries of the territory which she now rules: a territory ten times larger than the old thirteen states hemmed in between the Mississippi and the Atlantic.

It is proposed in the following pages to describe the principal features of this exodus. In executing the task, two principal objects have been aimed at — first, to present at one view, however imperfectly, a record of events which has hitherto been divided arbitrarily into fragments: secondly, to test the present colonial policy of England by the light of past experience.

A great change has of late years come over both writers and readers of history. As in other sciences isolated facts must be patiently accumulated before generalization is attempted, so in the science of history there was necessarily a period during which facts were stored up without comment. The first histories were ballads and chronicles; to them succeeded the dignified school—men who detailed the movements of camps, who delighted in battles, sieges, and court millinery, but left untold the real life of the nations of which they treated. It is only in comparatively modern times that the real objects of history have been understood. Voltaire led the way in France: in a single sentence he has summed up the great change which he was the first to effect. He said that his aim was rather to discover what society was like, how men lived in the privacy of their families, what arts were cultivated, than to recite in the ordinary fashion of history a mere record of disasters, combats, and human wickedness.* He was followed in his own time by Turgot and Montesquieu, and later by Michelet, Sismondi, Thiers, and Guizot. In England his ablest follower has been Lord Macaulay: whoever would appreciate the influence of that great writer on the method of history of our time, has only to compare the historical works which have appeared since he began his labours— Mr. Carlyle's works, Mr. Buckle's Introduction to the History of English Civilization, Mr. Motley's account of the United Netherlands, Lord Macaulay's own Essays, and his noble fragment on the English Revolution—with the standard histories of the eighteenth century.

But the works of these authors relate almost entirely to Europe: other great writers have treated as exclusively of American affairs; but we look in vain for a work showing the connection between events in the old world and the new. The truth

* Essai sur les Mœurs, Chap. xxxi.

seems to be that the history of the American continent has hardly yet passed out of the stage of chronicle writing. Many works of great interest have been written describing the Mexican and Peruvian conquests, the rise of the American republics, and of our own settlement in Canada. But these are episodes in the story, not the story itself. No writer has as yet disregarded the fictitious boundary line of the Atlantic, and given us the old and new world in the same picture, the action of Providence working through physical laws and human nature on America and Europe contemporaneously. Ample materials are to be found in political and military chronicles, in works on political economy, in books of travel, in books on geology and physical research, in plays, in romances, in pictures; but to write such a story according to the requirements of modern historical science, would be the labour of a lifetime, and demand qualities to which the writer of these pages lays no claim whatever.

If a complete history of this subject should ever be composed, the historian's most difficult task would be to weave the disjointed fragments of the great epic into a connected whole, and to show the relations of its various parts to each other. He would trace each great event in the new world to its far-off cause in the old, and follow each revolution in the old world to its results in the new. He would mark the inter-relation of politics and social history among the Spaniards, French, and English, in Europe and in their American plantations. He would sketch the development of national character in each people of European descent that now inhabits America ; and show how in each case that character was moulded by the course of events, the tone of thought, and the literature of the metropolis. He would describe not only events themselves, but the national life, temper, and peculiarities which produced them. He would narrate the causes which in the fifteenth century brought about the discovery of America, and the European revolutions which, in the sixteenth and seventeenth centuries, gave an impulse to discovery and colonization. He would paint the early establishments of the Dutch, the French, and the English. He would describe the planters, the temper in which they worked, the scenes which met them in the wilderness, their habits of thought and speech, the school in which they were formed, their idea of honour, of the duties and obligations of life. He would show how the character of each emigrant was moulded by the men, the time, the circumstances among which he lived. He would show that every man who landed in the new world, was, according to his own calibre, a specimen of the present stock. Every man who quitted the shores of Europe, were he Spaniard or Frenchman, Hollander, Englishman, or Dane, carried with him the characteristics of his native land, and, so far as his influence went, stamped his imported character on the colony of which he formed a part. The Spaniards might be a little less rough than the French, the French a little less rough than the Hollander, the Hollander a little more polished than the English. But each nation was originally hewn out of the same quarry of barbarism, and the roughest was also the hardest, the most durable of all. The English character was made of sterner stuff than the others, showed more distinct individuality, far greater aptitude for the work of founding nations.

The national peculiarities adverted to were still further encouraged by the widely different course of events in England and in France. In the first, a series of fortunate circumstances weakened the power both of the crown and the nobles; the form and the advantages of monarchy were preserved, while all that was real of power, or valuable in freedom, was given into the hands of the people: in the second, the aristocracy became completely independent of the crown; great lords, each in his own domain, kept state like sovereign princes, made war upon each other at their own discretion, and held the power of life and death within their own dominions. In England, the Norman invasion placed the disposal of all lands and dignities in the hands of the conqueror: the aristocracy thus early became completely amenable to the law, or, at any rate, subordinate to the king: too weak to cope with the monarch by their own authority, they were forced to make alliance with the people. The Great Charter, which limited the power of the crown, was an advantage to freemen of all ranks; the barons, without the assistance of the commons, would have failed to obtain it from King John: the result was that the people, feeling their own importance, acquired that tone of independence which is impressed on all our civil and political institutions. To these circumstances we owe the steady and enterprising spirit for which our countrymen have long been remarkable: they have enabled us to maintain for centuries liberties which no other nation has been able to acquire. In France the great seigneurs monopolized power: the feudal system invested them with such authority that the people were never able successfully to resist or even to curb it; the rights of self-government were never conceded to the *bourgeoisie*: the habits of the French lower classes became more obedient, as the English became more haughty and self-reliant. While in England an independent yeomanry sprung up, and municipal institutions carried self-government even into the most minute proceedings of society, the French, divided into two great classes, the noblesse and the bourgeoisie, had nothing really corresponding either to an independent class of yeomen or to municipal rights. The English Parliament gradually became possessed of supreme power; the French States-General fell entirely into disrepute.

Nor is it less necessary to examine with attention the stormy history of Spain. During many centuries that country was the seat of religious war: an intimate connection existed between the church and the crown; between them they monopolized power. During the long period of conflict with the Moors, it was absolutely necessary that there should be in each district one leader, and that he should be implicitly obeyed. Any division in a Christian camp would have been followed by the victory of the infidels and the extermination of the conquered. The general of each army of the Christians, along their gradually widening frontier, erected, in the territory he had wrested from the Moors, an independent monarchy, which he ruled with despotic power. The clergy of the religion which he was fighting to uphold, gave, in their turn, all the countenance that could be afforded by religion to his authority. The reverence thus inculcated, springing originally from necessity, became a part of the national character; it was encouraged by the priesthood till it became an article of faith. To such an extent was the spirit of loyalty carried, that the nobles, far from arrogating undue power to themselves, vied with the people in paying homage to the priesthood and the king. Popular institutions theoretically existed among the Spaniards in great perfection, but attachment to political rights among the body of the people was overmastered by the two stronger passions of loyalty and devotion.

In the fifteenth century, all the independent kingdoms into which the Iberian peninsula was divided were united in the persons of Ferdinand and Isabella: to them the whole loyalty of the people was transferred: a nation animated by such a spirit could not fail to become formidable as conquerors: as long as the rulers were able, the state, directed by a single mind, was strong, vigorous, and prosperous; but a policy which relied on the personal qualities of rulers ceased to be successful when its execution was intrusted to incompetent hands, and the guidance on which the people leant was withdrawn. The Reformation, which agitated the public mind in Europe, had little effect in Spain; indeed, it increased instead of diminishing the power of the church and of the crown. The succession of weak and imbecile monarchs which followed Philip II. ruined Spain, because the people had no habit of self-government to supply their defects.

The widely divergent characters of England, France, and Spain gave to the settlements which they founded characters equally divergent. Each of them adopted a commercial system, very similar in its main features; but that system was received by the colonies of each in a different spirit. In the Spanish and French possessions, perpetual interference blighted all feeling of national independence; they submitted with apathy, as though they considered their case to be without remedy. The Canadian settlers, recruited from the labouring portion of the French agricultural population, could hardly be expected to bring with them any exalted notion of liberty: each succeeding arrival tended to debase rather than to raise the feeling of independence amongst them. French nationality was kept alive, but emigrants offered rather a caricature than a copy of the mother-country. It was far different in the English colonies: there the right to personal liberty was undenied, or at any rate was always claimed. The population was constantly recruited from a country where the question between liberty and prerogative was being tried on a large scale. Those who emigrated considered themselves martyrs to liberty; they were not disposed to allow the standard by which it was measured to be lowered in America. The French and Spanish settlers sank below the level of their respective metropolis. The English settlers afforded a model which the patriots at home were never tired of praising. The result was that in the free states of Virginia and New England the people rebelled, the down-trodden emigrants of France and Spain submitted: such a population was not to be relied on even for self-defence. The fate of a single battle handed them over as contented subjects of an alien power. The Spanish colonies, though treated with far greater harshness than those of either of the other nations, remained in helpless bondage till long after their tyrants had lost their power to control them: the British provinces, at the first symptom of a desire to coerce them, shook off at once and for ever the yoke of the mother-country.

Since the American War of Independence, the colonial possessions of Great Britain have been very largely increased in Australia and New Zealand, as

CHAPTER I.

well as in America. Colonies which had then no existence exercise, through independent legislatures, all the rights of self-government. The relations which ought to exist between their communities and our own have long been a subject of debate among our statesmen: recent events have attracted public attention to the subject, and rendered it somewhat less difficult of solution. Matters of the greatest import, involving the very basis of the political relations between Great Britain and her colonies will, at no distant time, present themselves for settlement. Upon these, every Englishman interested in public affairs must make up his mind.

First in importance among these subjects of controversy, is one which strikes at the very root of our system. The broad issue has been boldly raised whether colonies have any assignable value at all. If that were once fairly answered in the affirmative, if it were decided that it was expedient at all hazards to prevent the dismemberment of our empire, there would probably be little difference of opinion as to the proper course to pursue. But such is not the case. Sir George Cornewall Lewis has laid down the doctrine* that when free trade is once firmly established, one of the principal, indeed, as some think, the only reason for retaining dependencies, will be removed. Some who accept the views of which Mr. Goldwin Smith is an exponent, argue that the possession of extended empire is a direct source

* Government of Dependencies, p. 230.

of weakness, and would resign without a scruple the whole of our colonial possessions: others, without going so far as to disapprove of the possession of colonies, are, nevertheless, convinced that our present position will not always be tenable—that sooner or later our colonies will demand their independence, and that our duty will then be to bid them " Godspeed," and let them go. So wide-spread is this belief, that our whole colonial policy is based upon the assumption that our colonies will at some future time desire to become independent nations; and that we have learned the lesson taught by the war of American independence too well to prevent them even if we could. But we stop half way. If we are convinced that our colonies will some day leave us, we must not be content to acquiesce passively in the fact, we must act upon it energetically: the manner in which we assume a basis of action without acting on our belief, paralyses and vitiates our whole colonial system. If ultimate separation be inevitable, our first care should surely be to secure an amicable, not an unfriendly, separation. There is little chance that the main errors of former days will be renewed. No modern statesman will attempt either to monopolize the trade of our colonies, to interfere with their internal affairs, to tax them without their consent, or to retain them by force if they should desire to leave us. But it may nevertheless reasonably be doubted whether under our present system the separation, when it comes, will be amicable. Old difficulties will recur, old enemies present themselves with new faces. In avoiding acknowledged faults, it is not unusual to fall into errors equally dangerous. We are not likely to err on the side of harshness: in these days, we talk much more of the duty which England owes to her colonies, than of the advantages which she may derive from them. One by one, the last rags of the commercial system have been torn away. We receive no tribute; we expect no commercial advantage in the ports of our own colonies that we do not hold by merit and not by favour; yet we undertake the burden of defending them against attack. It is on this ground that certain politicians exclaim against colonies; that they denounce them as a useless expense, and would do away with them altogether.

Historical facts reproduce themselves whenever similar conditions recur. We therefore naturally turn to history to see if past events will afford us a standard by which we may measure the danger. At first sight it would appear that there was little in common between the condition of colonial affairs now and before the commencement of the American war. We draw our knowledge of American history principally from the writings of Americans, or from those of Englishmen who belonged to the party favourable to American independence. We are so convinced that the attempt to coerce the thirteen colonies was unwise and unjust that we do not sufficiently study a history that presents many lessons to the student besides the trite one that it is impossible to govern unwilling colonies by the sword. No writer can for a moment defend the war, but systematic attention to the arguments on one side of the question, and systematic ignoring of all that can be said on the other, have deprived us of the historical lesson which an impartial examination of facts on both sides would convey. No doubt, if the popular estimate of the political state of the old thirteen colonies were correct, there would be little analogy between their position before the war of independence and that of British America at the present time. On the one hand, according to the prevalent belief, was a country ground down by commercial restrictions, governed by men alien in birth and feeling from the men over whom they ruled, deprived of its liberty, and goaded into rebellion by taxes imposed without its own consent. On the other, a people governed by their own laws, living under institutions framed and worked by their own inhabitants; imposing, by admitted constitutional right, their own taxes, and acknowledging a mere nominal supremacy of the parent State.

But it can be shown that the position of the thirteen colonies was far nearer to that of British America at the present day than is generally supposed. Long before the time of the American war the thirteen colonies were in all but the name independent. These pages will advance proof that ever since the English revolution they had steadily resolved on actual independence. Circumstances at last arose which made England appreciate the fact that her

CHAPTER I.

American dominions had escaped from her grasp. No experience had then taught her the impossibility of reclaiming them. Foolish advisers, national self-conceit, and an obstinate king, stirred up the English people to attempt oppression and revenge. The result was defeat, and hatred, which yet exists, from the people whom they had failed to subdue. The issue of the quarrel has obliterated its commencement. Few have realized how wise and beneficent the legislation of England had been—regard being necessarily had to the state of political science at the time.

It must be acknowledged that the policy we now pursue is different from any that the world has seen before. It has grown up by slow degrees, and after repeated experiments. After the fall of British power in the thirteen colonies, it became necessary to devise some scheme of legislation for the territory recently conquered from the French. English statesmen deduced an erroneous lesson from the American Revolution. They attributed the rebellion of the thirteen colonies to the insolence of liberty unwisely conceded and fostered into license by the freedom of British institutions. They hastily concluded that it was dangerous to permit colonies in any case to govern themselves. The ostensible cause of the American Revolution had been the interference of England with the powers of provincial assemblies. In reality the Americans did not resent interference with the power of their assemblies, but interference with labour: but this was not understood. It was generally believed that if the colonies had been ruled with a firmer hand they would never have rebelled: in order to make sure that the Canadians should never have an opportunity of resenting interference with their legislature, it was determined not to permit them to have any legislature at all. A governor armed with absolute power represented English authority. This plan succeeded very well so long as the large majority of the inhabitants were Frenchmen; but men of British descent began to pour into the country. It had been the intention of the government to keep Canada as French as possible. The framers of the Quebec Act thought that they could arrest, in the case of Canada, that desire for independence which the United States had successfully asserted. For this end the old French law was retained with all its complicated obscurity, and lands were held by seigniorial tenure. At the time of the cession, the territory now called Upper Canada was a wilderness. It was gradually settled by loyalists who fled from the rebellious colonies, and by English emigrants from home. A legislature was established towards the close of the last century, in which the French had a large majority. The province, against the advice of Mr. Fox, was divided into two—Lower Canada being almost entirely French, and Upper Canada as yet sparsely settled with men of English blood. After the peace of 1815, there was a large influx of English, chiefly old soldiers who settled on their military grants. The new comers quarrelled

1791

with the French. The latter, alarmed for their nationality, formed an active and united opposition. The result was the Canadian rebellion.

1838 The Earl of Durham was sent out to investigate the causes of discontent: his report is the great charter of colonial liberty. The legislatures of the British provinces were all one after the other assimilated, as far as circumstances would permit, to that of the mother country. It was decided that the governor, representing the constitutional power of the crown, should act by the advice of a cabinet composed of members of the legislature, and directly responsible to the people.

Earl Russell was in 1839 at the head of the Colonial Office. There was at that time considerable excitement on the subject of what was called responsible government; but the term was by no means thoroughly understood by those who were most anxious for its establishment. Earl Russell made the first attempt to give some shape to their vague ideas, and to carry out the reform desired by the colonists. It could not be expected that a veteran statesman would proceed otherwise than cautiously, in a course involving the almost entire abandonment of the traditions of his office. His policy, regarded by the light of after experience, may appear overcautious; it ought rather to excite admiration of his courage. It was a grave experiment to leave to their own devices a community in which the ashes of civil discord still smouldered, and which for the last two years had been held in check by martial law. If the experiment succeeded, he had only carried out a reform for which a whole people were clamouring; if it failed, he alone would be held responsible. Earl Russell conceded only a part of the demands addressed to him: for the time, he refused to sanction the responsibility of the local governments to the assemblies.

Lord Sydenham became governor-general. The insurrection was too recent to permit him to make further concessions than those which had been provided by Earl Russell. During the administration of his two successors, Sir Charles Bagot and Lord Metcalfe, a much nearer approach was made to a really constitutional system. Our relations with the United States were at that time so threatening, that it was considered necessary to vest the supreme civil and military authority in the same hands. Lord Cathcart was appointed. As a purely military governor, he did but little to forward the constitutional question. The Oregon dispute was at last happily arranged; and the Earl of Elgin, then chiefly known by his successful administration of the government of Jamaica, was appointed to the viceroyalty of Canada, with instructions to establish a purely constitutional government, on the model of that of England.

At the close of Lord Elgin's administration, responsible government was in full force in all the North American colonies; but it retained—indeed it still retains—a tentative or experimental character.

Even Lord Elgin's care had not been able to prevent outbreaks which threatened its stability. During the last few days of his administration an incident occurred, which was only prevented from becoming serious by his tact and temper. He had determined to dissolve his parliament: he announced his determination from the throne. The Speaker of the Assembly, in reply, questioned the constitutional power of the viceroy. The writer of these pages watched the expression of amazement, almost of consternation, which overspread the countenance of Lord Elgin as he listened to this unexpected announcement. It was impossible not to see that the interest involved was one of far deeper import than the mere words conveyed. It raised the whole question of the relations of Great Britain with her colonies: it told of a gigantic power given over to inexperienced, it might be to incapable, hands. Responsible government, as now established in British America, confers by law precisely the powers which the old thirteen colonies attempted to arrogate to themselves before the war of independence: the right of veto is reserved to the crown, but it is a right in name only.* If the political condition of British America justifies us in retaining it in a state of pupillage, we have gone too far in renouncing altogether our control over its affairs. If it cannot safely, or with advantage, be so retained, the system contains the germ of serious dispute when the time for separa-

* See Appendix, No. 1.

tion arrives. Virtually, British America is independent; nominally, it is subject to our government. The loyalty of the British American population is beyond dispute: it has been often tried, and often exhibited. Their affection for the person and rule of our sovereign cannot for one moment be doubted by any one who has lived among them. But that is not the question. If all the possessions of our Queen could be fused together, and made, in the strict sense of the term, one empire, then no danger would arise; but difficulties which need not here be referred to lie in the way. We must deal with things as they now exist. Several legislatures, each armed with supreme authority, sit on either side of the Atlantic. The deliberations of each are controlled by a common sovereign. The only difference which exists between the authority of each within the dominions it represents, is, that the British American assemblies are bound to make no law inconsistent with that of the Imperial Parliament; and that the veto, which is vested by the constitution in the sovereign, is practically exercised by ministers who are responsible to the Parliament of Great Britain alone.

Putting loyalty altogether on one side, it is highly probable that some question may arise on which the legislature of one of the high-spirited provinces of British America may differ from the Imperial Parliament. What is then to be done? A hackneyed phrase represents the answer which would generally be made. "Whenever the colonies wish to terminate their connection with the mother-country, they will be allowed to go in peace." In leading articles and in speeches on colonial subjects, we are often reminded that we have learned by experience the impossibility of retaining an unwilling colony by force. No doubt we have. Few would wish in such a case to see coercion tried. But the remark, for all that, is a dangerous half truth—worse, because less easily combated than an open fallacy.

In what form, and whence, is a demand for separation likely to arise? Again, historical analogy will help us to an answer. It was not actual oppression, such as that which in our day has existed in Naples and in Poland, that alienated our colonies in the eighteenth century. There were faults on both sides, but tyranny was not the fault committed by England. Our colonies left us in consequence of a feeling stronger than any that mere harsh legislation would excite: their secession was the irresistible development of a free people. It needs but to look around to see that the present relation of England and her colonies cannot be final: they will not always remain in the position of colonies: every Englishman must hope that a great and independent national existence is before them; but while England recognizes the necessity of ultimate separation, does she use the influence of her present position to prepare them for the change? To assert, as many writers have done, that the advantages of the connection are all on the side of the colonies, and the burdens on that of the mother-country, is merely to beg the question at issue. But it is undeniable that English supremacy is simply nominal. The Crown exercises no control over their laws. It has conceded every point upon which difference of opinion has arisen. Little reflection is required to see that this must some day come to an end Suppose a not improbable case : some point arises upon which it is necessary to refuse concession : the colonies resolutely demand it : angry passions are excited on both sides : public feeling, both at home and in the colonies, is divided upon the merits of the matter in dispute : what would be the result? A party in England would demand the continuance of our old plan of concession ; another would consider it better to let the colonies withdraw than yield to them. A party in the colonies would raise a cry for independence : another would advocate an abatement of their demands for the sake of retaining British protection. In a very short time the immediate issue would disappear, and independence become the main question. A point of such importance ought only to be decided with absolute unanimity. In a case like that I have supposed, it would furnish war-cries to four angry factions at least. It is easy to see that a wish for separation has a natural tendency to gather strength, while a party expressing contentment has a natural tendency to decrease, inasmuch as it is far easier to persuade men that they are ill-used than to keep them contented. Demands would be made on both sides in loud, possibly in insulting tones. Would it not then be too late to discuss such a measure as it should be discussed—calmly, deliberately, with exchange of banquets and speeches, good wishes, firing of salutes, and a thousand international courtesies?

It is obvious that the colonies will desire to enjoy the advantages afforded by connection with Great Britain, so long as they can do so without incurring inconveniences greater than the advantages. They will in no case leave us of their own accord until their interests and those of the mother-country seriously clash. To say that our colonies will be allowed to withdraw without molestation whenever they please, is virtually to declare that the manner of separation is to be left to chance, as it was in the case of the thirteen colonies; and that the time of it is to be fixed, as it was fixed in their case, only by the occurrence of some accidental quarrel. If that course be adopted, it is morally certain that the separation will be accompanied by a rupture of friendly relations; and our descendants have every prospect of living with the British Americans of their time on the same footing as we now occupy with regard to the Federal and Confederate States. Surely we might learn thus much from experience. The manner and time of separation should be decided by statesmen, and on statesemnlike grounds. The independence of British America might then become a subject dear to the pride of both nations, the occasion of goodwill that would last through generations.

CHAPTER II.

THE FIFTEENTH CENTURY.

State of America before it was known to Europe—Causes which led to the Discovery of America—Rise and Development of Knowledge, Arts, and Science in Europe.

LESS than four hundred years ago the shores of the American continent were an unbroken solitude, except when some migratory tribe might chance for a time to linger within hearing of the unnavigated sea. No ship broke the monotony of the Atlantic; and if the winds and waves, at long intervals, cast upon the shore fragments of some wrecked galley whose workmanship excited the wonder of the savage inhabitants, no tradition of its builders existed to explain whence it came. The nations of the east and west were each ignorant of the existence of any other continent than their own: it was reserved for Columbus to balance the egg upon its end —to show the way that was so easy to follow, and " to give to one half of the world a knowledge of the other."

America, previous to its discovery by the Spaniards,

had no general name. The nations of Europe, of Asia, and of Africa, barbarous as many of them were, far removed as were even the most advanced from our present standard of civilization, had yet that degree of knowledge which made them recognize each other's existence, give and accept generic and distinctive names, recognize the instinct of association which Providence has implanted in human minds, and which distinguishes reason from brute intelligence. One of the most remarkable circumstances relating to the early history of America is the complete isolation of each petty tribe. Each was ignorant of the very existence of any other nations than those they met in their hunting journeys. They had no distinctive name for the lovely land in which they lived. Their mythology was rude and picturesque; their innumerable languages were poetical; their expressions imaginative and rhetorical. Streams and headlands, mountains, bays, and rocks, had names wonderfully musical and significant; but in their nomenclature, as in all intellectual operations, they seemed incapable of generalization.

Everything which has now been developed existed in America. The materials which have since been so skilfully used in the cause of civilization, and which have caused material prosperity to advance with giant strides, were already in existence. God's gifts were there in profusion; and, in order to turn the wilderness into a garden, there lacked but the labour of man. The indolent savages who dwelt there were content to pass through life as their fathers had done, knowing neither the refinements nor the luxuries of civilization, sympathising neither with its sorrows, its virtues, nor its noble aims.

The vegetation of Carolina and Louisiana was as luxuriant then as now. Pine forests, from which an immense revenue has since been drawn, already clothed the slopes of Maine and New Brunswick. The great lakes and the large navigable rivers, which now carry upon their waters an incalculably valuable commerce, were in readiness for the requirements of man. Iron was stored in the Nova Scotian rocks; coal in the New England hills; gold in the placers and streams of California and New Columbia. All these requirements of a civilization which was to increase with unexampled rapidity, waited till the appointed hour should reveal them to the eastern world.

The wilderness was peopled by races of men whose origin can never be certainly known. Whether they migrated, in the infancy of history, from the cradle of our race, and gradually peopled the whole continent from one stock or tribe, or whether, during the course of ages, accident cast offshoots from various races upon its shores, has often been argued, but can never be set at rest. The discovery of America was one of the most important revolutions of the world.

No great invention has ever been the work of one unassisted mind. The success of the discoverer has been to the genius of others like the gem upon a ring—the crowning glory of an elaborate work.

The proof of the circulation of the blood was the demonstration of a proposition, of which every postulate and axiom had been for ages fiercely questioned. Newton watched the fall of the apple, which determined his theory of gravitation, with eyes taught by the experience of many ages and many men. Vaccination was but an advance of the theory of inoculation—the steam-engine of Watt but the realization of the idea entertained by Solomon de Caus. Electricity, the latest wonder of science, was dimly known to Thales twenty-two centuries ago. In like manner the discovery of America was a necessity of the age in which it was made—a result, not of the genius or the labour of one man, however renowned, but of nature's immutable law of progress. It would have been made within a few years of the time at which it actually was made, if Columbus had never been born. The thinkers, the natural leaders of the people by right of genius and by power of will, led the way; but every unit of the masses that crowded half-civilized Europe played, albeit unconsciously, his part in it. The history of the discovery of America is the history of Europe.

Could the discovery have been made earlier? The civilization of Europe under the Roman empire was more complete and perfect than that of Europe in the fifteenth century. Trajan and the Antonines, heirs of the conquests of Augustus, ruled in Europe over all the countries which lie west of the Rhine and south of the Danube. The entire shores of the Mediterranean — Asia Minor, Syria, Egypt, and Africa, as far west as the Pillars of Hercules, obeyed them. In all these lands, from Britain to the Euphrates, the Roman language was spoken, Roman legionaries kept guard, Roman proconsuls bore sway. Foreign nations sent embassies to petition for the honour of being recognized as subjects—and sent in vain. " Education and study inspired the natives of the Roman provinces with the sentiments of Romans: Italy gave fashions as well as laws to her Latin provincials :"* Greek and Roman literature was studied in the schools : Spain produced Columella, the Senecas, Lucan, Martial, Quintilian. It cannot be denied that the state of society was less rude throughout Europe in the second century than the fifteenth. Why, then, should the discovery have been then impossible? The Romans, masters in almost all arts, had neglected one. They had done little for navigation. The galleys of Antoninus differed little from those of the Liburnians with which Augustus had fought at Actium ; nor did the latter differ much from the ancient and unwieldy ships of the Phœnicians : yet it was not the size or the build of the Roman vessels that made the ocean impassable to them. If the military and colonizing spirit of the Romans had taken a purely maritime direction ; if, instead of contenting themselves with the safe navi-

* Gibbon, ii. 61.

gation of the Mediterranean, their energies had been devoted to the sea, there is no reason to doubt that their cultivated intellect would have done what the not more highly cultivated intellect of the Genoese did when a small part of the ancient learning had revived.

The Romans always looked to the sea with a certain terror. They ventured upon it no more than absolute necessity demanded. The discovery of America was actually made in ships not larger or more strongly built than the galleys of Antoninus. Many of the English adventurers in after times crossed the seas in vessels not larger than that in which the Apostle Paul was cast ashore at Melita: the 'Squirrel,' in which Sir Humphrey Gilbert sailed to Newfoundland, was but fourteen tons burden. The only book-learning which was accessible to Portuguese and Venetian discoverers was drawn from the well-known pages of Ptolemy and of Plato. Centuries before the time of King Ferdinand, Roman schoolboys had heard of the Island of Atlantis, beyond the Pillars of Hercules, and of the Atlantides behind them, larger than Libya and Asia together. Roman and Greek philosophers were acquainted with many remarkable properties of the magnet: there is no reason why they should have failed to discover its polarity, if only their attention had been turned in that direction. The spirit was wanting: the time had not come, nor the man, else America might have been added to the world fifteen instead of four centuries ago.

Could it have been discovered at any time during those ages of darkness and despair, when the Roman civilization had been beaten down, and the blackness of barbarian darkness had replaced it?—when Alaric and his Goths, and after him Herules, Gepids, Ostrogoths, and Lombards had passed into Italy over the passes of the Carnic Alps, and sacked Rome?— when waves of barbarians, issuing from the north-east, had broken out over the height of land between the head waters of the Rhine and Danube, and passed down the Alps to the sea?—when the Visigoths, driven back by the troops of the Empire, had rolled along the sea-coast into Spain, where they trampled out the degraded and effeminate Roman provincials, and established there a state of things which, though instinct with the life of a younger and nobler civilization, was as yet pure barbarism, and no more?—was it possible, with the false Franks in possession of North Gaul, and the Roman-Britons cut off from the Empire, crying for assistance to the power that was a power no longer, like effeminate slaves, as the conqueror's ignoble policy had made them? No. It might have been possible at one time in the history of the world, when the Roman race was brave and noble, pure and true, but hardly then, when the ancient name for valour had become in the mouths of degenerate descendants a mere synonym for taste. It was necessary that ages should elapse, that Europe should slowly reamass the old learning, and shake off the slough that deformed her; that her young nations should rise purified by suffering, and should replace the old power with one founded on the firmer basis of Christianity.

The early form of Christianity itself presented another obstacle. The barbarians at first adopted a part only of its doctrines, and intertwined them with Pagan superstitions. A system of cosmogony arose, compounded partly of oriental mythology and partly of the mysteries of the Christian faith—a system so wild and fanciful that any such attempt as that of Columbus would have been impossible while it held dominion over the minds of men. The world, according to the popular belief* of the middle ages, lay in concentric circles round Hell, which was situated in the centre of the earth. Satan there, seated on his burning throne, presided over an eternity of punishment. Above Hell lay Purgatory, where souls destined for ultimate beatification were purged and cleansed. Still higher was Limbo, a place neither of joy nor suffering, where dwelt virtuous men, who lived before Christ, and unchristened children. The surface of the earth was divided into three continents, Paradise being understood still to exist in the remote east, as the abode of the disembodied spirits of the just: a bridge communicated between it and Heaven. The earth was surrounded by the elements of water, air, and fire, each peopled by its independent races—elves, gnomes, fairies, sylphs, naiads,

* Lord Lindsay, Christian Art., I. xxxi.

and other similar beings. Beyond the region of fire, continually soaring upwards, were the spheres of the seven planets, all of them influencing the lives of men, the firmament, or eighth heaven of stars, the crystalline, or ninth heaven of pure ether, the whole encompassed by the empyrean, the first work of creation, and the residence of the throne of God.

Even had it been found possible to discover a man free from the terrors which the thought of invading unknown spheres would invoke, such a man would never, in that stage of learning, have succeeded in overcoming the preliminary obstacles which would oppose his start.

Europe was long a mere aggregate of rude tribes independent of each other. It was unconnected by ties of diplomacy or mutual interest. Each nation remained in a state of isolation. Each occupied itself with its internal affairs or quarrels, and, unless strong enough to make an inroad into a neighbouring state, none knew or cared about its nearest neighbours.

The barbarians established utter chaos on the ruins of the Roman power. Gradually, and with infinite labour, something of the old civilization was restored. The once highly cultivated fields, which had turned into marsh and moorland, were gradually again reclaimed. Monks, the great civilizers of the dark ages, pursued their labour of love. Hermits fled into the wilderness and died in the odour of sanctity. They were canonized. Their bones collected as precious relics, attracted penitents to worship at their shrines. Churches, rude and humble at first, rose on the site of their tombs. These gradually merged into stately piles as they were enriched by the liberality of successive generations of benefactors. Christian men, quiet spirits who felt themselves out of place among the turbulence and misrule of the lawless world outside, settled down there to read, to pray, to reclaim the lands around from the wilderness, to spread around them the knowledge of such useful arts as they themselves possessed. Schools and libraries arose round the abbey church. Learning, of which the monks were the sole repositories, brought to them the power that intellect naturally wields over mere force, and further increased their means of usefulness. The number of these establishments was very great. Every one of them was a centre of civilization. Then followed the institution of chivalry. The feudal system spread from the Tagus to the Vistula. Rude and imperfect as was that system, it was, nevertheless, an advance in civilization, a vast scheme of polity, which supplied many of the wants of the rude people among whom it arose. Although the rules of chivalry, inculcating respect for the weak and regard for the oppressed, were in many respects admirable, they were more favourable to manners than to liberty. For the first time an hereditary aristocracy arose, and power, residing exclusively in the hands of the nobles, rendered them masters of the state. The sovereign was but an unit among them. He possessed only a nominal supremacy. Even the degree of law and order which feudal supremacy implied was the result of "centuries of mere obscure slaughter, discord, and misendeavour."* In the infancy of European history you may read in doggrel Latin of nomade tribes wandering at will over the land,—the loves and hates of petty chieftains,— the muscular strength of one, the barbarous murder of another. Appalling revenge, turbulent misrule, and hard knocks fill these quaint records of a time out of joint. It is difficult for us, children of a milder age, to picture to ourselves the unreasoning ferocity of theirs. The records of the world's wisdom, which have accumulated since, and which shed their influence on our every action, had then no existence. The learning of Greece and Rome was an object of scorn to the untutored conquerors of the Romans; the splendid literature which the descendants of those conquerors were to compose, was not yet begun. The very languages in which it is couched were yet unformed.

In this state of society, when the chieftains acknowledged no right but that of superior force, it was not likely that the sovereignty should be much respected or even much coveted. For generations the family of Hugues Capet held the real power of the French monarchy, and disposed of the crown at will, without condescending to seize it themselves. This contemptuous indifference is a curious

* Carlyle.

comment on the state of a monarchy which its own vassals thought not worth having, even when it lay at their disposal.

The case of France will apply to most of the contemporary kingdoms of Europe. With the exception, perhaps, of Spain, the monarchy was in the same condition in all. It is true that to the crown belonged a right to homage and feudal superiority; but the lawless chieftains over whom the possessor of the crown held feudal power attached no value to an abstract idea. It was of little moment to the princes of Lorraine and Auvergne what potentate from the banks of the Seine claimed over them a barren sway. They made war on each other, or, if it so pleased them, on the king himself without scruple of conscience or thought of treason. Feudal rights were so intermingled, that a powerful prince often held some feof from a petty baron. The king of Lorraine might owe homage for part of his territory to a poor knight, and for part to the feudal lord of the realm, and respect them both in much the same degree. Now and then a clear-headed man like Charlemagne might arise and discern in his abstract right a means of assisting his scheme of universal dominion; but even after the Crusades, when monarchy generally was improving in power and repute, the domain of Louis VI. was hardly thirty leagues square. It was almost lost among the vast dominions of his vassals: Montfort, Coucy, Puisset, and a host of well-known names hemmed him in and forbade him to ride, without a strong guard, five leagues from the gate of Paris.

This state of things continued till the fifteenth century. Each country remained in a state of political isolation. The forces at the command of a monarch were mere levies of his tenantry and his vassals. They depended upon their individual prowess, instead of organization and discipline, for their success. They were only bound to remain for a short stated period. The armies consisted only of cavalry; no gentleman could appear on foot.

Meanwhile, the long wars which were carried on between England and France gave employment to men who gradually formed a class apart—that of professional soldiers. Towns and fortresses had to be invested and garrisoned. The feudal nobles, who were accustomed to retire whenever the termination of their period of military service, or their own caprice dictated, were not to be relied upon. The kings of France began to keep a regular army on foot. The vassals of the nobles were no match for men who were constantly disciplined and trained to war. The invention of gunpowder contributed still more to render useless the prowess of individual knights. The more warlike of the nobles entered the new service: neighbouring nations imitated the institution established by Charles VII. Every country in Europe took bands of mercenaries into its pay. To them the whole art of war was gradually confided. A deadly blow was thus struck at the feudal power; and the king, who owned and directed the allegiance of the army, became proportionately powerful.

Louis XI. followed with more resolution and ability in his father's steps. Charles had outwitted the nobles; Louis alternately braved, persecuted, and cajoled them. He put them to the torture, executed them, or shut them up in iron cages. He fomented jealousies among them, so that they could not combine, and then so overawed them with his mercenaries that they dared not rebel. The example he set was too inviting not to find followers. Henry VII. of England adopted his policy, and set himself systematically to overturn the power of his nobility. He could not do this with the iron hand of Louis; but he did it by enlarging the liberties of the people, and by pitting the commons against the aristocracy. Henry could not overawe his country with a standing army; but he could become nearly despotic by making himself a popular sovereign.

The feudal government remained longer in its integrity in Spain than in either of the other western nations. The Visigoths established there institutions similar to those of the other barbarians. For some time Spain appeared to advance in the same direction as the rest of Europe; their progress was suddenly checked by the invasion of the Moors. Within three years the Mahomedans had conquered the whole country, except the almost inaccessible region of the north-west. Pent up within the narrow limits of Asturias, the Christians relapsed into barbarism. Three-fourths of the country held the Mahomedan religion. Arabic manners and laws were introduced, together with the splendour and love of art which the caliphs had begun to cultivate.

But the Moors held Spain only as a conquered country. Gothic institutions had taken too deep root there to be easily eradicated. Gothic nobles, who had fled into the mountains rather than yield to the Moorish invaders, began by degrees to make head against their power. These reconquests were effected at various times and under various leaders. Each chief erected the portion of territory which he recovered from the enemy into a separate kingdom. In process of time a petty monarch, surrounded by all the insignia of independent sovereignty, established his throne in each city of note. There were as many kingdoms as provinces. It was not till a long series of conquests and intermarriages had swallowed up the smaller principalities, that the country became divided into the two more powerful kingdoms of Castile and Arragon. These, in their turn, were united by the marriage of Ferdinand, the hereditary prince of one, with Isabella, the chosen queen of the other.

From that time the political constitution of Spain assumed a regular appearance. Thence must the progress of her laws and manners be dated. The invasion of the Moors was but an episode. Their government and their religion were alike unpopular. A considerable portion of the population retained a fondness for the customs and laws of their ancestors. They were ready and willing to resume the one and to recognize the authority of the other. Lands continued to be held on the same tenure; the same privileges were claimed by the nobility; the same authority was exercised by the Cortes as before the advent of the invaders.

Up to this time the princes of Europe had been too busy in watching the gradual organization of their kingdoms to have leisure for foreign expeditions. Indeed, it was not known or surmised that there was anything to discover. Science was but little cultivated. Geographical knowledge was little sought after. Restless spirits had plenty of employment at home, and no need to look abroad for adventures. But when society began, in some degree, to settle down, and learning to revive a little, old problems began to be mooted again, and to acquire a certain degree of importance.

Constantinople fell before the onset of the Turks. Greek literati, flying from the cruelties of their conquerors, and attracted by the encouragement which Cosmo de Medicis had given to learning at Florence, passed into Italy, bringing with them the ancient literature of which they alone till then were the depositaries. Public schools were instituted at Florence for the study of Greek. The facility of diffusing their labours by the newly-discovered art of printing stimulated the learned to fresh exertions, and in a few years the cities of Italy vied with each other in the number and elegance of works produced from the press. Learning passed the Alps, and gradually remodelled the whole European society. Thenceforward the principal states began to acquire the strength and acquire the form that they have since maintained.

During the time of the Crusades, large fleets had been required to convey the vast armies which hurried to the holy wars, to keep open their communication with their bases of operation, and to supply them with provisions and warlike stores. This trade fell principally into the hands of the Venetians, the Pisans, and the Genoese. The manufacturers of silk, after having passed from Greece into Sicily, at length took up their principal position in Venice. The Lombard merchants extended their traffic through Europe. Fostered by immunities and privileges, they became masters of the purse and of the commerce of the nations in which they settled. Trade was not, however, entirely confined to Italy.

During the anarchy of the middle ages the Hanseatic towns had formed themselves into a league similar to that of the Lombards. They soon shared with the Lombards the trade of Europe, and almost monopolized that of the Baltic, as the Venetians did that of the Mediterranean. They had factories in Bruges, in London, and in Novogorod. Hemp, flax, timber, corn, hides, copper, formed the staple of their commerce. It was natural that a league formed for protection against disorder should find its influence decline as feudal anarchy disappeared. Dissensions arose among the members of the league which gave an opening, of which the English and Dutch were not slow to avail themselves.

Ghent, Bruges, and Antwerp contributed cotton, cloth, and tapestry to Europe. The English exported raw wool, reserving only a small quantity that was made into coarse cloth for home consumption, and received in return the finished manufactures of the Belgian looms, and the silk stuffs of India and the Levant. The fine arts followed the course of more solid industry. Flemings and Italians lived in comparative refinement before the neighbouring nations had acquired even the most necessary arts. The inhabitants of London and Paris crouched over fires lit on the earthen floors of their apartments, without even a chimney to carry off the smoke; while the burghers of Bruges and Ghent, Venice and Genoa, furnished their stately dwellings with paintings and tapestry, and adorned their cities with noble architecture.

During the preceding centuries learning was entirely in the hands of the clergy. To them alone was the education of the young intrusted. Schools were confined to chapels and monasteries. Learning was denounced as dangerous to piety, and unfit to be communicated to the laity. The poets and orators of Greece and Rome were consigned to oblivion or denounced in unsavoury terms. But when at length the learned persons who had studied among the Arabs opened schools in the chief cities of Italy, their example was followed by others in France, England, and Germany.

Before the invention of printing, knowledge spread but slowly among the body of the people: science was concealed beneath the veil of dead languages: the scarcity of parchment, and the expense of transcribing, rendered books so dear as to be within reach of few. The most useful invention made before that of printing might have remained unknown or been forgotten: gunpowder and the mariners' compass might have been lost to the world: the discovery of the New World might have been delayed, and the fortunes of the Old World changed. It was reserved for the genius of Guttenburg and Schæffer to do away with this great obstacle. Now, that thought could be transmitted with rapidity, and brought into contact with many minds, it was only necessary to make its expression free: learning revived, and with learning curiosity and free thought.

Events were also rapidly tending to bring the great discovery within the range of possibility. Printing had afforded the means of circulating with great rapidity any discovery of natural science or any speculation which might arise as to secrets of nature as yet undiscovered. One thing more was wanted—experience in shipbuilding and an improvement in the science of navigation. When these had been acquired, it would be possible for the first great thinker who should doubt the correctness of the then received cosmogony, or who should find reason to believe in the existence of land to the west, to realize his dream.

It happened that two comparatively insignificant states, Portugal and Venice, were just at that time making rapid strides both in shipbuilding and in navigation. Though they were deprived of the honour of discovering he Western World, they certainly contributed more than any other nations to the knowledge upon which the discovery was based.

At the close of the eleventh century, Alphonso VI., the king of Leon and Castile, having, by the assistance of Henry of Burgundy, rescued the northern provinces of Portugal from the invading Moors, gave Henry his daughter in marriage, and with her the rescued provinces as a dower. Henry contented himself with the title of Count; but his son enlarged the acquisition which his father had made, and assumed the style of king of Portugal. John the Bastard, some three centuries later, formed the first navy which was seen in Europe. His third son, Henry, who took a large share in the expeditions planned by his father, added to an adventurous disposition a large share of such learning as was then attainable. He devoted himself to the study of astronomy, which had been preserved in considerable perfection among the Arabs. To the school of astronomy which he founded at Sagres, belongs the credit of utilizing, and applying to the practical benefit of navigation, the discovery of the magnetic needle which had long been known in Europe.

Circumstances forced the energies of Portugal into a maritime channel. Unable to cope with Spain, and, therefore, shut out from any participation in the ambitious views which were entertained by other nations, she directed her energies more to the sea than to the land. Her kings had early driven the Moors out of their dominions, and acquired power and glory by their success against the infidels: their power was not circumscribed within the narrow limits which restrained other feudal princes. They had the command of the national forces, and could move them at will. Centuries of war with the Moors fostered the adventurous spirit of the nation and fitted it for discovery and conquest. The succession to the crown had been long in dispute, when John I., in 1411, obtained secure possession of the throne. He at once saw that his turbulent subjects must be employed abroad if he would prevent them from disaffection at home. He fitted out expeditions for discovery. He encouraged the study of the sciences cultivated by the Arabians. Geometry, astronomy, and navigation became objects of serious attention. In successive voyages, Cape Non, Cape Bogador, and ultimately the Cape of Good Hope, were passed. Settlements were founded on the coast of India. The

Azores were colonized, Madeira was planted with the vines of Cyprus and the sugar-canes of Sicily. The wonders narrated by the Portuguese adventurers disturbed European society to its centre. Bold spirits, who had before nothing to occupy their minds or their hands but murdering one another, now found excitement in commerce.

Venice, in the fourteenth century, was nearly overthrown. All the cities of Tuscany in early times formed themselves into republics, of which Florence, Venice, and Genoa were the most remarkable. In course of time most of the free cities of Tuscany were conquered by the Genoese; Venice and Lucca were the only two which still retained their independence. The great bone of contention between the Genoese and the Venetians was the possession of the Mediterranean trade. Towards the end of the fourteenth century, the former of these states, under Peter Doria, penetrated to the very midst of the lagoons of Venice. The city itself would have fallen if Doria had followed up his success. His procrastination gave the Venetians time to rally. They fitted out a fleet with great rapidity, and sallied forth against the enemy. But their efforts were ineffectual. The battle which ensued gave the Genoese the command of the sea. They formed establishments in the Adriatic Gulf and the Eastern archipelago. They acquired by treaty from the Sultan liberty of commerce in all the ports of Syria and Egypt, and the privilege of sending envoys to Alexandria and Damascus. Gradually they extended their boundaries by land: they seized the Trevisan March from the Cararas, and conquered Dalmatia from Sigismund, King of Hungary. They seized Vicenza, Verona, Padua, Cremona, and other cities from the Milanese.

India was the emporium of the world, and Venice held the key of India. Venetian navigators, trading with the ports of Syria and Alexandria, bought up the commodities which Jewish and Mahomedan merchants throughout the East collected and transported overland from the shores of the Red Sea and the Persian Gulf. All Europe depended upon them not only for the commodities which they derived from the East, but for manufactures of which they alone possessed the secret. The revenues derived from these sources enabled the doges of Venice to keep on foot armies which were sufficient, for some time, to contend with the powerful monarchies beyond the Alps, and often to dictate terms to Europe. The Venetian navy was formidable not only from its extent but its constitution. It was a favoured service, and contrasted strongly with the land forces. The doges feared to trust their own subjects with arms, and never admitted them into the armies which the state kept in pay. The army, therefore, consisted solely of mercenaries. It was officered by prominent captains among the "Condottieri," who, in the fifteenth and sixteenth centuries, made a trade of war. The navy was differently constituted. The nobles were encouraged to trade

CHAPTER II.

and to serve on board the fleet. They became merchants and admirals. They increased the wealth of the country by their industry, and its power by their valour.

The discoveries of the Portuguese made Venice tremble for its power. With the trade of India would depart their European pre-eminence, and the monopoly of Indian trade could not long be carried on overland when a path was open to it by sea.

Already Vasco de Gama was endeavouring to persuade his king that such a route existed. Genoese and Venetian geographers were startled to find that the theory was one which they could not deny. Many of their adventurers crowded to Lisbon; among them Christopher Columbus. Columbus married in Portugal, and for some years traded with the Canaries and the Azores. It is an old story how, in these western voyages, he saw canes of an enormous size floating upon the waves; how westerly gales cast pieces of carved timber upon the coast at Madeira; how the sea drifted corpses with strange features ashore at the Azores.

From all these indications, Columbus argued the existence of a country to the west. The roots and trees cast up by the waves resembled those which had been described by Ptolemy as the products of the Indies alone. While Gama was feeling for a passage to India by the east, Columbus determined to try for a passage by the west.

Thus did the master mind of the century collect

the light which glimmered around him and focused to a point. Thus did the seething caldron of Europe boil over. Thus—

> "Like a steed unbroken
> When first he feels the rein,
> The furious river struggled hard, and tossed his tawny mane,
> Then burst his curb, and bounded
> Rejoicing to be free;
> And whirling down in mad career,
> Battlement and plank and pier
> Rushed headlong to the sea."*

---

* Macaulay.

CHAPTER III.

DISCOVERY OF AMERICA TO TREATY OF NUREMBURG.

[1492—1530.]

The Discovery—Spanish Conquest—Views and Proceedings of England, France, and Spain—Rise of Diplomacy—History of Europe—The Reformation.

TREACHERY and cowardice prevented Portugal from equipping Columbus for his discovery. Tedious negotiations ensued with Genoa, England, and Spain. The Spaniards, occupied solely by internal politics, and by their contest for supremacy with the Moors, had not yet turned their attention to maritime discovery. It was not until the Moors were entirely driven out that Columbus received a commission from Ferdinand, and went forth to the discovery of America. Eighteen years had he laboured at his darling project, and won it at last with one day to spare. His crew were mutinous, his provisions exhausted. Three days more he asked for, then he would go back. Two passed without incident Next morning his ships would be directed homewards, and he would be doomed to face again the sneers of those who had sneered so long. But Columbus was born for success. When the day dawned on that memorable morrow, he was gazing on the mountains of a new world with a smile of triumph on his lip, and honour on his name for ever.

He gave the world a sight of the rich heritage of the west. He lived long enough to see Spaniards, Englishmen, and Frenchmen establish each a foothold on the land to which he had shown the way, and begin interminable disputes about priority of discovery, and rights which in good truth were one and all of the slenderest. Then died in 1506, leaving to the world, which he had benefited, an untarnished name; and the memory of his chains and his humiliations as a commentary on the text "Put not your trust in princes."

No sooner were the western islands revealed, than all the adventurous spirits who had won laurels at Malaga and Granada flocked to their shores.

The time was rich in incident; it was the most picturesque period of Spanish history. The warriors whom Ferdinand had led to the conquest of Granada had barely time to rest from their labours when religion, zeal, and avarice called them to a new field. Every Spaniard hoped to carve out a new province with his sword, and to plunder the hoarded wealth of Indian dynasties, the meanest subject of which was in the habit, it was said, of wearing the richest jewels and gold without knowing their value. It was supposed that, as the adventurers advanced to

CHAPTER III.

climates more and more under the torrid influence of the sun, the productions of nature would be sublimated to more rare and perfect qualities.* Jayme Ferrer, a learned lapidary, who had traded to the Levant, wrote to Columbus. He declared that he had gathered the testimony of Indians, Arabians, Ethiopians, natives of every land whence come precious stones: all agreed that gems and spices are to be found in greatest abundance among black races, and on the equinoctial line.

The Indians, too, had a legend of the fountain Bimini,† the swimmer in which would be for ever young. Ponce de Leon, brave soldier but weather-beaten, and hard of feature, wandered long—six months, says Ramusio—searching for the magic fountain, and found it not, only lighted upon a coast which he called "Fiorita," and the moderns call Florida. Ponce de Leon, after the way of the world, forsook the solid enjoyments of his viceroyalty of Hispaniola to pursue a shadow, and to die miserably by an Indian arrow in the land whence he hoped to draw the means of immortality.

1512

1519 Cortez followed in his steps. Restless, chivalrous, and adventurous, his youth wasted in broils and intrigues, political and amatory, in Old Spain, he nevertheless brought genius and a clear head to help him in his romantic conquest of Mexico.

---

* Navarette. Coleccion, tom. ii., Doc. 68.

† In questo tempo si divulgò quella favola del Fonte, che faceva ringiovenare et tornare giovani e freschi, i vecchi.

In 1513 Nunez de Balboa took possession of Darien. He had received from the Indians of Darien an account of a great sea, a few days' journey to the south. This he rightly conjectured to be the ocean of which Columbus had always been in search. Eager to be the first discoverer of countries which report alleged to abound with gold, Balboa determined to cross the isthmus with his troops. In the face of almost insurmountable obstacles he at length effected his purpose, and claimed the sovereignty of the Southern Ocean for the crown of Castile.

Magellan led the way through the Straits which bear his name; and in 1522 the ships under his command—though he himself was murdered by the savages—completed, for the first time, the circumnavigation of the globe. In the previous year Pizarro had conquered the kingdom of Peru.

By this time the subject of American conquest had laid firm hold on the Spanish mind. Colonization, or rather Spanish lust of gold, speedily seized on the land round about the Gulf of Mexico. Cortez, Pizarro, Valdivia,—brilliant conquerors, no doubt, in the unequal strife in which they engaged with the savages—carried on their operations without loss of time, but have left no very solid memorials of themselves. Havoc and devastation marked their path: strange stories of their glory and their prowess struck awe and wonder among their contemporaries: but not till they had disappeared came the era of the peaceful colonist, whose labours should consolidate the dominion of which they only traced the landmarks.

Pope Alexander VI., profoundly ignorant of the nature of the discovery made by Columbus, was perfectly ready to grant the new territory to any ally whom such a boon would gratify. Geographical science was vague at the Vatican. It may be that the sovereign pontiff, in his secret heart, inclined to the opinion held by the most learned of his predecessors, that the earth was not really round: at any rate, he could not perceive how a boundary drawn towards the west could injure any prince whose dominions lay towards the east. To remove all possibility of prejudice to the rights of either ally, he decided that the transatlantic possessions of Spain should have an eastern limit. It should run from pole to pole, one hundred leagues westward of the Azores. So, said he, shall the west belong to the King of Spain : the land that he has discovered shall be his in perpetuity : " Civitates et castra in perpetuum tenore præsentium donamus." The King of Portugal, however, entertained more correct notions of the earth's form : Vasco di Gama had been to India round Bartelemi Diaz's " Stormy Cape," rechristened by the Portuguese, John II., Cape of Good Hope : now that Columbus had sailed, or thought he had sailed, to India by way of the west, and that Ferdinand had obtained the grant " in perpetuum " of his discoveries, Portugal felt bound to remonstrate. The pope yielding to this new pressure reconsidered his former decision, and decreed that the boundary should be removed four hundred and seventy leagues further west. He would impose a western instead of an eastern limit on Spanish discovery.

There were others, beside the pope, upon whom the new discovery imposed the necessity of acquiring fresh ideas of geographical science. Experience had confounded the wisdom of the Council of Salamanca. It was shown that although the earth was spherical, a ship might sail down-hill to the end of the world, and yet be able to sail home up-hill on the other side. Cardinal D'Ailly * had proved equally wrong, notwithstanding the supposed authority of the fourth book of Ezra, in asserting that the ocean covered but one-seventh of the surface of the globe. The great deed was accomplished: the miracle of miracles had been performed. " A Castilla y a Leon, nuevo mundo diò colon."† What, then, was the limit of discovery? For men to whom so much had been possible, what was the boundary of possibility?

Ere Columbus had reached the mainland, two other nations had obtained a settlement in America. John Cabot, by order of Henry VII., had undertaken a voyage of discovery, and had landed at Labrador: and Pedro de Cabral, sailing for India with a fleet of thirteen vessels from Portugal, accidentally discovered the coast of Brazil. Cabral entered a harbour which he called Porto Seguro. He erected a cross and took possession of the country in the name of the

* Imago Mundi, quoted by Humboldt.
† Inscription on Columbus's monument at Seville.

CHAPTER III.

King of Portugal; and despatched a vessel to Lisbon with an account of the discovery he had made. Cabral's fleet proceeded on its voyage to India; but two felons, of whom he had a large number on board, were left behind to learn the language of the natives. Expeditions were soon after sent out from Portugal to the new discovery, and disputes occurred with Spain as to its limits. It was at length settled that Portugal should possess the country from the river Amazon as far south as the river Plate. Succeeding expeditions failed to find gold or silver mines: though the soil was fertile and the climate healthy, spices could be more easily grown in the Eastern Islands; so that for a long time Brazil was only used by the Portuguese as a penal settlement.

The English adventurer, John Cabot, was armed with all those exaggerated powers which afterwards became a matter of course in similar expeditions. One-fifth of the gains of the enterprise was reserved to the crown. Absolute power of life and death was bestowed on the adventurer "over all barbarous and heathen countries" which he might be strong enough to subdue. Cabot left no journal of his voyage. " He gave England a continent, and no one knows his burial-place."[*] His son, who was with him, gave Ramusio an account by word of mouth, which that author has handed down in the third volume of his collection of travels. Cabot himself thought that he was on the direct

* Bancroft's History of the United States.

road to China, and entertained no suspicion that he had found a continent. It would appear, too, that he was an indifferent disciplinarian; for his crew would not let him proceed to China, though he was exceedingly anxious to do so. "I should have gone there," he exclaims, "had it not been for the malignity of the master and crew."* It has taken three centuries and a half of patient exploration, and the sacrifice of many a valuable life, to prove the untruth of Cabot's dream —"di poter passar per quella via alla volta del Cattaio orientale." The material obstacles of cold and hunger, unfortunately, oppose a far more constant and insurmountable obstacle to a north-west passage to Cathay than did the master and crew who turned John Cabot back, and whose "malignity" the disappointed mariner so quaintly deplores.

He landed on St. John's day upon the island of Newfoundland, which he called St. John. The sailors, with less reverence, named it Baccalaos, which was, and is to this day, the principal matter you hear of there, "baccalaos" being the native name for codfish. Pietro Martire, who calls Sebastian Cabot his "dear and familiar friend," prefers, in treating of the island, to write "Baccalaos;" so does Lopez de Gomara. History says not whether Cabot brought home any dried "baccalaos." He certainly introduced turkeys, excellent birds, but evidently misnamed. The French call them "coqs d'Inde;" and as the French, in common with Pope Alexander VI. and other learned per-

* Discorso del Ramusio, vol. iii., delle navig. e viaggi.

CHAPTER III.

sons, considered America and India to be identical, their name is intelligible. So is the "Welche hahn" of the Germans; for as turkeys were brought to Europe by an Italian, the name of the Italian bird is not unreasonable; but the Turks can prove no right, direct or indirect, to the honour accorded them by the English. Cabot called Labrador, Primavista. It is supposed that the name Labrador was given it by the Portuguese slave-merchants in after days, " on account of the admirable qualities of the natives as labourers." *

The rights of England to priority of discovery on the American continent depend on Cabot's voyage. It is therefore natural that French historians, writing at a subsequent period, with a view of establishing the claim of France to the whole country, should endeavour to cast discredit on his veracity, and insinuate that he never went there at all.†

1504 The French established fisheries on the Labrador coast, and it was through the hardy Breton fishermen who resorted there that she claimed, in the following century, her prior right of discovery. John Verrazzano went out in 1523, by command of Francis I. But small results ensued; and Francis being taken
1523 prisoner by Charles V. at Pavia, and being therefore
1525 unable to continue the liberality upon which the Florentine adventurer had counted, Verrazzano withdrew from his service, and never returned to France ; some

* Picture of Quebec.
† Paris Documents, vol. ix. p. 2. Champlain's Abregé, &c.

say that he was hanged as a pirate by the Spaniards. Charlevoix says he and his crew were killed and eaten by the savages; so says Ramusio, "furono arrostiti e mangeati." All agree that he never returned. Thus Spain, England, and France almost at the same moment hastened to establish a foothold in the Western world. Times were changing; order was arising out of chaos; right instead of might was becoming, in theory if not in practice, the fundamental maxim of society. Many an adventurous spirit, who chafed at the limits which he saw narrowing around him, fitted out a ship for the Western Indies, or enlisted as a gentleman adventurer in some expedition to find a north-west passage to China.

Various motives prompted these expeditions: some went to search for gold: some—but that was at a later time—fled from religious persecution, or were urged by proselytizing zeal: some went from mere adventure, or to escape from the growing restraint of law. No one thought for a moment of colonization, as we understand the term. Each leader established a plantation, or built a fort, as a base whence he might pursue his operations. Some of these settlements became colonies in after-times; but in the first half of the sixteenth century no one had any idea of establishing new and independent states, such as the Dorians, in ancient times, formed in Italy and Sicily; or the Ionians and Æolians in Asia Minor, and on the shores of the Ægean Sea. A time came, long afterwards, when colonization was reduced to a system, quarrelled over by ministers, patronized by kings, fashioned into one of the regular wheels of statecraft, and made the object of a definite policy.

But as yet Europe was but a chicken breaking the shell which had confined it, struggling only for room to develop itself. Spanish, French, and English went unconcernedly on. Their adventurers, armed with preposterous powers, planted settlements haphazard, and with them goodly seeds of discord for the time to come.

Yet it was curious to observe with what vigour the national character of each was impressed upon these infant colonies. Men's minds in a rude state of society differ more from each other, and exhibit stronger individuality, than they do in times when civilization has reduced every one to the same dead level of outward good-breeding. While Columbus and Cortez were at work in the south, and Cabot and Verrazzano in the north of America, events were proceeding with lightning rapidity in Europe. The thirty years which had elapsed since the discovery of Columbus had sufficed to give form and colour to the change which even in his time had begun. The old theory of government was annihilated: it was replaced by one which came from beyond the Alps, as, indeed, in those days did all inventions which substituted intellect for brute force. The Italians invented the theory of the balance of power. Italy had early been subdivided into a number of states, of which none was sufficiently powerful to overawe the rest, nor any so feeble as to be entirely disregarded. The fundamental principle of political equilibrium which they by common consent adopted, was, that no state should become so powerful as to be able to resist a combination of the whole. Rules were invented by diplomatists which were gradually digested into a code of international law. While the rest of Europe was still torn with a thousand contending factions, the polished Italians learned to rely rather on their jurists than on their soldiers.

The decay of feudalism in Europe gave to law an importance which force only had possessed before. The policy as well as the learning of Italy passed the Alps. The new doctrines of statecraft were eagerly studied by the western and northern nations. Before that time, states, feeble and isolated, ignorant of each other, occupied with their own interests and quarrels, distracted by internal dissensions, could have no diplomatic relations. Each prince was continually engaged in war with factions and powerful vassals. Europe was paralyzed in detail; no united action was possible: the power of government was crippled. A great conqueror might for a time overrun neighbouring states; but military operations usually were conducted without unity, and were without permanent effect. Now constitutions, better organized, were gradually introduced: feudal disorders began to disappear: permanent armies replaced temporary levies. Kings, who had command of the national forces, were able by their means to hold the great feudal leaders in check. Freed from domestic invasion, they had leisure to form views of aggrandisement and conquest. Diplomacy came into play: alliances of many states against a powerful neighbour became common. In many cases embassies, treaties, and guarantees formed a satisfactory substitute for an appeal to arms.

The new development of political science was first directed against the house of Austria. Charles V., who obtained the crown of Spain in 1516, united, as the representative of the family of Hapsburg, the authority of various sovereigns. He had inherited the Low Countries from his father: the Spanish succession had fallen to him from his maternal grandfather: he succeeded to the Austrian dominions of his paternal grandfather. He espoused the daughter of Emanuel of Portugal; and in right of Isabella added the kingdom of Portugal to the already enormous dominions which he transmitted to his son.

Charles was the contemporary of a group of princes, each of whom exercised a great influence on the age in which he lived. It was perhaps fortunate that they reigned contemporaneously, and that the power and genius of one, thus pitted against the other, prevented any great and permanent disarrangement of power. Henry VIII. ruled in England, Francis I. in France, Leo X. at the Vatican. Each, when he mounted the throne, was in the flower of his age. Indeed, most of the reigning princes of Europe were young. Charles ascended the throne when he was sixteen years old. Henry was at that time twenty-four; Francis, twenty-two; Louis of Hungary, ten; Leo only thirty-nine. Their courts, except that of Charles, were witty, licentious, and luxurious.

Most of these princes were extravagant: the English king was the only one free from pecuniary embarrassment. Charles especially was in great straits: the American mines were not yet highly productive: Naples was unprofitable: the Low Countries were turbulent, and their contributions to his treasury uncertain: he was indebted to Henry VIII. for the money which enabled him to go to Spain to assume the government of his grandfather. On a subsequent occasion, when he was manœuvring to obtain the election to the imperial crown, an important courier was stopped for want of funds to pay his journey.* The loans of Henry VIII. were not without solid motives: he expected to be able to get Charles completely in his power. Charles had not yet received the imperial crown; but already his grandfather, "Maximilian the Moneyless," was offering the reversion of it to the highest bidder. Francis would gladly have obtained the nomination; but he was no better off than the King of Spain. Maximilian offered it to Henry; but he, aware that he could not hold it if he got it, and that even if he paid the money he was unlikely to get it, declined the offer. Not till

* Michelet, Hist. France, viii. 49.

then did Maximilian remember that he tenderly loved his grandson, and offered him the reversion— for a pecuniary consideration.

The finances of Leo were dilapidated. He had been elevated to the pontificate principally on account of the supposed pliability of his temper. Great was the astonishment of the holy college when they witnessed the creation of thirty new cardinals at a stroke. Never had such a step been ventured by former pontiffs. But Leo received a handsome sum from each of his new dignitaries, and so strengthened himself by their aid, that he could afford to disregard the indignation which he created.

The court of Francis was even more extravagant and more needy than those of his contemporaries. It was occupied by a constant succession of fêtes, hunting parties, and tournaments. In this time of early youth, the king's hawks and mistresses left him little time for state affairs. But he was skilled in manly exercises, for which he was well qualified by his handsome person and commanding stature, He was a better wrestler than our King Henry, whose heels he tripped up so skilfully at one of their meetings that the English king lost his temper, and was with difficulty restrained from following up the encounter with his fists. Francis considered himself pre-eminently fitted for a military leader. The great ambition of his later life was to curb the power of Austria. But the Flemish usurers who crowded the court of Spain kept him quiet for a time. They gave him large subsidies under the pretence of bringing about a marriage between Charles and a princess of the blood royal of France. The money was convenient. The king had need of it to pay for his hunting parties; but he was too clearsighted not to perceive the motives of his purveyors, and he broke away when he was strong enough.

Thus did the necessities of her princes for a time keep Europe at peace.

It was not the theory and forms of government only that were changed. A revolution of greater moment was rapidly coming to a crisis. In Saxony and in Switzerland two men were asserting opinions that attacked the fundamental doctrines of the Church. They called in question the authority of the pope himself. Leo disregarded the growing schism till it absolutely forced itself upon his attention. When too late he convened a Diet at Spires, and peremptorily ordered that no change should be made in the teaching of the church. Luther and Zuingle protested; and the schismatics, Protestants henceforward as they were called, were now fairly committed to the struggle which ended in the Reformation.

This was unquestionably the most important revolution of the sixteenth century. Its effect is especially discernible in the history of colonization. It is hardly too much to assert, that its influence is directly visible on every colony which subsequently to its occurrence was sent out from any nation of Europe. The New England colonies were peopled by

CHAPTER III.

men who fled from the persecution of James. France had her Protestant exiles in Florida, and her colonies for the spread of Catholicism on the St. Lawrence. The persecutions of Philip II. goaded the Dutch into the assertion of their national independence, and enabled them to extend their territory to the shores of the Hudson. The Swedish colony on the Delaware was founded by Gustavus Adolphus, to be, as he said, "a security to those whom wars and bigotry had made fugitives."* A large portion of the Portuguese settlements in Brazil were entirely in the hands of the Jesuits. The Spanish colonies became the scene of persecutions as dreadful, and religious quarrels as deadly, as any that raged in Europe. They were the centre of Catholicism in the new world. By their help the bloody drama of persecution which Philip performed in Europe was re-enacted beyond the seas.

The political effects of the Reformation were very considerable. The freedom of opinion, which was the grand characteristic of the reformed faith, was not an unmixed good. It was impossible to strike at the root of the Church of Rome, containing, as it did, so much that was venerable, without convulsing society to its centre. Liberty degenerated into licence. The ambition of princes, the turbulent spirit of the disaffected, assumed the mask of religion. Wars and factions arose in Germany, France, the Low Countries, Switzerland, Hungary, and Poland.

* Argonautica Gustaviana.

Everywhere the march of the Reformation was stained with blood. The papal authority was powerless to restrain these excesses. Princes took advantage of the commotion, to increase their own importance by adding spiritual authority, as heads of the church, to their temporal authority as sovereigns. The clergy ceased, in the Protestant states, to have a controlling influence. Liberty of opinion, and the absence of all authority in matters of faith, though they gave new energy to science and thought, allowed men long accustomed to leading-strings to fall into excesses of which previous ages had given no example. Readers of Lord Macaulay's Essays will remember the rapid and vigorous parallel which he draws between the Reformation and the French Revolution. He points out that both, in the endeavour to eradicate error, shook to their very foundations the principles on which society rests. In both frightful cruelties were committed —masses of property were confiscated. In both cases the spirit of innovation was at first encouraged by the class to which it was most likely to be prejudicial. Philosophy developed itself under the patronage of the grandees of France. The revival of learning was hailed with pleasure by the heads of the church. Old landmarks were destroyed. Religion replaced in men's minds the power which in quieter times is exercised by patriotism. Common faith was a stronger bond of union than common nationality. Both the French Huguenots and the French princes

CHAPTER III.

of the League thought it no disgrace to invite foreign soldiers into France. While the power of the Church of Rome was thus energetically assailed, and the spirit of insubordination was yet young, an order arose in the bosom of the Catholic church itself which was destined in after days to play a prominent part, and which acquired peculiar importance in the history of colonization.

1534 Ignatius Loyola founded the order of Jesuits. In the midst of universal insubordination they were distinguished by implicit obedience. They abjured all individual action to become machines in the hands of the general of their order: they soon spread over all the Catholic states: they filled every court with their emissaries : they planted missions in every clime : no long time elapsed ere they surpassed in power and in wealth every other religious society. They became one of the main instruments of the papal power. The very name of a Jesuit carried with it a sound of terror : they were looked upon by Protestants with hatred and apprehension ; and the zeal which marked the exercise of their mysterious authority gave ample grounds for mistrust and dread.

The Protestant movement continued, from the beginning, steadily to increase. Before the close of Charles's reign it had embraced many of the principal nations of Europe. Denmark, Norway, Sweden, 1530 Prussia, and Livonia had embraced the "declaration" submitted to the emperor by Luther. England, the United Provinces, and the Swiss adopted the doctrines of Calvin. In Hungary also, and in France, Bohemia, Silesia, Transylvania, and Poland the new faith made considerable progress.

The Reformers gradually became so important that the party they favoured or opposed could never be an object of indifference. They were alternately courted and persecuted by Charles. It occasionally happened that an alliance with some rigidly Catholic sovereign was necessary to his schemes : this he could only obtain on the condition of detaching himself from the Protestants. The fact of their aid being so often in demand, and the tenacity and unanimity with which they afforded it, raised them in importance far more than any persecution could depress them; they therefore, on the whole, largely increased both in power and in number. Almost every nation that embraced, or in any way countenanced the Reformation, sent in after times colonies to North America. A sketch of the events which marked its progress is therefore necessary.

I have already observed, that soon after the accession of Charles V. to the throne of Spain, the English king had, in consequence of his great wealth, been able to assume the position of arbiter among the candidates for the imperial throne. His influence thrown into the scale of Francis or of Charles, would greatly affect the course of affairs. But the judgment of Henry was not sufficiently mature to enable him to maintain the position which events had thrust upon him. Haughty, fierce, and impetuous, he was unable to follow out a policy which would have better suited the cold-blooded calculations of a Louis XI. than a prince of the Tudor blood. Charles became the successful candidate; and by his success laid the foundation of an enmity with Francis that gradually deepened into personal animosity.

Nothing is more amusing in the story of these endless wars, than the constant outcrop of anger and spite, jumbled up with strange freaks of generosity, which this personal quarrel between the two princes exhibits. They challenged each other to single combat, and were only prevented from a 'duel à l'outrance' by the exertions of their attendants. They gave each other the lie. When the dauphin died, Charles accused Francis of having poisoned him. Yet, with whimsical inconsistency each constantly threw himself absolutely upon the honour in which he had publicly declared his disbelief. On one occasion, Charles had occasion to pass rapidly from Spain to the Low Countries to chastise the men of Ghent. He demanded a safe-conduct from Francis, and passed through his rival's dominions with scarcely an attendant. When the emperor was driven ashore at Provence, Francis went without any precautions on board his galley, and gave him a good supper and a steady bedstead to refresh him after the inconveniences of his galley cabin and swinging cot.*

As soon as it was known that Charles was actually elected emperor, Francis prepared to attack the do-

* Aigues mortes, 1538.

minions of his rival. Both courted the alliance of
Henry. Each endeavoured to outbid the other for the
favour of Wolsey. Charles offered him the papal
throne: so magnificent a proposal was not to be refused: Henry was induced by his minister to join the
emperor. But Wolsey never received his promised
reward; the non-fulfilment of that promise was long
a thorn in the emperor's side.

After the sack of Rome by Bourbon, Henry VIII., 1527
who till then had remained in amity with Charles,
joined Francis in defence of the pope. Henry had
his own reasons for wishing to stand well with the
holy see: his marriage with Catherine had become
intolerable to him, and he foresaw his need of the
pope's assistance in the matter of his divorce.
Charles, however, supported his aunt, and countermined all his rival's attempts.

Now the Protestants for the first time appeared as 1530
a political body. The emperor at Augsburg had
condemned the declaration of faith, and had named a
time, within which the Protestants were commanded
to conform to the doctrines and ceremonies of the
church. The Protestants assembled at Smalkalde, and
there concluded a league of mutual defence. John
Frederick, Elector of Saxony, and Philip, Landgrave
of Hesse, declared themselves chiefs of this union,
and called upon the kings of England and France for
assistance.

The league, from its very commencement, became
involved with matters purely secular. Charles had

formed a scheme of continuing the imperial crown in his own family. He obtained for his brother Ferdinand the dignity of King of the Romans. Plausible reasons were not wanting to give a colour to this proceeding. The emperor was often away from Germany : the growing disturbances on the subject of religion, and the aggressive spirit manifested by the Turks under Solyman, afforded a good excuse for conferring upon a prince whose interest as well as his duty it would be to meet these disturbances, the power of doing so with effect. The Protestants were fully alive to the fact that a steady and powerful government was not the one best suited to the development of their religion. They saw clearly that it was their interest to combine against the emperor's design. The election, however, took place, and the Protestants despatched ambassadors into England and France to demand assistance and protection. Francis willingly complied with any request that could tend to humble the emperor. Henry, disgusted at the interference of Charles in the affair of the divorce gladly joined the French king.

At this moment Solyman took occasion of the disunion which existed, to march his troops into Hungary. The emperor quickly perceived that he was in no condition to face disunion in the empire, the hostility of France and England, and 300,000 Turks to boot. He came to a hasty accommodation with the Protestants.* It was agreed that no person should

* Nuremberg, 1530.

be molested on account of his religion, that a stop should be put to all processes begun by the imperial Chambers against heretics, and that the sentences already passed to their detriment should be considered void. On their part, the Protestants promised to assist with all their forces against the Turks.

A league which could thus dictate its own terms, and avail itself with such dexterity of the course of events, necessarily occupied an important position. The German Protestants, who had hitherto been looked upon only as crazy religionists, were henceforth considered as a political body of no small consequence.

The Treaty of Nuremburg was no sooner signed than Charles received intimation that Solyman had entered Hungary with 250,000 men. The imperial army assembled near Vienna. They were commanded by the emperor in person. The campaign was indecisive. But, during a subsequent raid against the Moors in favour of the deposed king of Tunis, Francis took advantage of the emperor's absence to reassert his long dormant claims on Italy. The war which then began occupied the attention of the emperor for several years; and it was not until 1544 that the Peace of Crespi left him at liberty to turn his attention from France to renew his persecution of the Protestants.

CHAPTER IV.

FROM THE TREATY OF NUREMBURG TO THE ACCESSION OF ELIZABETH.

[1530—1558.]

Spanish, French, and English Adventurers—The Reformation in England and other European Kingdoms.

CHAPTER IV.

THE necessities of Charles made him easily accessible to any who would pretend to help him out of his embarrassments. His Low Country dominions grudged him subsidies for wars in which they had no interest: in Spain the Cortes crippled his power, and doled out the supplies with a careful, if not with a parsimonious hand : gold had come from America sufficient to whet expectation, and to rouse cupidity, but not to aid him sensibly in his wars. He was therefore quite ready to catch at any chance of emolument that presented itself. Madrid had by this time worked itself into excitement. The courtiers swore that Cortez was not the only Castilian whose luck or whose talents could found a kingdom. Cortez, it is true, had discovered Mexico ; but had not Nunez de Balboa heard of countries to the south, richer than Mexico? Where was the city of Manoa, the city of prophecy, whose streets and whose very dust were gold? Where was the fountain of perpetual youth? The talk was of nothing but patents and privileges, galleons and caravels, cannons and pateraroes.

Patents and privileges the emperor granted with no sparing hand. Many a bold adventurer went forth, armed with such smattering of learning as he could gather from the shadowy oracles contained in the pages of Aristotle, Strabo, Pliny, Seneca, and Eratosthenes. Many failed, and perished miserably. But where the many fail a few succeed. A young soldier, who had worn the yellow jerkin and wielded a pike among the veterans of Italy, sailed with a single vessel to Tierra Firme, and lighted on Peru. Flouted by the Governor of Panama, Pizarro had come to court, and effectually tickled Charles's ears with his tales of gold. Governor, captain-general, "adelantado" of all the countries that he had discovered and hoped to conquer; supreme authority, civil and military; such were the proud titles with which the nameless bastard was dignified, and with which, accompanied by a hundred and twenty men, he went forth to conquer a kingdom. Landing at Nombre de Dios, he hurried to Panama. Here he obtained three small vessels, and increased his army to a hundred and eighty men.

In 1528 he sailed; in 1532 came news of his complete success. Private adventurers came home with many thousand *pezos* as the share of each. Treasures such as were never before dreamed of poured into Spain. Charles had spent a great deal more than he could afford on his coronation at Bologna. His campaign against Solyman had drained his treasury; he had been obliged to throw the burden of his army on his allies, and to persuade the Italian states to keep up an army for themselves, while he disbanded his own. The emperor's delight at his new acquisition was therefore unbounded. More encouragement than ever was lavished upon adventurers. Every day his ministers were besieged with proposals for new expeditions to the West.

Francis, who wanted gold and silver mines quite as much as his rival, and who could not bear to be outdone by him, lost no time in sending out an expedition of his own. He, too, pitched upon a man whose fortune and genius made him the founder of a kingdom. This was a gentleman of St. Malo, Jacques Cartier. There is a picture of him now at St. Malo. Rather a Jewish cast of face, square head, and high but wrinkled forehead; hair closely cropped; short curling beard, and mustachios bristling fiercely over a firm, clear-cut lip; slightly underjawed; eyes bright and quick; a man of iron nerve and prompt resolution. It was not his fault that his countrymen misgoverned the empire that he founded, and threw it away. He did his duty well, and left a splendid legacy to France. Five years ago, a namesake and descendant of Cartier the discoverer occupied the position of first minister of the crown under the parliamentary government of British Canada.

Cartier founded Quebec; and a few years afterwards La Nouvelle France was erected into a viceroyalty under Jean François de la Roque, Seigneur de Roberval. Hochelaga, Saguenay, Newfoundland, Belleisle, Carpon, Labrador, La Grande Baye, Baccalaos, were the names mentioned in the patent. Loaded with dignities, the Picard gentleman, with Cartier second in command, set out on his expedition in confident expectation of finding gold and silver mines.

Most strange of all the expeditions was that of the discoverer of the Mississippi. Ferdinand de Soto left Hispaniola, accompanied by a numerous band of horsemen, besides infantry. How horses were stowed in the small vessels of that period it is difficult to understand. It is, however, on record that between two and three hundred cavalry disembarked in the Bay of Spirito Santo. Portuguese volunteers in burnished armour, and Castilians "very gallant with silk upon silk," joined the adventurer as soon as the news of his voyage was told. Chains to bind their captives; bloodhounds to hunt down the natives; stores of food, and pigs which they might turn loose to breed in the woods, were among the munitions with which the expedition was furnished. Gallant freebooters in quest of fortune, men ferocious with avarice, bound on whatever path rumour might indicate as leading to the residence of some wealthy

CHAPTER IV.

prince, or wherever the signs of the natives were interpreted to indicate the existence of gold.

The ships which brought the adventurers to the Florida shore were sent back. "Death or success!" says the "Portuguese eye-witness."* Then follows a narrative of disaster, leading up to a climax of suffering and death. What a romance underlies the formal phrases of that eye-witness! We get a glimpse of terribly real life. We see the adventurers' dismay at the swamps and forest solitudes. Desertion of Porcallo, who had lavished his fortune in magnificent equipments. One guide after another, who fails to lead them to the golden city, torn to pieces by bloodhounds, burnt alive, cruelly slain in nameless ways. Now, the passion for play takes possession of their souls; the hot-blooded Castilian desperadoes quarrel eagerly over their dice. Now and then a blow—a gleam of Toledo rapiers in the moonlight, a few passes, carte, tierce, a stumble or somewhat too wide a parry of an eager thrust, a wicked blade leaping in like a tongue of flame right over the tardy guard, and then, a shallow grave among the tree-roots. Yet the solemn ceremonies of the church were observed in the forest, the ornaments which the usages of the church enjoined were carried on every saint's day in procession. Gold was to be found at all hazards, and by means fair or foul; but Christianity was to be carried too at

* 1557. Translated by Hakluyt; also Vega, and Ensayo Chronologico.

the sword's point. The adventurers wandered on fighting with the Indians, decimated by sickness, silken bravery in rags, rags giving place at last to skins, and mats of ivy. After four years and a half of wandering, three hundred and eleven men reached Cuba, the remnant of six hundred who had been chosen from many candidates as the flower of the chivalry of Spain. De Soto's miseries had ended the year before beside the Mississippi, which he had discovered.

Europe soon rang with the name of gold. In our own days we can remember two crises of "the gold fever." We can recall the feverish haste with which crowds of treasure-seekers hurried off to the diggings. The discovery of America, and the accounts which the Spaniards spread abroad of the wealth of Hispaniola, operated much in the same manner on Europe in the sixteenth century. The excitement was as great among the maritime nations then, as it has been among the travelling nations since. News did not spread so quickly, but its slower progress was compensated by the exaggerated form which it assumed. Science was less widely diffused, and left room for superstition to step in and hold its magnifying glass over facts. The historians of that time, writing with the subsequent light of experience, all condemn the extraordinary excitement which existed. Herrera is of opinion that "the mines were devised by the evil spirit to lure the Spaniards to destruction." " Les demandes ordinaires qu'on nous fait," says

CHAPTER IV.

l'Escarbot, "sont : Y a-t-il de l'or et de l'argent ? La plus belle mine que je sache, c'est du bled et du vin avec la nourriture du bestial." It is possible that this passage may have been in the mind of the Duc de Sully when he wrote in his Memoires the sententitious phrase, " Pâturage et labourage valent tout l'or du Perou ?" *

It has been before observed that colonization was not the object which the Spaniards proposed to themselves in America. They came not to colonize but to garrison. They were military adventurers; and, like other armies, were not accompanied by women. Their wealth, even their subsistence, was obtained by the labour of the natives, whom they reduced to slavery immediately on their arrival. Their only care was for gold; and " Fortune realized in some measure the extravagant hopes of her votaries, and in the discovery and conquest of Mexico and Peru, she gave them something not unlike the profusion of the precious metals which they sought for." †

Each of the *conquistadores* had a district allotted to him ; and the wretched inhabitants were given up to the unrestrained exercise of their owners' cupidity and violence. Skill and capital were alike wanting, but their place was filled by the vast numbers who were compelled to labour in the mines. The mortality was frightful, and indeed the expenditure of life, looking at the matter from the lowest point of

* Mémoires du Duc de Sully.
† Adam Smith, Wealth of Nations.

view, was so wasteful as to call for prompt legislative interference from home.

The tenure upon which the discoveries of the Spaniards were held from the pope was the spread of the Roman Catholic religion. Little as the title thus conferred was in reality cared for, it was one which could be conveniently asserted, and which was constantly kept in the foreground. The popes at a very early period* gave over the direct control of the Spanish American Church. Alexander II. and Julius II. resigned their right to tithes and presentation to benefices; but the emancipation, far from being a benefit to the unhappy natives, deprived them of the protection of a power which would often have stood between them and their temporal superiors. The Church was thus placed in the hands of men who used it solely as a political engine. It certainly was not less formidable under the temporal than under the ecclesiastical rule. In 1533 the Inquisition was introduced into the Spanish settlements, and from that time forward equalled, if it could not surpass, the terrible cruelties of its European prototype.

The islands of the Spanish main soon felt the merciless severity of Spanish rule. In little more than a century the entire native population was destroyed. No record of barbarity is equal to that which they endured. "What are all the desolations of the most savage tyrants of Greece and Rome to the massacre made by the Christians of Spain in the

* Pope Alexander II., Bull of 1501.

CHAPTER IV.

conquest of the New World? for on a very moderate computation, this conquest was effected by the slaughter of ten millions of the species."* The Indians were distributed by lot among the Spaniards, and forced to labour in the mines. Those who resisted were hunted down. Dogs were trained to tear the fugitives in pieces. The descendants of these animals—the loose-jowled and blear-eyed Cuban bloodhound—are still seen in a few English country-houses. Captives were driven into the water and baptized; then their throats were cut to prevent apostacy from the faith. Nor was ferocious fanaticism the only cloak for cruelty. Indians were murdered by the Spaniards from simple wantonness, or to keep their hands in use! †

Bartolomé de las Casas,‡ bishop of Chiapa, wrote an account of these fiendish excesses to the Prince

* Edwards, West Indies, vol. i.
† Pietro Martine.
‡ Bartolomé de las Casas was born in Seville probably in 1474; and in 1502, having gone through a course of studies at Salamanca, embarked for the Indies, where his father, who had been there with Columbus nine years earlier, had already accumulated a decent fortune.

The attention of the young man was early called to the condition of the natives, from the circumstance that one of them, given to his father by Columbus, had been attached to his own person as a slave while he was still at the university. He proceeded to Hispaniola, and from this moment devoted his life to their emancipation. In 1510 he took holy orders, and continued in the Indies as priest, and for a short time as bishop of Chiapa, nearly forty years. Six times he crossed the Atlantic in order to persuade the government of Charles V. to ameliorate their condition. At last, but not until 1547, when he was above seventy years old, he established himself at Valladolid, in Spain, where he passed the remainder of his serene old age. His works were voluminous; the earliest of them, the "Breve Relaçion," was written in 1542.

of Asturias, afterwards Philip II. His book is in size little larger than a pamphlet; but as a record of cruelty, it is hardly surpassed by the ghastly relations of the Book of Martyrs. It may well be supposed that the words of the good bishop, who earnestly exhorted the prince to intercede with his father on behalf of the Indians, fell unheeded on ears which could hear unmoved the cruelties of Alva and Requesens, and the details of the Bartholomew massacre. He told of wives outraged, of children taken by the heels from their mothers' breasts, and dashed against rocks in sport; of wagers as to who among the Christian warriors would cleave an Indian in two with the fewest blows. The savages artificially flattened the heads of their children in such a manner that the skull would almost turn a sword-cut. Las Casas told how the cudgel players of Spain were fond of betting that they would smash an Indian's skull with one blow of a pikestaff. He told of gallows, on which every morning thirteen victims were hanged, in honour of Christ and his twelve apostles. He told of fires, at which, day by day, a like number were slowly roasted. "I saw," he says, "five of the principal caçiques roasting before a slow fire. Their screams disturbed the captain. He ordered them to be strangled. The lieutenant—I know his name and his family in Seville—gagged them with his own hands, 'that they might not lose one iota of their torture!'" "I have seen," exclaims the bishop, "all the things I have told you, and an infinite number more." This reckless waste of life soon caused a scarcity of labour in the mines. The natives of neighbouring islands were kidnapped, and sent to share the fate of their brethren. In Jamaica, as in Hispaniola, the natives were at length completely exterminated. Caves are even now occasionally discovered full of human bones, the remains of aborigines who preferred death on the hill-side to the tender mercies of the Christians.

Esquemeling, who wrote a history of the buccaneering expeditions in which he and his lawless comrades engaged, says that he had found in these hiding-places heaps of human remains; and that, in his time, the island of Hispaniola was infested with large numbers of bloodhounds,* which ran wild in the woods.

---

* Esquemeling accounts quaintly enough for the presence of these bloodhounds. His sympathies are apparently completely with the Spaniards, and he appears hardly able to understand how the mild proceedings adopted by them failed to reduce the refractory natives to "civility." "But here the curious reader may perhaps inquire how so many wild dogs came here. The occasion was, the 'Spaniards' having possessed these isles, found them peopled with 'Indians,' a barbarous people, sensual and brutish, hating all labour, and only inclined to killing and making war against their neighbours, not out of ambition, but only because they agreed not with themselves in some common terms of language; and perceiving the dominion of the Spaniards laid great restrictions upon their lazy and brutish customs, they conceived an irreconcilable hatred against them, but especially because they saw them take possession of their kingdoms and dominions; hereupon they made against them all the resistance they could, opposing everywhere their designs to the utmost; and the Spaniards finding themselves cruelly hated by the Indians, and nowhere secure from their treacheries, resolved to extirpate and ruin them, since they could neither tame them by civility, nor conquer them with the sword. But the Indians, it being their custom to make their woods their chief places of defence, at present made these their refuge whenever they fled from the Spaniards; hereupon those first conquerours of the New World made use of dogs to range and search the

These dogs destroyed enormous quantities of cattle, and so nearly exterminated the race of wild boars, "that the hunters of that island had much ado to find any." Monsieur Ogeron, the governor of Tortuga, in 1668, sent to France for a store of poison to destroy them. "Horses were killed and empoisoned, and laid open at certain places where wild dogs used to resort: this being continued for six months there was killed an incredible number; and yet all this could not destroy the race, or scarce diminish them, their numbers appearing almost the same as before." Instinct taught the bloodhounds to hunt in packs. Esquemeling, and a French buccaneer of his acquaintance, once heard them coming through the woods, and took refuge in a tree, whence they looked on while the pack ran into a wild boar, and killed him. As soon as the boar was dead, the whole pack lay down, and waited till the hound who had first gripped the enemy had

---

intricatest thickets of woods and forests for those their implacable and unconquerable enemies; thus they forced them to leave their old refuge, and submit to the sword, seeing no milder usage would do it; hereupon they killed some of them, and quartering their bodies, placed them in the highways, that others might take warning from such a punishment; but this severity proved of ill consequence, for instead of frighting them, and reducing them to civility, they conceived such horror of the Spaniards, that they resolved to resist, and fly their sight for ever; hence the greatest part died in caves and subterraneous places of woods and mountains, in which places I myself have often seen great numbers of human bones. The Spaniards finding no more Indians to appear about the woods, turned away a great number of dogs they had in their houses, and they finding no masters to keep them, betook themselves to the woods and fields to hunt for food to preserve their lives; thus by degrees they became unacquainted with houses, and grew wild. This is the truest account I can give of the multitudes of wild dogs in these parts."—*History of the Buccaneers*, i. 25.

satisfied his hunger, before they presumed to begin their own repast.

The early establishment of the Portuguese in Brazil differed materially from the romantic expeditions of the Spaniards. Discovered by chance, its development was in a great measure left to chance. For many years it was employed only as a penal colony, where the criminal population of Portugal were landed, and left to take their chance of being eaten by the savages, or becoming chiefs among them. Rendered desperate by their situation, and hardened by crime, these men led the most turbulent and dissolute lives. The natives were at first kindly disposed towards the Portuguese. But quarrels soon arose, in which several of the convicts were killed. The Portuguese then began, in retaliation, a system of cruelty not surpassed by the atrocities of the Spaniards. They massacred old men and children in the villages, and carried off the able-bodied men as slaves. After a time, the criminal population of Brazil was joined by a large number of victims who had been condemned for heresy by the Inquisition. The new arrivals were men of industrious habits, and exemplary lives. The bad repute of Brazil began to disappear, and the success which attended honest industry attracted settlers. When the first governor-general was appointed, the country had already made considerable progress. A kind of feudal tenure was established. The country was divided into hereditary "captaincies," which were granted to grandees in Portugal who had rendered service to the crown. The captains were bound either to go to Brazil in person, or to send out colonists. They possessed complete authority, both civil and military, within the limits of their grants. Martin de Sousa received in 1531 a grant of all the region round San Vincente, extending about fifty leagues along the coast. His brother, Pedro de Sousa, had also fifty leagues in two allotments: one part, San Amaro, to the north of San Vincente; the other, Itamaraca, near Pernambuco. Joam de Barros, the historian, obtained the captaincy of Maranham. Duarte Pereira was made captain of Pernambuco. Pedro de Goes was captain of the region watered by the Rio Parnaiba. Francisco Coutinho obtained the district which lies between the river San Francisco and Bahia. Jeorge Correa had the grant of the Capitania dos Ilheos. Porto Seguro, with its regions of sea-coast, was given to Pedro Tourinha. The captaincy of Spirito Santo fell to the share of Vasco Coutinho.

No settlements were as yet formed by the crown; the governors of the various *capitanias* made war and peace with the Brazilian tribes, issued laws, or imposed taxes at pleasure. It may easily be supposed that despotic authority thus granted was grievously abused: the crown of Portugal soon found itself obliged to resume the powers it had bestowed: the feudal lords were left in possession of their lands, but a governor-general was appointed to superintend, and in some degree to circumscribe, their authority.

CHAPTER IV.

1548

The first governor-general was Thome de Souza. He arrived in the Bahia de todos los Santos in 1549: in the previous year, the Inquisition had banished the Jews from Portugal, where the honourable character they had borne in Europe procured them advances of money from the merchants with whom they had formerly transacted business. They imported sugar-canes from Madeira, and established sugar-plantations in Brazil. Up to this time, sugar had been used only as an article of medicine. It soon became an article of luxury; and the rapidly increasing demand for it greatly enriched the enterprising persons who had commenced its cultivation.

With De Sousa's arrival in Brazil commenced the first royal establishment. Within a few months, a hundred houses were built, and the erection of a cathedral was begun: batteries were traced, and a wall built round the town of San Salvador, which was thenceforward the central capital of the Brazilian provinces. All necessary supplies were imported from Portugal. Several young ladies of good birth were sent out to be given in marriage to the civil and military officers, and were handsomely dowered by the queen, who presented them with cattle, brood mares, and negroes from the crown estates. The first Brazilian bishop was appointed in 1552, and was killed by the savages shortly afterwards.

1549 The governor-general was accompanied by Father Manoel de Nobrega, a man high in estimation among the Jesuits. Nobrega was the contemporary of St. Francis Xavier, and his rival in disinterested exertions for the good of his fellow-creatures. He was soon reinforced by a considerable company of his order, who soon spread themselves over the country, and obtained a commanding influence over the natives. They instructed the children of the aborigines, who readily learnt to speak Portuguese, and whose extreme fondness for music made them eager to join in the choral services of the church. The fathers found it comparatively easy to make the natives sober, to heal feuds, to make each man content with one wife; but the task of eradicating the cannibal propensities of their neophytes was more difficult: no Brazilian could understand why the flesh of a captive taken in battle should be an unlawful banquet. The Jesuits were opposed in their efforts by priests who had already settled in the country. These men exacted fees for every clerical act; they maintained that it was lawful to enslave the Indians, and themselves joined in the slave-trade. The Jesuits performed all the offices of religion gratuitously, and laboriously and diligently devoted themselves to the task of raising both their own countrymen and the aborigines in the social scale. There will be occasion to describe the Jesuit establishments more fully when speaking of the social and political condition of Brazil: they became in after times the founders in Paraguay of one of the most remarkable republics that the world ever saw. But before that time arrived, the schism, which was then beginning in the church, was destined to convulse Europe, to wrest a large portion of it from the spiritual control of the pope, and to exercise an ever-present influence over the history of colonization. The scene of that schism lay at this time in Europe: to it, therefore, our attention must now be turned.

While the emperor, Charles V., was employed in his Turkish and Italian wars, the Protestant leaders were not idle. The obduracy of Clement with respect to the marriage of Catherine of Arragon induced the king of England to throw off his spiritual allegiance to the Roman see, and gave him an opportunity of introducing the Reformation into England. A visitatorial commission was appointed to inquire into the state of the monasteries and religious houses: so many disorders were brought to light, that their abolition was decreed, their vast revenues secularized, and Henry VIII. was declared by Parliament the head of the church on earth.

Though the English people acquiesced in the Reformation, it met neither with the enthusiastic support nor the violent opposition which it encountered elsewhere. There was a small number of zealous Catholics, and a small number of equally zealous Reformers, but the great body of the people cared far more for ease, and a quiet life, than for abstract points of doctrine. On the Continent, Protestantism was another name for personal freedom: in England, though the royal power appeared almost despotic, the liberty of the people was secure, or at least was never systematically violated. The Tudor kings held their power directly from the people; the English armies, formidable as they were to a foreign foe, could not for a moment have been depended upon if directed against the liberties of their countrymen. From the highest to the lowest they were not so much soldiers as Englishmen: they were attached by the peculiar forms of English land tenure to the soil; the association between the peasantry and the nobles was almost patriarchal in its simplicity. There were no mercenaries in the king's pay: he could take up no quarrel that was not an English quarrel, and wage no war that was not approved by his people.

The king then dared not govern but according to the laws of the realm: provided he kept within them, the people allowed him to deal as he chose with those who immediately surrounded his person. The noble who ventured into the perilous circle of the court, or entered on the game of ambition, did so at his own risk :—he staked his fortune or his head; and the people at large cared little whether he lost the one or the other. But the king who could dispose of a minister or a favourite at his pleasure was certain to repent it if he attempted to oppress a class.

The ease with which the Reformed was substituted for the Catholic religion, proves clearly that the great body of the people cared little about the question.

CHAPTER IV.

Had the matter involved the alternative of rendering homage to a true or to a false God, they might have understood it and been interested. But this was not the case: the ceremonies and forms of religion were but slightly changed; and it was not easy to induce minds, unaddicted to intellectual exercise, to feel interest in questions of abstract doctrine. When, therefore, the people were informed that the Pope of Rome had behaved unhandsomely to their king in the matter of his divorce; that a foreign sovereign claimed a right to depose their English monarch, to excommunicate him, to give his throne to another— they were willing enough to join heartily in resisting such pretensions.

Persecutions and martyrdoms were left to zealots on either side; the mass of the people went to one side or another, as they were ordered. When Henry VIII. proclaimed the Protestant faith as the established religion of the kingdom, there was no great disturbance; that faith was allowed to remain unmolested under Edward VI.: but when Mary recurred to the old religion, the body of the people felt little emotion. Under Elizabeth the Protestant form of worship was again restored; but the change caused little excitement: there were a few insignificant attempts at revolt, but they failed signally; they only served to prove that the masses looked on with perfect apathy, and cared for neither side of the controversy.

There is another reason for the indifference with which the change of religion was regarded. Cardinal Wolsey had long been preparing the way for a reform of the church, and had taught the people to expect and to acquiesce in it. It did not, however, come from the quarter whence he anticipated it, or in the manner which he intended. He was deeply attached to the church: and as he was far too clear-sighted not to perceive that some change was necessary, he determined to reform the church from within, in such a way as to sweep away abuses without endangering the fabric. As far back as the reign of Henry VII., the disorders of the clergy had been so marked as to call for the remedy afforded by an Act of Parliament.* But Henry VII. sat too insecurely on his throne to allow him to attempt a resolute reform. The statutes against the clergy remained in abeyance; and it was not until the chief power of the church was wielded by Wolsey that anything more was said upon the subject. That able prelate revived the question. Without doubt the compound of talent, honesty, and arrogance to be found in his character fitted him beyond all men to deal with it. But the temper of the times forbade disputes such as he opened to be closed again. It was not difficult to originate them; but, once started, it was beyond the power of any man, however able, to arrest their progress. Wolsey's well-meant attempts at reform stirred up a commotion which he afterwards vainly attempted to allay.

* 1 Hen. VII. c. 4. For the more sure and likely reformation of priests, clerks, and religious men, &c.

England was not the only one of the northern nations who at this time embraced the reformed doctrines. Christian II., king of Denmark, seized the crown of Sweden in 1520; and, by an imprudent act of cruelty, caused a revolution by which Sweden recovered her independence. Gustavus Vasa, who put himself at the head of the Swedish patriots, became first regent, and two years after, king. Under him, Sweden obtained an influence which she had never before enjoyed. Government, religion, finance, commerce, agriculture, received a new impetus; the assembly of the nobles was abolished, and a diet, composed of the nobility, clergy, citizens, and peasantry, was substituted in its room. The brothers, Olaus and Laurentius Petri, who were supposed to enjoy the entire confidence of Luther, were invited to preach the doctrine of the Reformation in Stockholm. The bishops and the nobility at once leagued themselves against Gustavus; the citizens and peasantry declared in his favour. A threat of abdication brought both bishops and nobles to his feet. Thenceforward he was practically absolute in the diet. The refractory prelates were punished in the way afterwards adopted in England; they were deprived of a large portion of their demesnes, which were annexed to the possessions of the crown. Their vast benefices were retrenched to an extent which rendered them powerless for aggression. They were excluded from the Senate. The ties which bound them to the court of Rome were broken, and they were compelled to ask confirmation of their appointments, not from the pope, but from the king. The Lutheran religion was thus introduced without difficulty into Sweden.

John Tausen, and others of Luther's followers, were invited to Denmark by Frederick I., the successor of Christian II. In a diet held at Oldensee (1527), the king made a public profession of his faith, and gave permission to monks and priests to marry in spite of the remonstrances which were urged by the bishops. In another diet, similar to that of Augsburg, held at Copenhagen in 1530, these articles were renewed, and the confession of faith presented by the Protestants was ratified. It was reserved for Christian III. to bring these changes to a close. The Catholic prelates had employed the time which elapsed between the death of Frederick, and the election of his successor, in strong efforts to compass the overthrow of the Protestants. The new king, desirous of annihilating the temporal power of the Catholics, planned, in conjunction with the principal nobility, the arrest of all the bishops. He then assembled the estates of the realm, abolished episcopacy, and suppressed the public exercise of the Roman Catholic religion. The castles, fortresses, and domains of the prelates were annexed to the crown. The other revenues of the clergy were appropriated to the support of ministers of the Protestant faith. of public schools, and of the poor. Monks and nuns were left at liberty either to quit their convents or to remain there during their lives. The revolution then set on foot extended to Norway, which had just been annexed by Denmark and declared a province of that kingdom.

It has been mentioned that as soon as Charles's attention was engaged with Solyman, Francis took advantage of his rival's absence to attack the imperial dominions. The struggle thus begun, occupied the exclusive attention of both princes. For a time the Protestant princes were not drawn into the dispute; but about the year 1544, events assumed a complexion which left them no choice but to engage in it. At the Diet of Spire, Charles made such large concessions, that he induced the Protestant princes to join him in his meditated attack on Francis; he gained the elector of Saxony and the landgrave of Hesse to his side; he persuaded the English king to march upon Paris, and himself took the field at the head of a large army. Before long, while Henry was still engaged in besieging Boulogne, Charles had found reason to believe that an alliance was in contemplation between Francis and the pope, which would have the effect of endangering his Italian dominions. Without consulting his allies, he hastened to sign a peace with Francis at Crespy. A secret article of this treaty bound the two monarchs to extirpate heresy from their dominions.

The year 1545 was spent in negotiations which the Protestants could not but mistrust. The Lutherans were persecuted with unrelenting rigour in the hereditary dominions of the emperor, who, at the same time, sent ambassadors to Constantinople, to make such terms with the porte as would prevent any danger or interruption from that quarter. The Protestants were not slow in perceiving and rightly interpreting these signs of the times. The peace between the emperor and the French king was not of long duration.

At the treaty of Crespy, the emperor had agreed to give his brother Ferdinand's daughter in marriage to the Duke of Orleans, Francis' second son, and to put Francis in possession of Milan, as a dower. But at the moment when the marriage was to take place, the duke died, and the emperor, who already began to regret the concessions he had made, peremptorily refused the request of Francis to remodel the treaty of Crespy in such a manner as to prevent him from suffering territorially by his son's death. About the same time an event occurred which threatened to embroil the emperor with the pope as well as with Francis. Pope Paul, who was always ready to aggrandise his family, bestowed upon a member of it the investiture of Parma and Placentia. Europe was at that moment in a state of indignation against the exorbitant power and ambition of ecclesiastics; and it was generally thought that the illegitimate birth of Peter Lewis was a matter of which the pope ought rather to be ashamed than thrust the fact so prominently before the world. The emperor insisted that both Parma and Piacenza belonged to the Milanese, and his ambassador refused pointedly to be present at the ceremony of infeoffment.

The confederates of Smalcalde naturally enough concluded that these two causes would involve the emperor in quarrels of sufficient importance to compel him to let them alone. But the extirpation of heresy was a matter of greater importance in the eyes both of the pope and the emperor than the investiture of two insignificant duchies. A council assembled at Trent; and the tone of its deliberations, as well as the preparations made by the emperor in the Low Countries, gave the confederates to understand that a strong confederacy was being assembled against them by the Roman Catholic powers.

By 1547 Charles had broken up the league of Smalcalde. He captured John Frederick, elector of Saxony, and the landgrave of Hesse, and compelled the rest to retire to their homes. Henry VIII. and Francis I., the kings of England and of France, died while the army of the confederates was still in the field. Charles selected Duke Maurice, a younger branch of the family of Saxony, as the successor of the elector, and invested him at Augsburg in 1548. The emperor was now at the summit of his power. He had grown old in the arts of government. Henry, Francis—all the rivals of his youth and early manhood—were dead. He had none but young and inexperienced monarchs to contend with. A minor sat on the throne of England. Henry II., who succeeded to the crown of France, was as far inferior to his father in intellect as in courage. His reign, a preface to the dreary wars of religion which devastated France, was disastrous for his people. Francis had at one time been anxious to induce Pope Clement VII. to join him in one of his wars with Charles. To cement the alliance, he had caused Henry, then a boy of fifteen, to marry Catherine de Medicis, a great-niece of the sovereign pontiff. Catherine was at the time of her marriage a year younger than her husband. Who that reads the history of these times remembers without horror her falseness, her cruelty, her systematic and calculated vileness? Yet the disgust with which historians record her character is as nothing compared to the loathing with which her husband himself regarded her. The tainted vitality which she inherited was transmitted to her children. Francis II. died at eighteen of a broken constitution; Charles IX. was the furious madman of St. Bartholomew; Henry III. was miserable, effete, enervated. Hated by her husband, Catherine was only kept upon the throne by acting with complete subservience to Diana of Poictiers, whose humble servant she consented to become.

No persecution of the Protestants took place during the reign of Henry II. When not occupied in frivolous amusement under the eye of his mistress, he was engaged in wars with the emperor, pursued with little vigour and leading to small results.

It was singular that the first blow to Charles's power should come to him from one whom he himself had promoted. In 1552, Maurice of Saxony concluded a secret treaty with Henry II., and advanced with such rapidity that he nearly surprised him at Innspruck. The credulous security of Charles V., during the time when Maurice was maturing his schemes, has puzzled historians. But up to the moment of declaring hostilities, Maurice was loud in his professions of attachment to the emperor. Granvelle, the prime minister, held the talents of the German princes in contempt; and often boasted that a drunken German was incapable of forming any schemes which he could not easily penetrate. The Duke of Alva alone found room for some hesitation; but it was not till the elector's schemes were ready for execution, that they were discovered.

Moreover, Charles had failed in the previous year in getting his son Philip named to the succession of the king of the Romans. Chagrin, and frequent fits of the gout, had almost paralyzed his bodily vigour: disappointment and bodily pain blunted his mental acuteness. Maurice marched with the utmost rapidity into Upper Germany. The towns opened their gates to him; the magistrates whom the emperor had deposed were reinstated; the Protestant divines preached once again in the churches whence they had been driven. The imperial garrison of Augsburg retired, and gave up the city to the elector. The castle of Ehrenburg, which commanded the only pass through the mountain, surrendered in panic. Leaving his cavalry to protect the mouth of the pass, Maurice hurried forward to capture the emperor, who was lying in indolent security at Innspruck, within two days' march of his victorious foe.

Nothing could exceed the astonishment and dismay of Charles when he heard that Maurice was at hand. He was unprovided for defence. His treasury was exhausted; the Cortes were not to be persuaded into advancing any more money; the usual consignments of treasure had not for a long time come to hand from America. Nothing remained but flight —flight by torchlight, in the midst of a fit of the gout, with his courtiers around him, some on foot and some on such horses as they could hastily procure. If it had not been for the mutiny of a regiment of Maurice's mercenaries, which delayed his advance for a few hours, the emperor, instead of pattering painfully through the rain in his litter, and getting half dead with pain and fright, over the Alps to Villach in Carnithia, would have been captured in his palace. Conditions of peace were at length agreed to at Passau in 1552. The principal articles of the treaty provided for the absolute security of the Protestant churches. It was agreed that a general council should assemble to draw up the articles of a permanent peace between the states of both religions.

This diet did not assemble till 1555; but a definitive peace was concluded in that year at Augsburg. It was agreed that both Catholic and Protestant states should enjoy a perfect liberty of worship, and that no reunion should ever be attempted by other than amicable means. The secularizing of the ecclesiastical revenues, which had been introduced into the states of most of the Protestant princes, was ratified; but one of the articles provided that every prelate or churchman who renounced his ancient faith to embrace the Confession of Augsburg should lose his benefice. This latter clause, known as the Ecclesiastical Reserve, did not pass without determined opposition.

1553   Charles was somewhat consoled for his miscarriage at Innspruck, when in the following year his son Philip, the infante of Spain, married Mary queen of England; but he adhered to a determination, which he had long been maturing, to abdicate his dominions in favour of his son. From the time of his accession he had devoted himself to the increase of his power. His authority and his position were both very different to what they had been at the commencement of his reign. His son Philip, who succeeded to his hereditary dominions, possessed at his accession Spain, the Netherlands on both sides of the Rhine, Franche Comté, Rousillon, the Milanese, and the two Sicilies. His influence was paramount in the smaller states of Italy. The imperial crown went to Ferdinand. Philip was, however, notwithstanding his disappointment with regard to the empire, the most powerful monarch of the time. Besides his European dominions, he possessed in America the empires of

Peru and Mexico, New Spain and Chili, besides Hispaniola, Cuba, and many other of the American islands. The gold mines of Chili, Mexico, and Potosi brought him in more wealth than was possessed by any other prince in Europe. His fleet was larger than that of any European power. His troops were better disciplined, and more accustomed to war and victory. They were commanded by the most experienced generals of the age. His intellect was not equal to that of his father; but he was industrious and tenacious of purpose in a surprising degree. His manners were haughty and disagreeable: even when he wished to please he was unable to appear gracious. When he first married Mary of England he would in all probability have obtained the power as well as the name of king, if his temper and manner had been such as to conciliate affection. But he kept the proud nobles of England standing uncovered before him without noticing them. Whenever he dared he surrounded himself with Spaniards. He was as unpopular in the Netherlands as his father had been in Spain. It was only in Spain itself that he ever obtained anything like regard or affection.

While the power of the king of Spain had thus increased, the other nations of Europe had diminished in importance. Whatever the faults of Henry VIII. might be, and they were not a few, he was a good Englishman, and a sturdy champion of the rights of England. He allowed no one to outrage her but himself. His successor, Mary, weak and unpopular, lost for England much of the importance which for the last fifty years she had enjoyed in Europe. At the beginning of the century, Henry had held the balance between the ambition of Francis and of Charles. Under Mary, commerce was neglected and oppressed. The troops of England were undisciplined and unused to war. Her navy languished.

Portugal, Denmark, and Sweden were in no condition to take any decided part in affairs. The pope, shut up between the duchy of Milan and the kingdom of Naples, was absolutely dependent upon Spain. France alone was able to cope with her. Henry II. was not either so warlike or of so pre-eminent a genius as Francis, but his military defects were counterbalanced by the crowd of distinguished generals who surrounded him. The situation of France was in her favour. She was not equal in extent to Spain; but her possessions were not scattered as were those of Philip, and the whole extent of her territories cut off both the Netherlands and the Italian possessions of Philip from Spain. The spirit of the French nation was essentially warlike. They had been long accustomed to war; and the chivalry which in feudal times had kept them in constant hot water, now served to animate them for united service to their country.

Philip endeavoured by every means in his power to enlist the English nation in his quarrels with

France. They looked upon his encroachment with suspicion, and himself with dislike. They steadily avoided any concession which, according to their ideas, contributed in any way to the aggrandisement of the Spanish power. Nevertheless, Mary so far prevailed as to succeed in raising 10,000 men under Lord Pembroke, whom she sent into the Low Countries to co-operate with Philip. Pembroke assisted the Duke of Savoy to take St. Quentin; but the Duke of Guise soon revenged the part taken by the English by laying siege to Calais, which had long remained in the hands of the English.

Mary died in 1558. Charles V. had died in retirement a few months before. Paul IV. ended his violent and imperious career within a twelvemonth, and Henry II. was killed in a tournament within a few weeks of the death of the pope.

The principal personages thus withdrew together. They left the stage to other actors and different passions. But the events of the last fifty years in which they had borne so conspicuous a part, had produced an ineffaceable effect on the history of the world.

CHAPTER V.

WARS OF RELIGION.

[1558—1570.]

Religious Quarrels complicated with Politics—Champions of the Catholics and of the Protestants—The Dutch—French Civil Wars.

CHAPTER V.

1558

QUEEN ELIZABETH came to the throne of England amidst the acclamations of her people. In the times of her predecessors, the landmarks between Protestantism and Catholicism had been gradually fixed. Each had enjoyed its turn of supremacy, and the dominant sect was always a persecuting sect. Each had its martyrs, each its colonies. But at length religious dissensions became complicated with disputes purely secular, and political ambition assumed the disguise of zeal for orthodoxy or for liberty of conscience.

The new force, of which Luther and Zuingle, Calvin and Melancthon, were at once the creatures and the exponents, was gradually measuring itself with the *vis inertiæ* of inaction. It ceased to be tentative in its character or uncertain in its aims. It assumed definite and even formidable proportions. It had emerged from insignificance, and was no longer either to be coerced or ignored. Sometimes it obtained the upper hand, then it persecuted its opponents. Sometimes it was forced to succumb to superior force, then it suffered persecution. But the struggle was always for the mastery, no longer for mere existence.

The events referred to in the last chapter settled the geographical boundaries of the reformed religion, pretty nearly as they have since remained. But even where the Reformation was rejected, it exercised great influence on the minds of men. Even in France, in Catholic Switzerland, and in Southern Germany, the Church of Rome had assumed a milder and more liberal character. In many parts of Europe it had been entirely successful. Denmark, Sweden, England, Scotland, and a great part of Germany, had thrown off their allegiance to the pope.

But though religion governed the alliances and decided the policy of Europe during the stormy century which succeeded, the issue was by no means exclusively religious. In the wars of Francis I., of Henry II., of Henry IV., and of Richelieu, it cannot be said that France was contending for Christian truth or civil freedom : she fought against external aggression ; she aimed at the humiliation of a rival. Austria and Spain, governed by sovereigns closely connected by blood, and in strict alliance with each other, were not only the representatives of certain religious opinions, but nations seeking territorial extension. It is true that the triumph of their principles was involved in their conquests, and that the fanaticism of Philip was not less real than his insatiable ambition; but the Holy League was only the war-horse that it pleased him to bestride in his fight for universal dominion: gloomy, cruel, gifted with dogged obstinacy, he strove not only for ascendency over material Europe, but over the thoughts of men. He could not bear that any should differ with him even in thought. Wherever opposition was offered to his opinion, or to his darling dream of absolutism, he retaliated with the rack, the wheel, the faggot, or the poison cup, even if his own son were the victim.

In the long religious wars, Spain and Austria espoused the cause of the Catholics; England and the Low Countries that of the Reformation. France, divided against itself, was prevented, during many years, from engaging in any other quarrels than her own. The contest eventually narrowed itself into a duel between England and Spain.

Philip, who had long anticipated the death of his wife, greeted Elizabeth on her accession to the throne with proposals of marriage. Her evasive, but not altogether unfavourable, reply gave him sufficient encouragement to induce him to hope, and to throw his influence in the scale to obtain advantageous terms for her at the general pacification of Château Cambresis. His friendly zeal declined in proportion as the vigour of Elizabeth's measures in favour of the Protestants increased. The treaty of peace was signed between France and England, at the same time as that between France and Spain; but from thenceforth deadly enmity took root in Philip's heart. He hated Elizabeth; he hated the Protestants. He had hoped to make liberty of thought in England quail before the tortures of the Inquisition. He had once nearly attained the crown of these realms, and a hope now arose in his mind that what he could not obtain by marriage he might conquer by force. During the rest of his life he clung to the idea with characteristic tenacity. He brought the vast resources of his kingdom to bear upon his design: for it Alva toiled, and Alexander Farnese exercised his extraordinary talents and not less extraordinary duplicity. For it he threw away one armada after another. Every weapon, threat, cajolery, force were exhausted in his vain attempt to seize the sceptre which ever eluded his grasp. The principal theatre of action was that part of the Spanish dominions which had belonged, in ancient times, to the crown of Lorraine. The Dukes of Burgundy had handed them over to the house of Austria. They thus came into the hands of Charles V. as an appanage of the German empire. He annexed them to the Spanish crown, 1519 and added Friesland, Groningen, and Gueldres to the estates to which he succeeded in Burgundy. The Low Countries at Philip's accession thus consisted of seventeen provinces. The treaty of Augsburg recognized their position as independent sovereignties. Keenly tenacious of their liberties, the states long and successfully resisted aggression. Charles had

CHAPTER V.

[1558—1570.

often been tempted to violate their privileges under pressure of pecuniary difficulties. The Netherlanders tried his temper as a good Catholic by their early adhesion to the Reformation. But he was a Fleming by birth, and he always retained an affection for the people among whom his earliest years were spent. It was reserved for Philip deliberately to invade their liberties, and to turn his enormous power to the subversion of their constitution.

The political condition of the Netherlands at the time of Philip's accession was the same as had existed from the fall of the Roman empire. The feudal system of the middle ages had coexisted with rude municipal institutions. The territorial aristocracy, the clergy, and the municipalities all possessed political power. Although the power of the people was not distinctly recognized, the municipal officers had common interests with the industrious citizens from among whom their ranks were recruited. Philip founded tyranny on maxims of policy and religion. Almost the first act of his reign was to order the extirpation of heresy in his American as well as in his European dominions.

The struggle that ensued exhibited the Church of Rome in a position which she had not before assumed, though she had long been tending towards it. In the middle ages, the Roman hierarchy had been revered as the protector of the poor. The church was the sole stepping-stone by which a person in the humbler ranks of life, however great his talents, could arrive at eminence. It was by her alone that men like Stephen Langton and Wolsey could hope to rise. All avenues of distinction—the court, the senate, and the higher ranks of the army —were closed against those who were not nobly born. The church alone opened her arms to the plebeian; and while her cardinals and other dignitaries held a place, at least of equality, with the noblest, they never forgot the order from which their strength was principally recruited. A strongly democratic spirit animated them, and kept them in a state of perpetual antagonism with the secular powers, whose cruelties against the weak and defenceless they were willing and able to curb.

But the church had gradually established a tyranny of its own. It asserted a spiritual absolutism which struck at the root of individual independence. The secular authority had also in many nations become a despotism intolerant of interference, and unwilling to submit its administration to discussion. The Reformation was the assertion of the right of free thought. The right of free action is a necessary corollary. Both despotisms, the spiritual and the temporal, were attacked at their very roots. The result was a political necessity—a close union between the monarchy and the priesthood.

Many thousand persons had been destroyed in the Netherlands by the orders of Charles. But cruel as he was, he had not pushed his tyranny so far as it was afterwards carried by his son. In his time the

CHAPTER V.

governors of the different towns had gradually allowed the penal laws agains Protestants to fall into desuetude. They saw no end to the desolation which their instructions, literally followed, would cause. Some, too, among themselves were inclined to the reformed religion. Persecutions had begun to depopulate the country. Many industrious traders had fled to the neighbouring states; and the representations of Margaret, queen-dowager of Hungary, viceroy of the Netherlands, had not been without effect. Charles was always happiest when in the land of his birth. In manner and feelings he resembled his own countrymen more than the stern and formal grandees of Spain. But Philip, educated in Spain, accustomed to the rigid etiquette of Madrid, speaking no language but Spanish, had small sympathy with the turbulent freedom of the Flemish burghers, and was rather disposed to resent than to encourage their familiarity. Charles had humoured the Flemings, and they had repaid him by affection. Philip determined to put them down with a high hand, and to crush their spirit to the dead level of the other kingdoms which he ruled with despotic sway.

He renewed the edicts against the Protestants. As an earnest of his sincerity, he threw his father's confessor into prison. He was hardly restrained from pronouncing a sentence of heresy against his father's memory. But the feeling of the Flemings at these evidences of their king's intolerance was as nothing compared to the horror with which they beheld the hated Inquisition established in their country. The foreign merchants who came to reside in the Netherlands; the Swiss and German troops whom both Charles and Philip had employed in their wars against France; and, lastly, the English, French, and German Protestants who had fled from persecution in their native countries, had diffused the reformed religion into every corner of the Netherlands. Philip's decrees were therefore directed against a very large portion, if not an actual majority of his Low-Country subjects. The penal laws ordained that whosoever should be convicted of having taught heretical doctrines, or of having been present at religious meetings of heretics, should, if they were men, be put to death by the sword; or, if women, be buried alive. Even recantation could not save persons once tainted with heresy from their fate. Tortures and the flames were the lot of any who had the daring to persist in their opinions.

Even in Spain and Italy the Inquisition had at first excited dread and indignation among the most attached to the Catholic church. The horror of the Flemings at the new tribunal may therefore be easily imagined. It struck at the root of their prosperity. Their main dependence was upon commerce; how could they expect the foreign merchants, most of them Protestants, who lived among them, to remain in a country where the exercise of their religion was forbidden, and their lives were at the mercy of the first informer who owed them a grudge?

On Philip's departure to assume the crown of Spain, the states eagerly watched the choice of a regent which he was about to make. Margaret, duchess of Parma, was eventually selected; and had the conduct of affairs been left to her good sense and kindly temper, the affections of the Flemings would not have been alienated. She, however, only governed in name: the real authority was in the hands of the severe and haughty Granvelle. The duchess soon found that she had undertaken an impossible task. Granvelle possessed all the power, while she incurred the odium of the violent measures which Philip's orders compelled her to adopt. Every day new assaults were made upon the liberties of the Flemings. The nobles, the gentry, and the populace alike clamoured for redress, which Philip haughtily refused.

But while discontent was thus smouldering in the Netherlands, the first war of religion broke out in France. Henry II. was followed by three sons in succession, each one more feeble and incapable than the last. Under them France was peculiarly exposed to the danger of internal feuds. Francis II., Charles IX., and Henry III., were each in turn under the control of their mother, and through her of the Dukes of Guise. These able princes were cadets of the family of Lorraine, a house *parvenu* and poor, aliens in France, and greedy, as younger sons of poor monarchs often are. They had long remained in obscurity: disliked by Francis I., they had thrown themselves into the hands of Diana of Poictiers; had made themselves her instruments for crushing the Duchesse d'Estampes; had performed for Henry before his accession many services which a prince in those days required, but which a king is not anxious to remember. Diana of Poictiers could not afford to lose friends: under the strange conditions of alliance in which she lived with Catherine of Medicis, the friends of the mistress were the friends of the wife; so Catherine and the Guises were close allies. During the reign of Francis I., Guise had married a sister to James V. of Scotland. James died; his widow became regent for her little daughter Mary. The Guises, who were absolute with their sister, married their niece Mary Stuart to the dauphin.* The brothers were twelve in number—gentlemen bold, resolute, with fortunes to make. They showed spirit. They had that quality which Mazarin always preferred in a general to any other,—good luck. Francis, the eldest, was an excellent bulldog—executed well any commissions in the way of fighting wherewith he might be charged—took Metz and Calais in an offhand, masterly manner. The brothers hung together. In the then disorderly state of France, an united party of twelve, with long heads and strong arms, were not to be despised at the time when the family of Guise was rising into power.

Protestantism in France was in danger of its very

* Afterwards Francis II.

CHAPTER existence. The reformers of other lands were at
V. least a recognized body. The German Protestants
had conquered a peace; toleration was secured to
them by treaty. Catholic Mary was dead in England; Protestant Elizabeth had her Calvinists under
the wing of royalty. In none of these countries
was there any immediate danger. It was evident
that persecution was in store for the whole Protestant world; but in no country was united action more
necessary than in France. The first move of the
1559 reformers was unfortunate: on the death of Henry II.,
Anthony, King of Navarre, and Louis, Prince of
Condé, his brother, who naturally enough looked upon
the Guises as aliens and interlopers, enlisted the
leaders of the Calvinists in their cause. As a natural consequence the leadership of the Catholics fell
to the Guises. The whole power of the kingdom
thus passed into the hands of Francis, Duke of Guise,
and of the Cardinal of Lorraine, the two uncles of the
queen regent.

If France was ruled by the Guises, they, in their
turn, were ruled by Spain. The gold of Philip,
however scarce it was for the immediate necessities
of his kingdom, was always ready for any cause
which promised the extension of the ancient faith, or
the extirpation of heresy. The appearance of wealth
produced by this ready liberality, added not a little to
the terror of his name. Had it been possible for
the politicians of 1559 to see the real state of the
King of Spain—his impotence for aggression, the

utter ruin of the finances of his kingdom—could they have read Granvelle's letters, in which he trusted that "The (French) machine would not yet go to pieces, till Spain was ready to profit by the scramble which would ensue,"* they would not have allowed Philip, by the mere terror of his name, to domineer over Europe. They did not know that the abdication of Charles V. had taken place in a hall hung with black for the death of Juana, Charles's mother, because money was so scarce that the black hangings were retained out of economy.† They did not know that in 1561, the king's courier was delayed on his journey to Rome for want of funds till Granvelle lent him money from his private purse. They had not seen the letter from Philip to Granvelle, in which Philip, conjuring Granvelle to raise him even a little money from the Netherlands, unfolded his dismal state of despair :—" For this year the expenses are ten millions, the receipts one million—nine millions of deficit."

The army of Philip was mutinous; its pay was far in arrear. The garrisons which held the frontier towns must have been disbanded if a little money had not opportunely come to hand from the Indies. The king was in daily fear that his troops would go over to France. Even the wages of his personal servants were unpaid.

Yet, amid all this poverty, what was the secret which made Spain so terrible? The answer is in one word—Unity. Other nations were divided against

* Granvelle to Philip II.   † Michelet.

themselves. England had its Catholic party, its Protestant party, its very large party of neutrals. France had her Huguenots and her Leaguers. Holland her obedient and her disobedient provinces. Spain alone was united :—she had burned up all her Jews; all her heretics. Her terrible Inquisition had made so clean a sweep, that to avoid persecution every one had become a persecutor—no one was left now to destroy. The Guises waited but for Philip's signal to begin the prearranged drama of persecution.

The Protestants demanded a conference. The Guises turned their demand into a trap to catch them. The conference was granted. The doctrines which they advanced were declared blasphemous. Spain and Rome sent embassies to protest against the scandal offered to religion. Philip gravely offered his assistance to the outraged faith. Many historians have spoken of this conference and its results as an evil brought upon themselves by the Protestants. They have believed that the clergy accepted unwillingly the demand of the Protestants, not seeing that in its minutest details it was a stratagem organized by Philip and his men. The meeting of Protestants for worship was forbidden : soon afterwards followed the massacre of Vassy. Coligny, Condé, Andelot, found it impossible longer to postpone an appeal to arms.

France, on the threshold of the civil wars that so distracted her, little thought whither events were hurrying. Neither Catherine nor Guise, Condé nor

Navarre, were more than puppets of circumstances. Neither of them read clearly the signs of their stirring time. One man alone—true Frenchman, true hero—stands in intellect and intelligence far above the crowd—Coligny. A mournful, grave man, far-seeing when no one else could see for the dangers and difficulties around him. One moment only before the first blow of the civil war was struck, he hesitated, shuddering at the vast misery which he foresaw. That moment past, he went straight and fearless on his path. A man of battles, he yet hated war. Victory did not exalt, nor defeat depress him. He, first of his countrymen, saw that the necessity of the age demanded external development, and devoted considerable attention to colonization.

Condé, the nominal chief of the party, was a much less noble character.

This "petit galant," as Guise calls him, on account of his diminutive stature and amatory disposition—this prince in miniature, was the pet and the destruction of his party.

> " Ce petit homme tant joli,
> Qui toutjours chante, toutjours rit
> Et toutjours baise sa mignonne,
> Dieu garde de mal le petit homme."

So sings a contemporary ballad. The heart of Condé was always with the luxury and easy virtue of Catherine's court. Brave as a tiger, he liked the fighting, but not the strict manners and opinions of the Huguenot camp. True, the strict morals did not last long. For the first few months the camp was like a convent — no oaths, no gambling, no debauchery. But after the armistice at Bauce this was all changed; sack and pillage characterized both armies alike.

With hesitation, under the pressure of stern necessity, the Protestants accepted the quarrel thrust upon them. The massacres of Vassy and Sens showed them that it was time for every Protestant to arm for hearth and home. Tours, Blois, Angers, were the first to rise. Then followed Normandy, Rouen, Dieppe, Caen, Poictiers. Half Languedoc, and many of the towns of Guienne and Gascony, had declared themselves for the Protestants before the year was out. Provence remained Catholic; Dauphiné armed for the Huguenots.

It may be left to the historian of these wars to describe the barbarity with which they were conducted. The Spaniards whom Philip sent to help distinguished themselves pre-eminently by their cruelty.

Coligny, patriot as well as Protestant, had till the last moment refused his consent to any application for foreign aid. But his army now saw their homes desolated, their wives and children outraged: they were obliged to return to defend each man his own homestead: he could resist no longer. Dandelot went into Germany, and another messenger into England to entreat for help. While these negotiations were in progress, Coligny held Orleans with the nucleus of an army. Outside its walls a frightful guerilla warfare of reprisals—cruelty for cruelty, not a pin to choose on either side.

Why linger on the details of the first campaign? One can but tell of opportunities lost by Condé, dupe and tool of the Lais of the Medicis, in her turn the willing puppet of Guise. The English succours lay at Havre; Condé, attempting to make his junction with them, was overtaken at Dreux, by Montmorency, constable of France. The heavy infantry of Spain, entrenched, according to their fashion, behind their baggage-waggons, secured the victory for the Catholics. Montmorency, however, remained in the hands of the Protestants. Condé was taken by the Catholics. Soon after Guise fell under the pistol of Poltrot.

The Huguenots thus gained two steps in advance. Guise was dead, and Coligny took the command of the army in name as well as in reality, *vice* Condé captured. Captured indeed in two ways—prisoner of war, and over head and ears in love with one of Catherine's well-disciplined maids of honour.

The power of the Guise family was never more firmly rooted than after the death of Francis II. The Cardinals of Guise and Lorraine held between them fifteen of the richest bishoprics in France. Joinville was Grand Master of the King's Household; Aumale Grand Huntsman; Elbœuf, General of the Galleys. The Minister of Finance was one of their creatures. The governments of Champagne and Burgundy were in their hands, and with them the command of the

1561

military roads into Lorraine and Germany. Henry, the son of the murdered duke, was but thirteen years of age; but he inherited, if not the genius at least the courage and the subtlety of his father. Till he could act for himself he was in safe hands. His uncles were quite capable of guiding him.

While Coligny was overrunning Normandy with his Germans, Condé, at the dictation of Catherine, signed a miserable peace. Such a document, dated from the enemy's camp, and signed by a chief who at the moment of signature was in that enemy's hands, was of course not worth the parchment on which it was written. Still the great soul of Coligny might well revolt at this twirl of the little political weathercock. He did not, indeed, repudiate the engagement entered into by his nominal chief, but he gave it no sanction. He was content to hold proudly aloof, and bide his time. "Le petit homme tant joli" forgot in his treaty to do anything for his late ally, Elizabeth. The Queen of England was not of a temper to be thus forgotten, and refused to surrender the cautionary towns. A campaign followed, in no way remarkable except in so far as it exhibited the nominal leader of the Protestants in the character of the humble servant of Catherine de Medicis.

Coligny had long foreseen the possibility of the utter rout and destruction of the Huguenots. Like a wise general, he determined to secure his retreat. Before the death of Henry II., he had sent an unfortunate expedition to Brazil. Now while yet his army lay shut up in Orleans, and the blood of the martyrs of Vassy and Sens was scarcely dry, he determined to found a Protestant colony in Florida. Thither, if the fortune of war should prove adverse, he intended to withdraw, to end his days away from the civil broils which rent his country.

The Brazilian voyage had been conducted by Nicolas de Villegagnon, a native of Provence and Knight of Malta. This adventurer was a brave and skilful seaman. He had been intrusted with the task of conveying Mary, the young Queen of Scots, into France, and had eluded the English cruisers by a bold and successful manœuvre. He had shown courage on many occasions, and was possessed of considerable learning. In an evil hour Coligny was induced to confide in him. Villegagnon had previously made a voyage to Brazil, and chosen a spot for a settlement; at Coligny's request, a vessel of two hundred tons and a store ship were fitted out by Henry II. A company was raised, composed of artificers, soldiers, and a considerable number of noble Huguenot adventurers. They had scarcely started, when a storm arose, so severe as to compel Villegagnon's ship to put into Dieppe. A large number of his noble adventurers, besides some of the soldiers and artificers, had already seen quite enough of naval adventure, and deserted as soon as they got into harbour. After a tedious voyage, Villegagnon arrived at Rio de Janeiro. The natives of this place had long traded with the French, and were

CHAPTER V.

on bad terms with the Portuguese ; Villegagnon was therefore permitted to land, and to establish himself on a great rock which stands in the centre of the harbour. His force consisted but of eighty men : but Villegagnon, with characteristic arrogance, formally took possession of the whole continent of South America for the King of France, and named it " La France Antarticque." He at once sent off tidings of his arrival to Coligny, and demanded reinforcements—amongst others, " some good theologians from Geneva."*

Coligny at once busied himself in providing for the wants, ghostly and bodily, of his colony. Calvin and his elders in convocation appointed Pierre Richier and Guillaume Chartier to this mission. Many respectable adventurers of the Huguenot persuasion were induced to accompany the ministers. Three ships were fitted out at the expense of the crown ; the command was given to Bois le Comte, a nephew of Villegagnon, who arrived safely in Brazil, having plundered every ship he met with on the way, whether they belonged to friend or foe. Villegagnon had now gained all that he could from Coligny, and considered it now time to throw off the mask and avow himself a friend of Guise. The Huguenots who had sought refuge from persecution in Antarctic France found themselves worse off than ever ; they demanded and obtained permission to return to France. Had it not been for this stupid treachery on the part of Villegagnon, the

* Southey's History of Brazil.

settlement at Rio de Janeiro would doubtless have been at this day the capital of a French colony, for a large body of industrious Flemings were only waiting for the report of the captain who carried back the Huguenots, to start for Brazil, and "ten thousand Frenchmen would have emigrated, if the object of Coligny in founding his colony had not been thus wickedly betrayed."* The Portuguese, jealous of their monopoly of the Brazilian trade, were accustomed to treat all interlopers as pirates; yet they permitted Villegagnon's settlement to remain for four years unmolested. The Court of Lisbon was nevertheless well aware of the danger, and at length ordered Mem de Sa, governor of Brazil, to attack and expel the French. The Portuguese commander arrived at Rio de Janeiro in the beginning of 1560. A desperate engagement ensued, in which the Portuguese carried, first the outworks which commanded the landing, and afterwards the rock in which the French had excavated their magazine. The besieged were so intimidated that they took refuge in their ships, and witnessed the total destruction of their stores and the demolition of their fort.

Coligny determined not again to confide in one who might repeat the treachery of Villegagnon. He selected for the command of his Florida expedition a Huguenot who had been proved faithful in many scenes of trial.

* Southey, Hist. Brazil, i. 278.

Dieppe, it has been already said, was in his hands. There he fitted out a small squadron, which he placed under the command of Jean de Ribault. Many of the Huguenot nobility accompanied the adventure, as well as a small number of veteran troops. Land was first made in the latitude of St. Augustine. The St. John's river—the San Matteo of the Spaniards—was discovered and called the River of May. The ships sailed along the coast, naming as they went the various rivers that they passed after the streams of France. America for a time had its Loire, its Rhone, and its Garonne.* They came upon the entrance of Port Royal harbour, which appeared to be the entrance of some magnificent river. Here a monumental stone was raised, engraved with the arms of France. Ribault determined to leave a settlement. Twenty-six persons were put ashore, and the leader sailed away to obtain supplies and reinforcements.

When he returned to France the Protestants in Europe were in great distress, and the promised reinforcements were not levied. The colony became insubordinate; Ribault's governor was killed in a mutiny, and the company, after incredible sufferings, managed to build a small vessel and return to France. As soon as the peace of 1562 gave Coligny a moment's breathing space, he bethought him of his American expedition. Laudonnière, who in the former voyage had been upon the Florida coast, was appointed to the command of three ships. Emigrants crowded to his

* Bancroft, i. 48.

standard. They already pictured to themselves a career of conquest, and a rich spoil which should rival the Spaniards in Mexico and Peru. This time the harbour of Port Royal was avoided, and the emigrants landed on the shores of the river May. The colonists, though gathered under the standard of religion, were a collection of scoundrels of the deepest dye. As soon as Laudonnière had withdrawn, they equipped two vessels and began a career of piracy.

Meanwhile, Philip had heard from Guise, or one of his creatures at the court of France, that the Huguenots had formed a colony in Florida. Spain had often tried to occupy that country, but had invariably failed. Large numbers of her soldiers had perished there. To allow a settlement there was to allow an encroachment on the commercial monopoly of Spain—to abandon some of her dominions to France. Worse than all, it would be to allow Calvinism to be planted over against her Catholic dominions.

Don Pedro Melendez de Aviles was commissioned to destroy the new settlement. He was named hereditary governor of a territory of great extent. Various commercial immunities were granted to him. He was to receive a salary of 25,000 ducats and a fifteenth of all royal perquisites. Melendez, on his part, was to invade Florida at his own cost with at least five hundred men, to introduce ecclesiastics, Jesuits, married men, and domestic animals. The enthusiasm of fanaticism was soon kindled; large numbers of adventurers offered themselves. Melendez landed on the coast and surprised the French garrison in their fort. Soldiers, women, children, the aged and the sick, were massacred alike. The number killed was estimated at nine hundred. The Spanish accounts give a smaller amount of slain, but do not deny the deed. Melendez put up an inscription on the place of the massacre, stating that the victims were slain, not as Frenchmen, but as Lutherans and enemies of God.

The court of France demanded no reparation for this outrage. But just after the battle of St. Denis a bold Huguenot of Gascony, Dominic de Gourgues, who had once been a slave in the Spanish galleys, and who had sworn undying revenge against them, equipped an expedition at his own charge, and murdered every soul among the Spaniards. He hanged his prisoners upon trees on the site of de Ribault's Fort, with an inscription over their heads, " I do not this as unto Spaniards and mariners, but as unto traitors, robbers, and murderers." So ended the first Huguenot colony of France.

Meanwhile in France, the wiles of Catherine had amply succeeded. Condé had succumbed to the arts which Catherine had found successful against King Anthony of Navarre, and which for a time were equally successful against his son. Condé had managed to estrange his friends, to displease Elizabeth, to divide the Protestant party : indeed, as a party, they almost seemed to be annihilated : their nominal chief was acting as honorary secretary to the queen-mother. He wrote and spoke at her dictation. He assured the German princes that all was going well.

The Protestants thus isolated from England were everywhere insulted with impunity. They languished under the shadow of peace, as more fortunate people languish under the shadow of war. Peace was death to them unless it were one gained at the sword's point.

Soon, a still worse apprehension than any that had yet existed came across them. Alva and Elizabeth, councillor and wife of Philip, met the king and his mother at Bayonne. None could yet know what passed there, but all might guess that such a meeting must be a portent of evil augury to the Huguenots. Coligny perceived that it was necessary to strike a decisive blow. The miseries he had witnessed, and the example of John Knox and the Scotch Reformers, had changed the veteran statesman, so loyal heretofore, into a republican. Royalty, represented by Catherine de Medicis, had become a thing contemptible in his eyes, a puppet which he might use as well as another. He determined to seize the king. He made known his intentions to Condé, who at last broke the bonds that detained him at court, and joined his old ally.

Then followed the battle of St. Denis. The Protestants wore the white badges which marked the Huguenot troops. Michelet tells how a Turkish envoy, who was posted upon a hill to witness the fight, seeing the numbers of the opposing forces—two thousand and seven hundred against twenty thousand—exclaimed that if his master had but "those white fellows," he would make the tour of the world. Coligny and Condé had at last escaped from Catherine's leading-strings, and led one charge after another with desperate bravery. Montmorency fell: for fifty out of his seventy-five years he had filled a great space in history. The victory was followed by a peace, which gave the Huguenots a moment's breathing space.

Three years before Granvelle, in despair of making head against the disaffection which he saw around him, had retired from his office in the Netherlands. Philip was much displeased at the defection of his favourite officer, which he attributed, not without reason, to the intrigues of Counts Egmont and Horn, and of the Prince of Orange. Philip issued strict orders that the edicts promulgated by the Council of Trent should be put fully in force. But it was not possible to do this without assistance. The French civil wars had sent many refugees into the southern provinces. Ministers of the reformed religion were to be found in every town of the north. Constant intercourse went on with the reformers of England and Germany. The printing-presses were full of books against the doctrines of the Catholics. The governors of many of the provinces had imbibed the new opinions. In spite, therefore, of the regent's strenuous endeavours to carry out the instructions of the king, she found that without laying the country waste, and perpetrating a general massacre, the edicts could not be enforced at all.

In some of the provinces the king's commands were altogether disregarded, and in some, where their execution was attempted, the Protestants were rescued by force out of the hands of the inquisitors, and the inquisitors themselves forced to fly from the enraged multitude.

Disorders broke out in several towns. The populace of Antwerp sacked the churches and monasteries, and turned the nuns out of the convents. Under a show of zeal for Protestantism, they indulged in private rapacity. Even the Counts Egmont and Horn saw that excess was indefensible, even as retaliation for the cruelties of Philip, and that it was the worst way in the world to obtain redress. The rioters were therefore put down with a strong hand; and the regent had soon the satisfaction of announcing to Philip that the disorders were quelled, and the country tranquil.

But the Duke of Alva saw in these disturbances an opportunity too good to be lost. The liberties of the Netherlands should be destroyed utterly. The king should be absolute there as in his Italian dominions. The states had never tolerated without remonstrance the presence of Spanish soldiers within their boundaries; they should now be ruled with military authority. The compact made the year before (1566) at Bayonne with Catherine de Medicis should be carried out to the letter. The Protestants should be utterly extirpated, and no heretic should raise his voice within the limits of the Netherlands. Alva therefore advised Philip to ignore the pacification which had followed the disorders of the Netherlands, and to intrust him with the government. No counsel could be more acceptable to Philip; and the duke was commissioned to lead an army into the Netherlands, and bring the refractory heretics to reason.

Alva immediately set sail for Italy, where he assembled an army of about nine thousand five hundred men, and passed through the territories of the Duke of Savoy, and then through Burgundy and Lorraine, recruiting his strength as he advanced. Three thousand Burgundian cavalry, and four thousand German foot made up a formidable array, with which he arrived at Brussels, in August, 1567. Early in the following year the Duchess of Parma, who had till then retained the title of regent, resigned her office. Alva at once commenced his persecutions. He threw Counts Egmont and Horn into prison. He erected a stronghold in Antwerp, and taxed the city to pay for it. He quartered his troops upon the inhabitants, and encouraged his "Council of Blood" to commit horrible excesses. Thousands fled to France, England, and Protestant Germany.* Numbers were seized ere they could make their escape, and tortured to death on bare suspicion.

Those among the nobility who had at first been

* Above 20,000 persons escaped at this time into France, Germany, and the Protestant provinces of Germany.—Watson, Phil. II., b. viii.

1558—1570.]

favourable to the exercise of Philip's despotic power, became disgusted at the unreasoning ferocity of Alva. They remonstrated, but in vain. The pope himself interfered, and exhorted Philip to moderation: but Vargas, a Spanish lawyer pre-eminent even among Spaniards for avarice and cruelty, who was Alva's deputy at the Council of Blood, encouraged the king to proceed, and his voice, and those of the inquisitors of Madrid, prevailed. Happy were they who, accused of heresy, were only hanged or drowned. By far the greater number perished on the rack, or in the flames, where their tortures were prolonged by the ingenuity of the inquisitors. Their tongues were seared with red-hot irons, and screwed in iron vices, to prevent them from uttering aloud that testimony to the truth which even the cruelties to which they were exposed would not otherwise have wholly repressed.

Britain afforded a refuge to these unfortunates. The fires of Smithfield were yet smouldering; but there was at that time an interval when the war which was waged with rack and faggot all over Europe was at rest in England. Elizabeth protected the Flemish exiles; and as many of them were skilled in the arts which made the Netherlands pre-eminent among the commercial nations of the world, the humane policy of the queen brought its own reward. Elizabeth, though not actually at war with Philip, still looked upon him with deep dislike. She dreaded the formation of a military despotism such as that of Alva's so near her own shores, and was not unwilling to give it a side blow. In common with all the Protestant chiefs, she had long watched with jealousy the growing power of the Spanish monarchy. When, therefore, the Prince of Orange, goaded to madness by the ruin of his country, took up arms against the Duke of Alva, she assisted him with money and advice, though prudence counselled her to remain as long as possible on good terms with him. All Europe was aware of the resentment of Philip at the miscarriage of his matrimonial schemes. Had he been pre-eminent in the councils of England, as he had been during the reign of Mary, the Low Countries would never have obtained their freedom. But all through the struggle they obtained indirect countenance from Elizabeth; and pending the time when she was able to—though not for some years—afford them open assistance, she stopped supplies which were on their way to the Duke of Alva, and thereby reduced him to the necessity of imposing taxes, which drove the people to extremity, and ultimately caused the downfall of his power.

Many of the Protestants had taken to piracy. They now exercised their lawless calling under the banner, and, as they alleged, under the patronage, of the Prince of Orange. That prince and his brother, Count Louis, had been at first very successful against Alva; but want of money and provisions soon drove them to disband their forces, and Orange, at the head of about a thousand, or twelve hundred horsemen, went to France to the assistance of the Calvinists. It was urgently required: the French Protestants, after the accommodation of 1568, were not allowed to remain long unmolested. The queen-mother had put Henry of Anjou in the place of Montmorenci: she now endeavoured to seize Condé and Coligny. But Tavannes, governor of Burgundy, to whom the order for this arrest was transmitted, gave timely warning to the Protestant leaders. Traversing the whole breadth of France, with scarcely an attendant, Condé threw himself into Rochelle. This city was the head-quarters of pirates, who gained their living by plundering Philip's gold-laden galleys. Soon the whole west, and the greater part of the south, declared for the Protestants. The queen of England supplied Condé with money and munitions of war. In March he was advancing towards the Upper Loire, to meet the Germans whom Orange and his brother were bringing to his assistance, when the Catholics met him at Jarnac.

Here Condé fell. He had been hurt the day before by a fall, and on the morning of the battle a kick from a horse had fractured his leg so that the bone came through the boot. Regardless of his wounds, he was in the thickest of the fight, surrounded by the enemy's cavalry, when a blow from behind smashed his skull. Anjou, coward, and cruel, condescended, it is said, to wreak indignities on the corpse.

Such was the strength of the belief of the necessity of royal birth for a leader in those days, that even after the death of Condé, Coligny was again passed over, and another prince sought after for the command: this time the choice fell on Henry of Navarre. Coligny obliged the Duke of Anjou to retreat, and invested Poictiers. It was relieved by Henri, son of the murdered Duke of Guise, who here, for the first time, appears on the stage. Coligny raised the siege. Queen Elizabeth sent men and money; but it was only to enable Coligny to rush again upon defeat at Montcontour. He was outnumbered, and routed. He himself was wounded, and directed a masterly retreat from his litter. Louis of Nassau charged again and again with the reckless dash of Condé; but nothing could retrieve the fortune of the day. Nevertheless the Huguenot hero was undismayed. He showed himself more powerful, and was more dreaded, after his reverses than before.

Catherine de Medicis had now got what she wanted. Her darling Henry of Anjou was victorious and famous; the Huguenots, as she thought, were crushed. She offered peace; but Coligny scornfully rejected her terms.

1569 He appeared before the gates of Paris, and compelled from the unwilling king an amnesty, in which the Huguenots were declared capable of holding all offices, civil and military, and were pardoned for all past offences. The edicts for liberty of conscience were renewed; and Rochelle, La Charité, Montauban, and Cognac were handed over to them as places of refuge. Rochelle kept the sea open for succours from England in case of a new war; La Charité preserved the passage of the Loire; Montauban commanded the frontiers of Languedoc and Querçi, and Cognac opened a passage into Angoumois, the Protestant stronghold.

The year 1570 was one in which it appeared for a moment that the landmarks so carefully and painfully raised were to be swept away. The Protestants had conquered peace; but still their party throughout Europe were in doubt and dismay. Coligny, blinded by his own nobility of soul, was becoming entangled in a web of court intrigue. Elizabeth was thinking of a French alliance, and exchanging portraits with the Duke of Anjou, the Catholic hero of Jarnac and Montcontour. Alva was treading out, as it seemed, the last sparks of liberty in the Netherlands. Philip was re-enacting the middle ages, and amusing himself with cannonading the Turks, taking care, however, to make his Venetian allies pull his chestnuts out of the fire: which they did at Lepanto, where they bore the brunt of the battle, and he got the glory. Catherine, systematically held up by history as the author and moving spirit of her time, was, in truth, but the puppet and toy of the Guises. They pulled the strings, and she bore the blame of their crimes—more than contented to do so if she might still be allowed to appear powerful before the world. She had but one passion—if any feeling she entertained be strong enough to call a passion — affection for her children. Her heart, shallow and base, perverted even that instinct: she loved her children, would make them great—but great only in her own way, and as she understood the term. She plunged them from their earliest days into debauchery that she might retain ascendency over their enfeebled minds and enervated bodies; then exercised every art of chicane and petty intrigue to set them up, puppets of a puppet, in high places before the eyes of men. She was all her life upon the side of the Catholics. Her Lorraine masters used her as a scourge of the Huguenots; but her heart was not in the task. In her perfect indifference to the religious part of the question, she would willingly have seen her son Anjou become the husband of Mary Stuart, chief of the Catholics, King of Scotland, and of France; and her son Alençon, the husband of Queen Elizabeth, and chief of the Protestants.

Such was the position of the political chess-board in 1570. The pope played the first move—excommunication of Queen Elizabeth.

Philip and Henry of Guise were shocked at this sudden move of Pius. They were afraid that it would startle Coligny, upon whom they were industriously working, before their schemes were ripe for execution. For a great wickedness was being brewed in France—such a one as was never heard of before nor shall be again till the end of time—a massacre of the Protestants throughout France. Force had been used in vain. Victorious or beaten, it mattered not—the Huguenots rebounded undismayed. Their lion-hearted leader, terrible even in defeat, ever turned again, and kept the enemy at bay. Treachery of the common kind, blandishments and wiles, even assassination, had failed. Coligny, who was a statesman as well as a hero, swept away their cobwebs with a strong hand, and a smile on his grave, massive face.

But the scheme now ripe for execution had been gradually maturing ever since the meeting at Bayonne ten years before. It was devised with such consummate art that even Coligny, who had seen the court break through five pacifications, whose head had grown white during years of active life, was duped. It seems incredible that this great statesman should believe the first words of affection uttered by his enemies, or be induced, on the faith of any promises, to trust himself within the walls of Paris. But the position of affairs at that time was such that even the most wary statesman might well be deceived. It appeared to be the interest of the king to keep faith. Coligny was, or thought that he was, necessary to him. Through Coligny alone could he gratify his hatred of his brother Anjou, of his uncles the Guises, of the court of Spain. Charles IX. had amply sufficient reason for his antipathy in each of these cases. Though in general subservient to his mother, he chafed under the thraldom from which he had not energy enough permanently to emancipate himself. He was at times a furious madman; but he had lucid intervals; and at such times he could bend his mother's will to his own, and carry out his projects in spite both of her and of his uncles. He knew that he was not his mother's favourite son; that she preferred the Duke of Anjou; that she counted the days till his death should place her darling on the throne. Anjou's good fortune had placed him, as the head of the army, in the position of Catholic hero and fortunate soldier: he was adored by the ladies of his mother's court. Charles knew that he was himself unfitted to excite admiration either as a warrior or as a lover. He therefore detested Anjou. He saw that the Spanish party, the party of his mother and of Guise, was opposed to him, and he hated it accordingly. He had been attached to his sister Elizabeth; and report accused the King of Spain of poisoning her. Nor could he forget the massacre of de Ribault's colony in Florida, though he was powerless to avenge it; so that he had no lack of motives for hating Spain. Again, at the time of the pacification with the Protestants, Catherine had proposed a marriage between Margaret, the king's sister, and Henry of Navarre. Whether Catherine was sincere or not, Coligny could not but perceive that the king himself was thoroughly in earnest — so much in earnest, that he wanted to kill Henry of Guise, who, as he thought, stood in the way of the marriage. The king gave other proofs of good faith: the Catholics of Rouen, having committed some excesses against the reformers, Charles carried out the terms of the pacification, and had them hanged. There was still another reason why the king should be true. The Low Countries had at length opposed such determined resistance to Alva, that Philip was obliged to disown and disgrace him. Charles determined to seize this opportunity of satisfying his old grudge against Philip, by attacking the Flemish dominions of Spain. But if he did, whom should he place in command of the army—Anjou? the king would rather die than appoint him. Coligny should command.

Charles was perfectly sincere in all this, and Coligny could not but perceive that he was so. Coligny's mistake consisted in believing too much in the stability of the king's mind, and in thinking that Charles and himself were a match in intrigue for Catherine and the Guises. He came to Paris, and assisted in the negotiations that ensued with England, Venice, Orange. This was just what Guise,* bribed with Spanish gold, required. He could counterplot the king and Coligny. He could mature his plan of the massacre, and all this by simply letting matters alone. All he had to make sure was this,

* Henry of Guise, called "Mucio" by Philip II. See Motley's History of the United Netherlands.

that Charles's project against the Low Countries should not be mature before his own plans for the massacre. Guise had to hurry his preparations, for Count Louis took the field, and seized Mons by a *coup de main* with the Huguenot soldiers who joined his standard, while Alva still imagined him to be " tennis-playing at Versailles." The Prince of Orange hurried his preparations, and had barely completed them, when he received intelligence that Brille had fallen into the hands of a marauder named William de la Marck. This adventurer was one of the maritime 'gueux,' or beggars, as they were called by their opponents; in other words, a Protestant fugitive, who, like many of his countrymen, had taken to piracy, under a commission from the Prince of Orange and in the name of the reformed religion. De la Marck and his followers had a year before taken refuge in an English port, whence he issued forth to plunder the treasure-ships of the Spaniards on their way up channel to the Netherlands. Alva had remonstrated at Elizabeth's " unkindness," as he called it, in allowing the enemies of his master to harbour in English territory. Though Elizabeth had no reason to love the Spanish king, or his haughty viceroy in the Netherlands, she had not yet heard of Alva's intended invasion of England, or of his correspondence with the Duke of Norfolk and the English Catholics. In order to avoid a rupture with Spain, she had desired the Count de la Marck and his followers to quit the kingdom. De la Marck obeyed, and with twenty-five vessels set sail from Dover, seized a couple of Spanish treasure-ships in his way, and possessed himself of Brille, at the mouth of the Maese, whence he wrote desiring the Prince of Orange to hasten to his assistance.

News of the exploit of De la Marck reached the Duke of Alva just in time to save a number of innocent victims whom he had condemned to death. Trade did not thrive under persecution; nor did confidence exist among the merchants: Alva's resource in this, as in most cases, was capital punishment. Seventeen principal burghers had been selected; the troops were under arms in the market-place, the gibbets were prepared, the cords and the executioners were ready, when a messenger arrived in hot haste to tell of the capture of Brille; and Alva, from motives of policy, reluctantly renounced for the moment the intended execution. The Count de Bossut, governor of Holland, who commanded the Spanish troops, endeavoured in vain to recover Brille. The townsmen opened the sluices and flooded him out of the country. He marched first to Dort, and then to Rotterdam; but as his troops behaved with the ordinary cruelty of the Spaniards, the whole province was soon in a blaze, and Zealand generally declared for the Prince of Orange.

By September the Prince of Orange was in Hainault with twenty thousand men. Here he was told of the massacre of St. Bartholomew. He heard how, on the night of the twenty-fourth of August, the Duke of Guise, who had so lately, at his king's command, offered the hand of good fellowship to Coligny, and promised to forget his ancient feud, had himself stood at the door of the venerable admiral's apartment, while an attendant foully murdered him. He heard how the king himself had fired upon the people, and with almost a madman's joy had shouted to the butchers to kill and not to spare. He heard that Guerchy was dead, and the amiable Teligny, and sixty thousand more of the bravest of his late companions in arms.

The intelligence was a stunning blow for the Prince of Orange. If anything could have added to his hatred of Alva or of Alva's master, it would have been their conduct on the receiving intelligence of the massacre. Philip offered public thanksgivings to heaven for the defeat of his enemies, and sent congratulatory messages to the French king. Men attributed the treachery which had just been executed to the dark suggestions of Alva. They reminded one another of the meeting at Bayonne, twelve years before, and surmised that the wicked plot had been then concocted, and had been ever since steadily kept in view.

But the Prince of Orange had other reasons for dismay. Among his army were many French subjects who had joined him when they believed their king to be favourable to his undertaking. Would they remain faithful to his standard now? He himself was acting under a commission from Charles IX.; and it was now certain that he had nothing more to hope for from that sovereign.

The prince felt that nothing was left for him but to show a bold front, and to endeavour by some signal success to retain the waverers on his side. He therefore marched with all despatch to the relief of Mons.

The course of action which Alva had adopted when William and his brother Louis had first attempted to rescue their country from the Spaniards, he now repeated. He avoided an engagement with the most consummate skill, and left want of funds and of provisions to do the work of demoralization on the army of his opponent. The Prince of Orange was forced to retreat. Count Louis capitulated; and the Spanish general, Frederick of Toledo, gradually recovered all the towns in the southern provinces which had declared for the Prince of Orange.

The massacre of St. Bartholomew, far from annihilating the French Huguenots, only rendered them more formidable. They crowded into the fortresses which remained in the hands of their party; and knowing that they could now put no more trust in the word of the king, defended Rochelle with an energy and success which entirely defied the best efforts of their opponents.

Elizabeth was deeply incensed at the conduct of

the French court. The French ambassador, who was ordered to excuse it to her on the ground that it was a political necessity, was received with coldness and neglect almost amounting to insult.* No one at court would speak to him or return his salutations. The English nobles were so eager to avenge the murdered Huguenots, that they offered to raise an army, and maintain it for six months on French ground at their own expense. But the queen, who was engaged in watching the warlike preparations of Philip, and who easily foresaw that she would sooner or later be dragged into the impending quarrel, contented herself with fortifying her coasts and putting her fleet in order. The militia was drilled and armed; and the German Protestants were called upon to join in preparations for a struggle which seemed imminent; and which, if once begun, would amount to a general European conflagration—a Protestant league against a Catholic crusade.

The enmity of the Catholic courts was not a matter of mere surmise. The Duke of Norfolk was discovered to be in communication with the Spaniards. Alva, as soon as he had reduced the Netherlands to obedience, had turned his attention to England. He engaged to land ten thousand men near London; Norfolk and Northumberland were to raise the Catholics of England. This had come to the knowledge of Elizabeth : it was therefore with great satisfaction that the queen perceived that, notwithstand-

* Carte. Fénélon's despatches.

ing the reverses which the Prince of Orange experienced in the south, he seemed fully able to hold his own in Zealand and the maritime provinces. She refused active assistance, but held out constant encouragement to the Protestants to persevere.

CHAPTER VI.

THE HOLY LEAGUE.

[1570—1603.]

Formation of the Holy League—Reaction in Europe against the Reformation—English Adventurers—Downfall of the League—French Discovery.

TILL now the course of the Protestant Revolution had been always in advance. It had experienced no check; it acknowledged no defeat. Persecution which would have crushed a weaker cause had but stimulated its zeal, and developed its energies. Country after country had thrown off the dominion of the pope. With the single exception of Ireland, all northern Europe was Protestant. Henceforth the tide turned. The Catholic reaction began. During the next two generations a great drama was performed—the history of the Holy League. At the very beginning new actors took a part in it.

Philip and Elizabeth held the purse-strings of their respective parties. Catherine de Medicis had already ruined two of her sons. She was now the evil genius of a third, and the tool of a second generation of the

Guises. Her new master, Henry with the Scar, son of the imperious and haughty Francis, surpassed his father in daring, in ambition, in violence, and in genius. He had been the principal mover of the Bartholomew massacre. He now appeared as the founder of the League. A traitor to his country, the centre of Spanish policy in Europe, while Spanish troops were starving, and Spanish generals dying broken-hearted through their sovereign's neglect, "Mucio," as he is called in Philip's ciphered letters, was always plentifully supplied with Spanish gold.

The new King of France, though he had acquired some reputation at Jarnac and Montcontour, had ,forgotten all that was manly in his character, in the Venetian Capreæ, where he loitered in luxurious seclusion after his flight from the Polish crown. The woman's dress, the bracelets, the earrings, with which he delighted to exhibit himself, showed the depth of degradation to which the royal trifler had descended. He surrounded himself with "mignons," whom he selected for their beauty, their ferocity, their skill in the niceties of the stoccado. He admired strength and daring, but he shrunk with unmanly fear from personal risk, or participation in rough scenes. This was the man whom fate had opposed to the bright and daring prince, the hero of Protestantism, Henry of Navarre, the man whose battle-horse was the Reformation, and who rode it manfully and well. Only, unfortunately for his fame, he dismounted ere the fight was won. But perhaps the most noteworthy of any was Alexander Farnese, Prince of Parma. The right hand of Philip in the Netherlands, chief of his projected invasion of England; a man of iron nerve and Italian subtlety of brain, he challenges the reluctant admiration even of those whom he did his best to ruin. If, on the one hand, stern fidelity to his king, stedfast adherence to his own standard of right, moderation in victory, manly bearing in defeat, clear-sightedness in politics, vigorous arm in action, marvellous fertility of resource, be qualities worthy of praise, Farnese demands it at our hands. If, on the other hand, to lie basely, habitually, unscrupulously, "upon his honour," whenever it suited his purpose, demand reprobation, we cannot judge too hardly of his character.

Though last, not least, William the Silent, "Father William," the greatest Protestant general of the age, the man who by his own personal influence made head against all the power of reaction, claims a foremost place among the statesmen of the time.

Here is a list, in chronological order, of the principal events in the history of the League, from the massacre of St. Bartholomew to the defeat of the Spanish Armada.

1573. A grand military spectacle in the Netherlands in which William the Silent gradually made head against the enemy. Then came the accession of Henry III. It was announced that the king would mediate between the Huguenots and the Catholics. He tried to do so, failed, and retired covered with confusion. The war, for a moment interrupted, was again resumed.

1576. The Escurial was startled by the announcement that the Spanish siege of Leyden had been raised, that Requesens was dead, that his unpaid troops had mutinied, that a horrible massacre had taken place in Antwerp. Such was the news from the Low Countries. From Henry of Guise came intelligence that the Protestant hero had escaped from Paris, had put himself at the head of the Huguenots, had been joined by Francis Duke of Anjou, and a German army under young Condé, and had forced from the king advantageous conditions of peace.

1577. The Cardinal of Lorraine, Catherine de Medicis, and Guise, lost no time in arranging details which they had long been meditating for forming the Holy League. It was to destroy heresy all over the world. It was to be supported by Philip in purse and person; by the pope, and all who were loyal to his power; by German lanzknechts; by Italian condottieri; by the assassin's dagger,* the poison cup; and by Mexican pistoles.

While the preparations were in progress for the war determined on by the League, there was much

* See conspiracy of Anthony Babington against life of Queen Elizabeth.— Camden; Murdin, State Papers, 412, 413. See also letter from Philip to Parma, Nov. 30, 1579, offering 30,000 crowns to any who who would deliver Orange dead or alive. Archives et Corres. de la Maison d'Orange Nassau, ap. Groen v. Trinsterer, quoted by Motley. Five attempts on the life of Orange, the last successful, were made in consequence of this offered reward. See Motley's Rise of Dutch Republic, vol iii., for original authorities cited therein.

CHAPTER VI.

wrangling throughout Europe, but little fighting. Prince Casimir and the army under his command, were dismissed by the Low Countries, whom Elizabeth had sent him to assist; the Prince of Orange became an object of suspicion to his friends; and Don John of Austria died.

In 1579, the Prince of Orange, with deputies from Utrecht, Groningen, Oberyssel, Friesland, and Guelderland, assembled for the purpose of signing the "Union" of the Netherlands. Meanwhile the King of Portugal had embarked with his army on a romantic expedition against the Moors. Philip took advantage of the occasion to seize the crown of Portugal, and other valuables which Antonio had left behind him.

1582. Spain, successful in the neighbouring country of Portugal, made a descent on Ireland, where the soldiers who took part in the expedition were deservedly hanged by Lord Grey. The Low Countries definitively cast off their allegiance, and transferred it to the Duke of Anjou. Five attempts were successively made on the life of the Prince of Orange. So well was the advice of Cardinal Granvelle followed, "poner talla de 30 o 40 mil escudos, à quien le matasse o diésse vivo, *como hazen todos los potentados de Italia.*"* The last attempt was successful.

In 1585 a deputation of Flemish plenipotentiaries performed the tour of Europe, offering the crown of the Netherlands to each sovereign in succession—

* Granvelle to Philip, Aug. 8, 1579.

which not one of them would accept. Philip meanwhile worked hard at his preparations for his English invasion, on which, for the next few years, he concentrated all the energy of his mind, until in 1588, the great Armada came, only to be destroyed by the providence of God, and the dauntless courage of the English seamen.

I have thought it necessary to bring to the reader's recollection the events which have just been enumerated, inasmuch as the wars of religion so materially affect the development of those states which, in the succeeding century, colonized America. These wars were, in fact, the great school in which the character of Europe was formed. It is not too much to say that no emigration went forth that was not in some measure affected by them, and that too when private interest or mere adventure appeared to be the sole motive power. During the sixteenth century, all the western nations were involved in the war of creeds, and their fortunes depended on the issue of the struggle. With the massacre of 1572, the main event of the contest was decided. The schism had spent its force: the reaction began. Protestantism wrested no fresh countries from the pope; nor did Catholicism recover those in which the Reformation was accepted. Each held its own ground. Protestantism was dominant in northern Europe. The party of reaction strove fiercely to dislodge it, but it has remained there unshaken till this day. Catholicism prevailed in the south; and

CHAPTER VI.

the schism made no further advances in that direction. But in central Europe, the land which lay in debate between the Reformation and the League, the ancient faith gradually regained its ascendency and remained mistress of the field.

The cause must be sought in the position which the two religious parties now assumed.

In the days of Calvin, of Luther, of Leo, the contest had been between men very much in earnest and men not in earnest at all. The papacy was apathetic. The Reformers were protesting against abuses, and were ready to shed their blood in defence of their opinions. The effects of the revolution, like those of all successful revolutions, went much further than at first sight they seemed likely to do. The Church which it opposed caught the infection of reform—there was a change within as well as without her pale. One class of reformers was anxious to hurl her headlong to the ground; another sought to furbish up the old armour which had been proved in many a desperate fight. The monastic orders were purified. Able men, whose lives were of undeniable sanctity, sat on the throne of St. Peter. The church became animated with a spirit of enthusiasm equal to, if not exceeding, that of the seceders from her communion. While the Jesuits worked the reaction with unparalleled devotion, their opponents began to quarrel vainly among themselves. In England, the queen persecuted the Puritans: in the Palatinate, the elector persecuted the Lutherans.

"As they waxed hot in faction,
In battle they waxed cold."*

The later wars of religion were hardly waged for the sake of religion at all. At length, religion ceased to be even nominally the moving spring of European wars. The great old leaders were dead. They left no successors. Plunder and pay among the common soldiers; private ambition and advancement among the nobles; —such were the motives of action. The first zeal of the Reformers had evaporated; the people saw nothing of its results but the ruin of their countries and themselves. The nobles asked themselves if the aim and end of long and bloody wars were that a few potentates should enrich themselves with the plunder of the church. A statesman like Orange might see that personal and political liberty was involved in the struggle for religious liberty; a statesman like Parma might see that, unless the Catholic religion was upheld, the tap-root of absolutism was cut, and the future ascendency of democracy insured. Orange, perhaps, was the only man who proposed to himself not liberty for Protestantism, but liberty of conscience for Protestant and Catholic alike. Many fought hard on either side for the triumph of their own faith; but Orange was the only one, so far as history gives us any clue, who divined in the sixteenth century the meaning of the modern word toleration. The original object of the contest had been

* Macaulay, Lays of Ancient Rome.

forgotten: now that Luther and Calvin were no longer at hand, the Reformers were divided among themselves. There were Lutherans, Calvinists, Flaccianists, Majorists, Adiaphorists, Brantionists, Anabaptists. Each of these, when not persecuted, claimed the right of persecution. William of Hesse and John of Nassau strove in vain for a "concordia" among the different sects. No one listened; and it was the personal character only of Orange that kept the whole machine from going to pieces. The struggle was centred at last in the Netherland provinces of King Philip. On them the King of Spain concentrated his attention; against them he directed his ablest generals, his bravest veterans. Upon that die he staked the cause of absolute power.

Included in the Netherlands quarrel was that of Philip with England. It was on English protection and help that the Low Country men principally relied: it was mainly as a base of operations, whence England might be enslaved and France crushed, that Philip regarded them. Elizabeth saw this plainly. She accepted the issue and the battle-ground. The names of the heroes whom she sent into the States sound, as Mr. Motley observes, "like a roll-call of the English chivalry." There was the lover of the Queen, Leicester—"her own sweet Robin;" Sir Philip Sidney, governor of Flushing, who died a hero's death at Zutphen. There were Audley and Essex, Pelham, Russell; there was Stanley, who, in sight of two armies, clung to a Spanish pike and was lifted clean over the parapet of the great fort of Zutphen, and, single-handed, held his own against an army till his soldiers scrambled over the walls. There was Sir John Norris, " the best soldier of them all," as Parma wrote to Philip.* There was Sir Francis Drake; "a fearful man to the King of Spain is Sir Francis Drake," as the great Lord Burleigh exclaims.† There was the hero of a hundred ballads, and of as many fights,

> " Brave Lord Willoughby,
> Of courage fierce and fell."

These, and many more like them, were sent by Elizabeth to help the men of Holland. For, although she long fought against the idea, although she hoped against hope that peace would be established and war avoided, events had hurried her into a position from which there was no escape. It was very evident to the grave Burleigh and the astute Walsingham that sooner or later a contest must take place with Spain, in the issue of which the very existence of England would be involved. To postpone this attack until England could be fully prepared became their principal object. It could only be effected by hampering Philip's movements in Holland, and cutting off his supplies from America.

As long as William the Silent lived, Elizabeth felt

---

* MS. Archives de Simancas (quoted by Motley), Parma to Philip, 30th Oct. 1586.
† Leicester Correspond., 199.

comparatively secure. The plans of Philip were not yet matured. The genius of Orange kept him pretty fully employed. It was only necessary to help unostentatiously, to send an occasional subsidy or a handful of men. The queen's well-known parsimony made her deal out these supplies with a very sparing hand. Her money was too hardly come by to permit her to waste it. In truth, her power was as yet very different from what it was afterwards. The historian of the Dutch republic gives a lively sketch of her position.*

"The England," he says, "of Elizabeth, Walsingham, Burghley, Drake, and Raleigh, of Spenser and Shakespeare, hardly numbered a larger population than now dwells in its capital and immediate suburbs. It had neither standing army nor royal navy. It was full of conspirators, daring and unscrupulous, loyal to none save to Mary of Scotland, Philip of Spain, and the pope of Rome, and untiring in their efforts to bring about a general rebellion. With Ireland at its side, nominally a subject province, but in a state of chronic insurrection; a perpetual hotbed of Spanish conspiracy and stratagem; with Scotland at its back, a foreign country with half its population exasperated enemies of England and the rest but doubtful friends; with the legitimate sovereign of that country

"The daughter of debate,
Who discord still did sow,"

---

* Motley, Hist. United Netherlands, i. 29.

a prisoner in Elizabeth's hands,—the central point round which treason was always crystallizing itself,"
—she never could be at ease.

There were two other reasons which made Elizabeth very unwilling actively to intervene in Flemish affairs. Her temper, like that of all the Tudors, was haughty and despotic. The Provinces, however good might be their cause, were in rebellion against an anointed king;—she sympathized with the cause, but she hated the rebellion, and would rather, if she could have done so safely, put down the rebellion than help it on. She was from policy, not from conviction, a Protestant. The Dutch were Calvinists, men with whose tenets she had no sympathy whatever. She was sincerely desirous of remaining at peace with Philip. All Europe was afraid of him. The Spaniards were considered more than human in their power and bravery. It was not till years of predatory warfare carried on by her bold pirates and adventurers had convinced Elizabeth that the Spaniard was in truth anything but invincible, that she in her heart believed the possibility of successful resistance. The quarrel was not, in her opinion, yet irremediable. The great tragedy of the Scottish queen, whose execution was to render peace with Philip even in her own eyes impossible, was yet in abeyance. At the last moment, in the autumn of 1587, when Philip had irrevocably and finally decided on doing all that lay in his power to dethrone and destroy her, she was ever catching at the hopes of peace with which the matchless duplicity of Alexander Farnese amused her credulity.

The murder of the Prince of Orange gave the first rude shock to the system of ostensible neutrality which she had proposed to herself. The crime of Balthazar Gerard irrevocably determined her future course. The story, so fraught with ruin to the Protestant cause, demands a word in passing. In 1583, the prince had shifted his quarters from Antwerp to the little town of Delft, which lay on the high road between Rotterdam and the Hague. A canal, overshadowed by tall trees, occupied the centre of the principal street. On each side was a roadway, beyond, houses with their courtyards and offices stretched back to the town walls. One of these houses belonged to the prince; it was a two-story brick building; it looked on to a court-yard which bordered on the street; along one side of the court, at right angles to the roadway, a narrow alley ran back to the walls. On the ground floor was the dining-room, and the principal entrance into the court. The entrance communicated by a covered way with a little hall, into which opened on one side the dining-room door, on another a deep archway with a door into the lane, on the third stairs which led to the private apartments above.

On Sunday, 8th July, 1584, the prince was aroused from sleep by the announcement of a courier from France, who bore intelligence of the death of the Duke of Anjou. The messenger was summoned to give details of the murder. He was a man of low stature, and meanly dressed; his complexion sallow; his general appearance furtive and disagreeable. He appeared to be somewhat under thirty years of age. His name he stated to be Francis Guion, son of a martyred Calvinist. Such was Belthazar Gerard—a man who for seven years had been sworn to assassinate the man who now lay before him unarmed and in bed. The summons to the prince's chamber was so unexpected that Gerard had not time to mature his plan; nor, indeed, had he funds to buy a weapon. He was indebted to the charity of Orange, who compassionated his forlorn appearance, for an alms, which he expended in the purchase of a pair of pistols. This purchase was made on the Monday. About noon on the Tuesday, Gerard concealed himself in the shadow of the archway which led into the lane. The prince, who was at dinner with his friends, came out conversing pleasantly with the burgomaster of Leewarden, his only guest that day. He had advanced to the bottom of the stairs, when Gerard stepped forward, and discharged his pistol. The assassin passed through the archway, and ran swiftly towards the walls. He was, however, arrested by the attendants. But the greatest statesman of the age lay dead in his own dining-room, with three bullets through his heart.

The states, deprived of the storng hand and resolute spirit of Orange, sought long and earnestly for a protector. Henry of France refused. Surrounded by his worthless minions, hopelessly entangled in the meshes of his mother's intrigues, sold to be a tool and bond-slave to Philip by the rival whom he hated and feared, but could not shake off, the poor king dared not, if he would, accept the protectorate of Philip's revolted provinces. Elizabeth, too, refused, for she was intent upon the Spanish quarrel, which had become inevitable. Nevertheless, she was compelled to declare herself. She sent Leicester with the title of governor-general to the states.

While the quarrel with Spain was thus brewing, England was quietly amassing the means by which danger could be repelled. She had no royal navy, but a strange spirit had taken possession of her merchants. It was a curious mixture—half fanaticism, half piracy. Bold explorers had aroused the maritime ardour of the nation. Zealots had infused into it religious fervour. To the temper thus nurtured we owe our colonies, our commerce, our existence. The sailors of Elizabeth crippled the resources of the Spaniard by their raids on the West Indian shores. They crushed his last huge effort in the great sea-fight of 1588.

It was still a mystery eagerly discussed by geographers whether fertile lands did not lie between Florida and the river of Canada. Winganditoia still awaited the discoverer, who was to re-christen it after the Virgin Queen. During her life no permanent settlement was made; but her adventurous mariners surely paved the way for the political and religious exiles of the Stuarts.

The intelligence of the nation was expanding.

Thought had been emancipated by the Reformation. The very nature of the authority exercised by the Tudor princes left individual action untrammeled. Spain alone could dispute with England the supremacy of the seas, and the dread with which it was regarded was fast diminishing before the increasing number of naval actions in which English sailors came off triumphant. The Spaniards held the markets of the New World. Fabulous accounts of the wealth which they drew thence were circulated and believed. There was not a merchant but had his imagination full of patents, and companies, privileges, monopolies, and settlements. The cruelties perpetrated by the Spaniards added religious zeal to the hatred with which they were regarded as the monopolists of the Indies. It must be acknowledged that Englishmen vied with their rivals in ferocity. The Spaniards were enemies of God and the queen. Massacres were committed by both on the most righteous pretexts. Zeal for the church on one side, zeal for the reformation on the other, sanctioned every excess. Behind the decent veil of religion each fought for and worshipped with unpitying cruelty their common idol—gold.

The English had preceded the French in their North American discoveries. It was not, however, until the viceroyalty of Canada had assumed considerable importance that any attempt was made from England to interfere with them.

Sir Humphrey Gilbert, of Compton, in Devonshire, 1580

was the first who started. He obtained a patent from the queen granting to him for ever such barbarous countries as he could discover, and giving him absolute authority therein both by land and sea. He was driven back; lost one ship and some of his companions; encountered severe weather, and of course had a fight with the Spaniards.

It was true that England was technically at peace with Spain; but the stubborn pride of the old English mariners never allowed them to throw away a chance of battle, even when the Spaniards were favoured with overwhelming odds. They staked their lives on the issue; they looked upon the ocean as debatable ground: it belonged to all alike. They laughed at the pretension of the Dons to monopolize the rich west. They had commissions from her highness the Queen of England; the patents and monopolies which she gave were in their eyes to the full as valid as those of the Bishop of Rome. If, in defence of their rights, they fell foul of a Spanish galley, or captured a gold-laden caravel, Elizabeth reproved them smilingly, and occasionally condescended to share the plunder. At peace with Spain! Why in every company some pious marauder could show wrists and ankles scarred by the cords which had bound him to the rack in the Inquisition; another could tell of a comrade burnt at an auto da fé at Lima; a third could describe how, chained and flogged, he rowed as a forçado in those floating hells, the treasure galleys of Panama; a fourth had worked in chains at Potosi; lust of battle, lust of plunder, thirst for revenge, love of adventure, all the wild instincts of semi-barbarism, made up a race of men who were little disposed to casuistry when they saw a Spaniard under their lee.

The discouragement of Sir Humphrey Gilbert was not of long duration. Sir George Peckham and Sir Humphrey's half-brother, Sir Walter Raleigh, who was then rising into favour with the queen, again equipped him. The queen herself sent him a token. " Her highness," writes Raleigh, " willed me to send you word that she wished you as great goodhap and safety to your ship as if she herself were there in person, desiring you to have care of yourself as of that which she tendereth." Gilbert endorsed the letter, " Received March 18, 1582." But the queen's good wishes were of no avail; he and his brave crew, mechanics, refiners of metal, tradesmen, and, as chroniclers have said, captured pirates, were lost at sea.

What an undertaking! To set out to take possession of a new world with such provision. Sir Humphrey's largest ship was but two hundred tons. The " Squirrel," in which he himself hoisted his flag, and in which he foundered, was only ten tons. That cockboat had need to be freighted with fearless hearts to try so much on such a slender chance.

Encounters took place wherever a Spanish ship or a Spanish garrison could be found. Raleigh alone sent out no less than seven expeditions. He procured a renewal of the patents of his half-brother—" Two hundred miles in every direction of such remote barbarous and heathen countries as were not in the possession of any Christian king." Such was the tenor of the patent which formed a model for most of the innumerable charters which were granted by the queen and her successors in following times. Raleigh's captains, Amadas and Barlow, returned with a a glowing description of the country in which they had landed. It was named Virginia, in honour of the spinster queen. Before the end of the century he had sent out no less than seven expeditions at the cost of 40,000*l*. Twice the small barques of his navigators were scattered. His adventurers perished by famine, by disease, by the hostility of the Indians. Twice the ships which came to arrest the colony found only a heap of bones and ruins, wild animals wandering amidst the deserted houses of the settlements, and clearings overgrown with the rankness of tropical vegetation. But neither treachery, war, famine, nor the deadly Indian scalping-knife dulled the energy or quelled the courage of these dauntless men.

Dreams and fables added to the real marvels of the tropics, and represented cities of pure gold and fountains of perpetual youth. The Spaniard was to be encountered on the sea, the Indian on the land. Freebooting and proselytism were to be followed in the name of the reformed religion. Adventurers said their prayers or sold their prisoners into slavery with equal zest.

The discovery of a new world was certainly an

event of sufficient magnitude to unhinge the equilibrium of the strongest mind, and to give a tinge of romance to the expedition of the most prosaic trader.

But the sailor of Queen Elizabeth's days was made up of contrasts. He was a robber; he considered himself a crusader. Wars of religion were raging in Europe; they were re-enacted beyond the Atlantic. The companions of Drake, Raleigh, and Grenville never hesitated, while in the Spanish main, to pillage a church or murder the officiating priests. The Spaniards delighted to grace an auto da fé at Lima or Vera Cruz by the burning of a batch of heretics. Each adventurer was a merchant in search of gold; he was a statesman burning to found a kingdom. He was a pioneer settler in an unknown land. He was a pirate ravaging an enemy's coast. His life was a series of abrupt transitions.

Sir Francis Drake was the type and mirror of these bold rovers. He was at the time of the great armada fight about five-and-forty years of age. Nearly forty of these he had passed at sea. He was a little bullet-headed man, with bright twinkling eyes and short curling hair. His complexion, originally fair, was burned to the colour of brickdust by many a year of sun and wind. He drawled his words with a strong Devonshire accent, and, as he said himself, "hated nothing so much as idleness."

Drake had been at sea ever since his boyhood. He was born on the sea-beach. His father's home was an old boat turned upside down. As soon as he could speak he went to sea, and served his apprenticeship in a coasting lugger. No sooner was that at an end than he went on a slaving voyage with old Hawkins, whom we met with a few pages back relieving Ribault's Florida colony from starvation. The hard old trader had a brush with the Spaniards, and Drake was captured. Escaping, he vowed, after the fashion of those days, eternal enmity to the Dons, and well he kept his word. Hardly had Magellan performed his celebrated voyage when Drake followed in his track. He went to California, and was the first Englishman to circumnavigate the globe. What treasures he amassed, what prisoners he took, what Spaniards he slew, what towns he sacked and burned in the Spanish colonies, need not here be recited. But he won wealth enough to make himself rich, to wear a gold chain and sumptuously embroidered clothes; he won honour enough to be the hero of song and story, and to attract the attention of the great Elizabeth, from whose sword he received the much-coveted knightly accolade, and rose up "Sir Francis."

In 1585 he had collected a small fleet and had sailed again to the Spanish Main, whence next summer he returned bearing tidings of wreck and ruin to the Spaniards, St. Domingo plundered and burnt, Carthagena almost annihilated, and a very pretty penny of prize-money to show as the result of his labours.

Again in 1587, the year when all Europe was in

expectation of the sailing of the great armada, Drake left protocols and embassies to those who understood the trade. His own course was plain; he called his bold comrades together, fitted out his ships and sailed for Cadiz, where lay the great galleys of Spain. There he burned and scuttled, sacked and hewed in pieces, the transports which Philip had toilfully collected for the war. Thence hastening to Lisbon harbour, under the very eyes of Santa Cruz, 1587 the English corsair plundered the royal fleet, and drove those which he did not burn to take refuge under the walls. He then took a run to Barbary and sold his prisoners to the " Mowers." When he returned, after a few weeks' absence, his worst enemy could not have accused him of "idleness." The prize he had amassed was enormous. But though he wrote modestly that "he had made a beginning upon the coast of Spain," he thought and said with all his might that the enemy would soon repair damages and seek revenge.

Elizabeth, however, was busy treating with the Prince of Parma, exchanging real vows and earnest strivings for peace, against polite diplomatic fictions, exceedingly downright lies on the part of the Italian statesman. She received Drake with frowns and discouragement. Not the less Sir Francis had "made a beginning," and the armada which was to conquer England could not come that year.

While events were thus ripening, while Philip was crouching for his spring, and Elizabeth's volunteers were arming to repel him, a sect was rising into importance to which the colonization of New England is mainly due.

The Reformation in Switzerland and Northern Germany had from the first struck at the doctrine as well as the supremacy of Rome. In England it was a social and political rather than a religious revolution. Henry VIII. burned those who asserted the pope's supremacy, but he also burned those who denied the doctrine of the real presence, or affirmed justification by faith. The English Reformation was a revolt against political vassalage, not against doctrinal inaccuracies.

But in the reign of King Edward VI. controversy arose. Bishop Hooper refused to be consecrated in Roman vestments. These vestments were the badges of religious party. Much of the efficacy of the sacraments were by the uneducated supposed to reside in them; the refusal, therefore, was one of great importance. If the reformers at the first had fixed upon badges of episcopal or priestly office which had no reference to the Church of Rome, this controversy might have been prevented. But from the beginning they had proceeded by compromise, even in the Liturgy, instead of rejecting the offices of the church, they contented themselves with altering and amending it. The death of Edward put a stop to the further alterations which he meditated, and the persecutions of Mary drove the Protestants into banishment. Romanism was the religion of the state, and the statutes against heretics which Edward had abolished, were directed anew against the reformers. The fugitives were hospitably entertained by the reformed churches of Germany and Switzerland. But here began the division which has never since been healed. Some among the exiles rejected the liturgy which Edward had established, and pronounced it a "remnant of Antichrist."* On the accession of Elizabeth they returned to England. Each party tried to establish the ascendency of its own views. The queen was for restoring King Edward's Liturgy: the exiles preferred the discipline and worship of the foreign churches. The bishops, many of whom had themselves been banished, made every exertion to keep the peace, declaring that they would use their influence at court to have all things set right. The queen, too, for a time winked at the secession which she could not wholly avert; but as her government became more and more firmly established, and adulation developed her imperious character with greater distinctness, she declared that she had fixed the standard, to which she intended all her subjects to conform. The bishops, in spite of their professions, soon followed her lead.

In 1564 the clergy of the several dioceses were invited to subscribe the liturgy ceremonies and discipline of the English church. The recusants obtained the name of Puritans, which in after time came to designate all those who, without actually separating

* Neale, Hist. Puritans, preface, vi.

CHAPTER VI from the church, refused to assent to its forms — the surplice, the cross in baptism, the ring in marriage, holy water, the use of instrumental music in public worship, they repudiated as derived from "the idolatries of popery." The queen hated and persecuted them; but in her council and court they had powerful friends — Cecil, Walsingham, Leicester, Essex, Warwick, Bedford, and Knollys. In their successful development in the next two reigns, they subverted the church, the peerage, and the monarchy.

As far as doctrine is concerned, the queen could hardly be called a Protestant. She admired the magnificence of the Roman Catholic ceremonies. In her revised Liturgy, transubstantiation was not explicitly denied. She retained images, crucifixes, and tapers in her private chapel. She favoured the invocation of saints. She sought the intercession of the Virgin. She insisted, as far as she dared, upon the celibacy of the clergy. It was her wish to keep the Church of England midway between the licentiousness of sectarianism and the acknowledgment of papal supremacy. This middle course pleased neither the Puritans nor the Catholics. The Puritans became utterly disaffected. The pope excommunicated her. Elizabeth looked on both sects with nearly equal dislike. The one was openly hostile to her throne, the other she considered mutineers in her camp. Active measures were taken to compel uniformity. The high commission was established to take cognizance of disputed points of doctrine. A court which founded its decisions upon the canon law instead of the statute law of the realm, naturally became extremely obnoxious to the non-conforming clergy. Neale, the historian of the Puritans, compares it to the Spanish inquisition. Ministers, he says, were brought by the pursuivants of the court from their distant benefices, and were imprisoned without bail and without trial. They were arraigned, not for inefficiency or immorality, but for baptizing without the sign of the cross, or for not wearing a white surplice. Catholic recusants were continually plotting against the queen. The laws made to guard against their machinations were turned against Protestant nonconformists. At one time a fourth part of all the beneficed clergymen of England were under suspension in the ecclesiastical courts,* and the royal prerogative was carried as high under Queen Elizabeth as ever it was under Charles I.† These severities rather increased than diminished the number of nonconformists. Men do not readily adopt a faith recommended only by penal laws, nor love a church which uses such weapons of controversy. The bishops began to lose credit with the people. The persecuted sect fled to Holland. Laws so unjust and so severe cannot be palliated or excused. It must, however, be remembered, that the government was dealing with men whose avowed wish it was to upset existing institutions by the sword. Both parties

* Neale, Hist. of Puritans.
† Lord Clarendon, vol. i. 8vo, p. 72, quoted by Neale.

agreed in asserting the necessity of uniformity in public worship, and of using the sword of the magistrate in support of their respective principles.

The great armada of Spain came and went: carcases of great galleons lay covered with tangle and seaweeds on the storm-swept rocks of the Hebrides, long after Medina Sidonia, with the shattered remnant of his expedition, had crept back to Spain.

Now that the inordinate ambition of Spain was no longer a cause of immediate danger, Protestant Europe could look calmly at the dying struggles of the league. Henry of Guise succumbed to the same fate as his father: he was assassinated. His brother, Mayenne, chosen by the confederates lieutenant-general of the state royal and crown of France, took the field against the two Henries—Valois and Navarre. Supported by the chief nobility of France, the two kings took Swiss and German mercenaries into their pay, and with forty thousand men advanced to the gates of Paris. While they were intent upon the siege, Henry of Valois, upon whose organization the presence of a friar produced, as he said himself, an agreeable sensation, died by the felon hand of Jacques Clement. Then the troubled state fell into the firmer hands of Henry of Navarre.

The prejudices which were entertained against the religion of Henry induced a large part of his army to desert him on his accession. He abandoned the siege of Paris, and retired into Normandy. Thither Mayenne led the forces of the League.

Elizabeth sent "brave Lord Willoughby" to the rescue. With this help and that of his Swiss and Germans, Henry conquered Mayenne at Ivry, and marched straight on Paris. But Parma, though suffering from disease, and maddened by accusations of treachery from the king whom he had so faithfully served, quitted the Low Countries, and with wonderful skill advanced by forced marches and raised the siege. Hardly had he returned to Holland when he again rushed back to raise the siege of Rouen. He died at Arras in 1592. It must be conceded alike by friend and foe, that Alexander Farnese, Prince of Parma, was, beyond dispute, the ablest general and most consummate statesman even in that court and generation where generals and statesmen so abounded.

CHAPTER VI.

1590

Then followed the abjuration of Protestant opinions by Henry IV., his coronation, and the absolute destruction of the League.

1593

In the meanwhile, Prince Maurice and Sir Francis Vere were gallantly holding their own in the Low Countries. They expelled the Spaniards from Gerstruydenburg and Groningen, and soon afterwards the decisive victory of Turnhout placed a number of other places in their hands.

1597

1595

Henry IV. had declared war with Spain two years before. He had driven the Spaniards from Burgundy. He now repossessed himself of Amiens. The English under Effingham and Essex attacked Cadiz, where a new armada was being fitted out for

1598

the reduction of England. A combined English and Dutch fleet surprised the war galleys that lay in the bay, and after an obstinate engagement obliged them to surrender or to run ashore. The land forces under Essex then sacked the town. So ended the second Spanish armada. Victorious at all points, Spain silenced, the League disbanded, Henry determined to lay the foundations of a lasting peace. He signed the edict of Nantes, which secured to the Protestants not only the free exercise of their religion, but a share in the administration of justice, and the right of being admitted to all employments of trust, profit, and honour. For the first time during six-and-thirty years the Huguenots were able to consider themselves secure; Philip, who wanted leisure to concentrate his attention on England and his rebellious provinces in Holland, was not unwilling to come to an accommodation. Peace was therefore signed between France and Spain at Vervins in 1598.

The disobedient provinces of the Netherlands offered a strong contrast to the condition of Spain. Though they had long been the seat of war, they were every year increasing in power and in riches. The obedient Netherlands were almost a desert: the manufacturing towns were deserted, and the fields untilled. Brabant, the Walloon provinces, and Flanders were completely desolate. The mouth of the Scheldt was commanded by Flushing, and Flushing was held for the republic by the brave soldiers of Elizabeth. Antwerp had been recovered for the king; but its commerce was annihilated—its docks and basins were empty. Its industrious population had migrated or had died of starvation. Ghent and Bruges, Valenciennes and Tournay, once so populous and so vigorous, had shared the same destruction. The Republic lay between them and the seacoast, and blocked up every avenue of trade. Agriculture was dying out of the land. Commerce was perishing of inanition. The pikemen of Spain and Italy replaced the weavers and clothworkers who had formerly crowded the towns. The peasantry, driven from their employments, made the fields and woods unsafe; the only trade was war. Towns were depopulated; wild beasts inhabited the deserted farmhouses. The dykes were neglected, and the water, toilfully excluded during the time of Holland's prosperity, resumed its old ascendency. Vast morasses replaced smiling farms and vineyards. Boars and wolves prowled even to the outskirts of the great cities. Pestilence, the natural consequence of uncultivated fields, smote the unhappy country. The spoiler and the despoiled were visited impartially with the evils that famine brings in its train. The silver of Potosi went straight to the centres of wealth and industry which had been formed in the disobedient provinces.

In the confederated states, the war paid itself over and over again. The leaders found time, amidst the more pressing avocations, to patronize and encourage schools and found colleges. The artisans of Flanders and Brabant transferred their industry to the cities of Friesland and Gueldres. The navy of the republic commanded the seas, and made itself necessary even to its enemies in Spain and Portugal. In the lifetime of Philip II., the mines of America were worked principally for the benefit of the enemies of Spain. Amsterdam, Leyden, and Utrecht became as celebrated for their lace, their tapestry, their cutlery, as Ypres, Brussels, and Valenciennes had formerly been. "War had become a benediction." The republic performed the carrying trade of Europe, and became the commercial emporium and granary of the west. It waxed rich and powerful. Its population was increased by emigrants from those provinces which, unhappily for themselves, still remained faithful to Spain.

The latter country was rapidly becoming merely the mint of Europe. Gold which came from Mexico and Peru was hypothecated before its arrival. The long wars of Charles V. and of Philip had exhausted the resources of the peninsula. Its agriculture had degenerated. The only trade was with America, and even that was in the hands of foreigners who found the capital, and carried it on under the names of privileged merchants at Seville and Cadiz. Manufactures likewise fell into decay. During the whole war with the Low Countries, a brisk traffic was kept up between the belligerents. The Spaniards were dependent on the Dutch for the necessaries as well as the luxuries of life.

At peace with France, Philip could now direct his

whole attention to the subjugation of his revolted colonies; but his efforts were ineffectual. The sturdy Netherlanders, whom his barbarities had failed to intimidate, were little disposed to return to their allegiance now that their star appeared to be in the ascendant. Nothing would henceforth satisfy them but complete emancipation from the tyrant's yoke.

The peace between France and Spain at Vervins, was immediately followed by a close alliance between England and Holland. Philip looked on at first with sullen indignation. He proposed to increase his armies; to subdue his rebellious provinces at any cost. But age and infirmities were creeping on him apace. His haughty and imperious mind was broken by years and by disaster. He resolved to make vicariously the concessions which he was ashamed to make in person. He made over the sovereignty of the Netherlands to his daughter Isabella, whose marriage with the Archduke of Austria had just been arranged. He did not live to see either the marriage or the disdain with which the Dutch treated their new sovereign. In 1598, September 13th, he died.

Albert, Archduke of Austria, immediately after his marriage, hastened to take possession of his new inheritance. The Dutch returned no answer to his entreaty that they would return to their natural rulers; on the contrary, they obtained money from Henry IV., and took into their service the veterans whom at the peace of Vervins, he had disbanded. The archduke collected fresh levies in Spain,

Italy, and Germany. With these he proceeded to encounter the allies under Prince Maurice and Sir Francis Vere. They met at Nieuport in the year 1600. For hours the fate of battle wavered:—the yellow-jerkined pikemen of Spain and Italy again and again withstood the impetuous advance of the allies; but at nightfall the Spaniards were beaten from the field.

Sieges, tedious marchings and countermarchings now took the place of active enterprise. The great Spinola, who commanded for the archduke, sat down before Ostend, according to the strictest rules of the military art. Money was expended in sums which even Mexico and Peru could not long continue to supply. Seventy thousand of the bravest warriors of Spain were killed beneath the walls. Times were changed since a Spanish general could by the mere terror of his name reduce a Dutch citadel to obedience. Day by day the besiegers became more hopeless; and Prince Maurice saw more clearly the approach of the time which should bring the recognition of his country's independence. For years the adventurers of Elizabeth had carried on a-predatory warfare with Spain;—had plundered his galleons and intercepted his supplies. Since 1589, when Drake and Norris had with small assistance fitted out a fleet to make descents in Spain and Portugal, every year had been signalized by some new exploit. In April 1589, Drake with eleven hundred gentlemen had marched up to Lisbon, and plundered the country. Of his eleven hundred he brought but three hundred and fifty back. In June of the same year sixty ships were cut out from their moorings in the Tagus. In 1592 the Earl of Cumberland, the corporation of London, and Sir Walter Raleigh, had combined to make a marauding expedition against the Spanish Indies, and had brought back a galleon from the Azores worth a hundred and fifty thousand pounds. In July 1595, sailed the disastrous expedition to Darien. Drake and the first captain under whom he served as a boy, old Hawkins, intended to plunder Panama, where was stored the treasure of Peru. But the season was sickly : the Spaniards were well prepared. Sir Thomas Baskerville, and a host of other gallant gentlemen died on the inhospitable shore. In September of the same year sailed the expedition of Howard and Essex, in which Cadiz was plundered and the ships in its harbour burned. In 1957, Raleigh and Essex sailed on a vain quest for the homeward-bound treasure-galleons of the Spaniards. In 1601 the Spaniards made a landing at Kinsale, and joined Tyrone and his Irish rebels; and Sir Robert Mansel with three sail had a brilliant and successful action with a Spanish fleet.

Nevertheless, the war between England and Spain began to languish. Philip II. was dead. Elizabeth was no longer the great and imperious princess "with the heart of an English king." She was but the wreck of her former self—a wailing, infirm old woman. " These troubles waste her much," says Sir John Harrington. "Everie new message from the city doth disturb her;—she frowns on all the ladies. The many evil plots and designs hath overcome her highness's sweet temper; she walks much in her privy chamber, and stamps much at ill news, and thrusts her rusty sword at times into the arras, in a great rage. Her highness has worne but one change of rayment for manie days, and swears much at those who cause her griefs. She often chides for small neglect, in such wise as to make these fayre maides often cry and bewail in piteous sort." Pitiful record of a great intellect dethroned! At length, while Spinola sat before Ostend, and Rimbach, Grave, and Sluys were falling before the attack of Maurice, news came from England that she was dead. The 25th March, 1603, was a sad day for England.

None felt the loss more keenly than the struggling states. They soon found that her successor, James I., was little likely to continue the war with Spain. Spinola became commander-in-chief for the archduke in the Netherlands, and three hundred thousand crowns a month were sent into Holland for the prosecution of the war. Yet the forces of the archduke barely held their own. It was not long ere Spinola discovered that it would be impossible to reduce the Netherlanders to obedience. Before the suspension of arms which he recommended took place, the Netherlands had achieved a position which enabled them to dictate its terms.

During the long struggle which was now drawing to a close, each of the belligerents had sent traders or colonists to the west. Before the close of the sixteenth century, the Dutch, the French, the English, the Swedes, the Danes, and the Spaniards had all, with more or less success, traded with, or settled beyond the Atlantic. During the war of independence the industry of the Dutch had never wavered. Their geographical and political position gave that industry an external impulse. Their citadels had been filled with mercenary soldiers; village, camp, and city were held by their oppressors; men could find no asylum but foreign exile or the ocean. The Zealanders took almost instinctively to commerce and to piracy. The two trades now so incompatible were then almost synonymous. The Spanish war was carried on in every clime. To plunder the Spaniard was not only a lucrative but a patriotic pursuit. The soil of Holland was kept with difficulty from being submerged by the ocean. Zealand was but a collection of fishing villages on the shore of the North Sea; the land was inhospitable; even had it been good and fully cultivated, it was not extensive enough to support the teeming population which resorted to it. For, while the obedient provinces were becoming depopulated, the provinces of the union were increasing; gradually their ships obtained the carrying trade of Europe, and carried the flag of the republic into distant lands. Amsterdam rose on the commercial ruins of Antwerp. It became the great emporium of the world. After the discoveries of Vasco di Gama, Lisbon might have risen to pre-eminence, had not the supineness of her merchants thrown away the golden opportunity. It was eagerly seized by the Dutch. Through the long struggle with Spain, Dutch vessels traded freely with Portugal, and distributed over Europe the wealth which Lisbon merchants had gathered from the East. But in 1594, the narrow-minded bigotry of Philip prohibited the intercourse which had subsisted between Portugal and his rebellious provinces. A moment of consternation on the part of the Dutch was succeeded by a resolve to beat the Lisbon merchant at his own weapons. Bukker of Amsterdam, and Leyer of Enkhuisen, formed companies to traffic with the East Indies. They met with distinguished success; their armed vessels put down by force of arms all efforts of the Spanish to arrest their progress. A few years later they were able to take their share in the colonization of America.

Meanwhile the English and French were not idle. As early as 1541 the advantages of the cod-fishery on the banks of Newfoundland were well known. They were protected by a special act in the first parliament of Edward VI., the preamble of which states that the navigation of the Newfoundland seas had long been burdened by exactions from the officers of admiralty. These exactions are forbidden in the body of the act. It is evident that the trade must have been of long standing, since the exactions spoken of in the act of 1548 had been levied so long as to be regarded almost as a prescriptive right. In 1578, the English vessels on the banks were about fifty in number. There were a hundred Spaniards, fifty Portuguese, a hundred and fifty French, and twenty or thirty Biscayan whale-ships. The English claimed the sovereignty of those seas, partly on the score of Cabot's discoveries, and partly on the strength of Gilbert's settlement in Newfoundland. The foreign fishermen generally acknowledged the claim set up by the English; and before the close of Queen Elizabeth's reign, more than two hundred English vessels and eight thousand English sailors frequented the banks.

French discovery, which had languished after the loss of Roberval's colony in 1542, revived with the return of peace. The same year which witnessed the signature of the Edict of Nantes, and the peace of Vervins, saw the Marquis de la Roche invested with the title and power of viceroy of New France. Lescarbot, the geographer,* describes the limits of de la Roche's government in grandiloquent terms:—
"Ainsi," says he, "notre nouvelle France a pour limites du côté d'ouest les terres jusqu'à la mer dite Pacifique, au deçà du tropique du Cancer; au midi les îles de la mer Atlantique du côté de Cuba et l'île Espagnole; au levant la mer du Nord qui baigne la nouvelle France; et au septentrion cette

---

* Edit. 1611, vol. i. p. 31.

terre qui est dite inconnue, vers la mer Glacée jusqu'au Pole arctique."

The traders of France had gradually crept inland, and had long carried on a peddling traffic with the Indian hunters.

De la Roche's expedition perished miserably by famine and pestilence, but private adventurers carried on the trade in peltries. Pontgravé, Chauvin, and La Chatte led expeditions, more or less successful, till, in 1603, Champlain sailed for the St. Lawrence and established the first permanent settlement in the magnificent province of Canada.

CHAPTER VII.

EUROPEAN MANNERS IN THE SEVENTEENTH CENTURY.

[1603—1648.]

State of Manners in France, in England—History of John Smith—Social Condition of Holland.

DURING the time which elapsed between the formation and the downfall of the Holy League, there was but little time for any attempt at colonization on the part of England and France. Spain was quietly and securely spreading her settlements over the southern portion of North America and the whole area of the southern continent; but, with the exception of Ribault's unfortunate expedition to Florida, and an equally unfortunate attempt of Raleigh, neither of her northern rivals had done anything on the coast of America but burn and destroy. Vast armies were constantly kept on foot. Adventurous spirits found fighting and excitement in plenty near home; and had no need to go across the seas to obtain their fill of either.

With the accession of James I. to the throne, a new era began. England withdrew from the Spanish war. France was enjoying a temporary lull in her

1603

intestine feuds. The Catholic reaction, triumphant in France, in Southern Germany, in Italy, in Spain, had almost entirely withdrawn from the contest in Holland and Northern Europe. For a time commerce and honest enterprise had leisure to expand under the fostering influence of peace.

It was no longer the warrior, but the statesman who ruled in France. "Dans cette époque," writes Michelet, in his notes on Richelieu,* " l'histoire de la place publique, du grand jour des révolutions, tombe du cabinet des princes ou des ministres rois." The great men of the sixteenth century were no more. The king was a man of contradictions and incongruities. Successive ministers, Sully, Richelieu, and Mazarin, pulled the strings of political· puppets; and, instead of appearing at the head of armies, and dictating peace at the sword's point, they were seen only by the beneficent effects of wise economy and good management.

Although the genius of Henry, and, in the succeeding reign, of Richelieu, prevented any active outbreak, France was still divided into two hostile camps. Henry, under the mask of Catholicism, concealed as great an attachment to freedom of opinion as he could avow with safety to his crown. He saw that the only thing which could restore the shattered state was unity. But Richelieu and Henry, though both agreed upon the object to be aimed at, differed in their way of attaining it. Henry

* Histoire de France, xi., 458.

EXODUS OF THE WESTERN NATIONS. 193

wished to employ and direct the energies of both opposing forces, and, if possible, by dexterous management to unite them. He would have taken the Protestants into the service of the state: he would have calmed their fears, utilized and directed their efforts: he would have employed the mariners of Rochelle in his navy. The Huguenot soldiers would have been absorbed into his army. A colony under royal patronage would have been established in Acadia. Dispersed on the sea in pursuit of Spanish galleons, or laden with the spoils of the Spanish colonies, they would have soon forgotten their factions and their cities of refuge. Rochelle would have been no longer Huguenot; but French nationality would have replaced religion. The immutable law would have asserted its power—that an opinion persecuted is an active danger, an opinion left alone is disarmed. But when Richelieu acquired power he adopted a different plan. He, too, sought unity, but he sought it through the destruction of one of the opposing forces. He succeeded in a great measure. Emigration commenced, and De Monts carried with him the life of Protestantism to Acadia. But even this refuge was not long permitted. The old faith was established even on the shores of Newfoundland and on the forest-clad banks of the St. Lawrence. The Jesuits were recalled to France.

The state of the European continent, desolated by civil war, imperfectly cultivated, accustomed for years to no law but force, was wild and unsettled. France was far before her neighbours in many of the requirements of civilization. The inns of other nations were mere rude caravanserais, where the traveller was obliged to carry with him every necessary of life. In Spain nothing could be procured at the roadside inns except vinegar, oil, and salt. The traveller was compelled to take his provisions with him, or to rely on such supplies as he could purchase from the peasantry on his route. These matters were much better ordered in France. The French hotel-keepers were appointed by letters-patent from the king. The licences thus granted were of different kinds: some took in only foot travellers, others only horsemen. The dinner of a foot traveller cost six sols, his bed eight sols. A traveller on horseback dined for twelve sols; his bed cost twenty sols.*

The minutest particulars were the objects of government supervision: a foot traveller was not allowed to dine or to sleep in the same style or at the same expense as a horseman. The horseman was not permitted to indulge in the simple fare of a traveller on foot. The inns in which the traveller dined but did not sleep were called "repues." Crows, snakes, horses, and other nameless viands were sometimes † served up. Inns where the traveller could sleep were called "gîtes," and were very often on a grand scale.‡ The innkeeper received the guest with the

* Ordonnance relative aux taux des hôteliers, 1579.

† Hist. de Sancerre, Jean de Léry; Chap. ix. Hist. de France, par Biguerre, liv. xxxv.

‡ Guide des Chemins de France. Charles Estienne, Paris, 1563.

greatest civility; but he had the right of marching him off to prison, or seizing his horse and goods for the non-payment of his bill. During the time of the League, the innkeepers were among the hottest of partisans: the traveller was obliged to be very cautious in observing whether the inn in which he lodged had the royal escutcheon of France or the cross of Lorraine. Every traveller, Royalist or Leaguer alike, was in those days, as a matter of precaution, disarmed on entering the hostelry.* After the Edict of Nantes the custom fell into disuse.

The roads of France were among the best of Europe. While the highways of England were but miserable swamps, impracticable for wheel-carriages and almost equally impracticable for horsemen, the French had made many broad, flat highways. In Bergier's History of the Great Roads of the Roman Empire,† the method of their construction is described. The breadth of the road was first traced by engineers and marked out by boulders of rock; on the hills it was paved; in the plains or swamps it was filled in with flint, gravel, or stones; ditches were run along the sides; and fruit or forest trees were planted at intervals along them. The roads radiating from the great towns were causeways made of earth and stones, raised several feet above the surrounding country. Along the course of the rivers great embankments served in many places both for dykes

* Registres du Parl. de Paris, 1563.
† Bergier, liv. ii. chap. 19.

CHAPTER VII.

against inundations and for highways :* the slopes reveted with grass or stone, like those of fortifications. The chemins de châtellerie, or roads leading to a castle, were built by great troops of villagers and artisans, who were summoned to work in the name of the seigneur. They were employed in the name of the mayor in the case of roads running from one town to another; in the name of the king for royal roads which went from one extremity of the kingdom to the other. These working parties were called "corvées," and were not paid. Often, however, the workmen received salaries, which were paid in Brittany by a tax on wine; in other provinces by the gabelle, or salt tax; and again in others by tolls received at turnpikes, which consisted, as at present, of long bars which went across the road, and were hoisted or lowered by pulleys. In some cases, the farmers of the tolls were charged with the reparation of the roads; in others, the reparation as well as the construction was made by "corvées."† The *itinéraires* of that period tell you that on such a road pavement begins at such a place, finishes at such another; that between such a town and another there is no great road. Then the directions run— go to the right above or below the villages. Keep to the hill, follow the valley, or go parallel to the ditches.‡

* Bouchel, Bibliothèque du Droit Français, under head "Turcies et levées."
† Bib. de Bouchel, ubi sup.
‡ Guide des Chemins de France, ubi sup.

Some of the roads are described in terms by no means reassuring :—Chemin du Diable, Rue d'Enfer. They indicate certain places with such warnings as the following :— Briganderie, Ancienne Briganderie, Passage Périlleux, Bois de Deux Lieux, Passe-Vite!

The French posts were thoroughly organized.* Postmasters of the king wore the royal arms upon their sleeve. Great seigneurs rode post with thirty horses, the king with a hundred. In Brittany there were no posts at all; the post-riders were forbidden to carry private letters, they carried only the despatches of the king.† The conveyance of private letters was in the hands, not of the government, but of carriers. A traveller would go from twelve to fifteen leagues a day; he might carry a small portmanteau behind him on his saddle, but if he had a trunk he was obliged to take a baggage-horse. He was invariably accompanied by a guide whose business it was to prevent the traveller from running off with the horse. The animal was branded with the initial letters of the town whence he started. On some of the great roads post carriages ran ; they had stuffed seats, were covered with leather outside, and were furnished with curtains to keep out the rain. Each traveller was allowed four pounds of luggage ; he could go from Paris to Rouen for seventy sous, from Paris to Orleans for seventy-five.

---
* Traité de police de Delamarre, liv. vi. art. " Postes."
† Ordonnance du 19 Juin 1464, relative à l'institution des postes.

CHAPTER VII.

Dress* was subject to sumptuary laws even more strict than the English laws of Elizabeth. Clerks and nobles alone were allowed to wear silk. It was only prelates, great personages, and soldiers even among the privileged class who could wear silk upon silk. Colours of stuff distinguished different ranks of life. Boatmen wore one stocking of one colour and one of another. The bourgeois was dressed in black, ecclesiastical dignitaries in scarlet; so were the nobles. Great gentlemen only might wear a red head-dress. The lowest class of the people dressed in white, as also did the nobles occasionally, but then they wore white velvet. The courtiers wore their sword far back, with the pummel on the loins; gentlemen of lesser station on the hip. Great nobles occasionally had their sword carried by a footman in livery. The dress of ladies was distinguished by equally minute peculiarities. Colours and stuffs marked rank as among the men. Only princesses and duchesses could wear double rows of diamonds. The noble lady and the bourgeoise were distinguishable even by their rosaries or their prayer-books. Manners were more attended to here than in any other country. Nothing was done without frequent salutation. You met the public executioner in the street—he was easily known by his dress: you took off your hat to him; "Heaven keep you out of my hands," was his

---

* Many "ordonnances relatives aux vêtements," quoted by Monteil, Histoire des Français.

answer.* Salutations were even counted by the parliaments and lawyers, and among seignorial rights, which could be enforced by law.† A great noble, a cardinal or a bishop, was addressed monseigneur; a knight, messire; a gentleman, monsieur; a magistrate, messire-maître; a lawyer or a doctor, maître; a monk, dom. The wife of a great lord, madame; the wife of a gentleman, or lawyer, or a doctor, mademoiselle. In Paris, as may be seen in the journal of Henry IV., 28 Mar., 1594, the term madame had descended to the wives of lawyers and doctors, and even to those of librarians and shopkeepers. Did any one sneeze, all present took off their hats and muttered a prayer. The rich carried a handkerchief in their pockets: it was the custom of the bourgeois to blow their noses with their sleeves. To intimate that a man had a considerable fortune, you said, "Il ne se mouche pas avec la manche."‡

But in no particular was etiquette more rigorous than in the matter of chairs and stools.§ The visitor, according to his rank, was invited to sit on a large armchair, a little armchair, a chair without arms, a bench, a chest, or a footstool. Politeness was carried as far as to furnish accused persons in courts of justice with a little stool called a sellette. In 1601, a gentleman of the court, François de Nagu, sieur de Varenne,

---

* The custom was kept up till the Revolution: see Monteil.
† Bouchet, verb. "saisie féodale."
‡ Recueil des Proverbes.
§ Traité de Civilité Puérile, par Saliat, chap. "visites."

was sentenced to be whipped in the Conciergerie for having refused to sit upon the sellette when on his trial.

Paris, at the end of the sixteenth century, was about as large as Madrid and Toledo together. The kings often issued decrees against the increase of the size of the town; but it was found impossible, in fact, to restrain it. It was divided into four principal quarters : the court, where was the Louvre, the Tuileries ; the quarter where was the Bastille, the Arsenal, which was full of arms, and the Temple, which was full of powder; the learned quarter, where were the colleges of the university; lastly, the religious quarter, where were situated the convents and hospitals. The population was about 400,000 ; a little more than London, and a little less than Constantinople. The garde bourgeoise, of which the army of the League was in its time principally composed, counted nearly 100,000 men. The hospital of the Hôtel Dieu already existed : there were generally 1000 patients. The number of poor was estimated at about 17,000.

As in London, thieves and disorderly persons associated themselves in companies under various slang names. These may be seen in the "Histoire de Francion." There was, amongst others, a company of murderers, who could be hired for the satisfaction of private revenge. Besides thieves, cut-throats, and murderers, there were a large number of turbulent scholars of the university : the apprentices were as disorderly as in London. Lackeys and serving-men were more disorderly still, and were constantly fighting in the streets. Pre-eminent among the lovers of disturbance were the young noblemen, to the full as ill-disciplined and as wild as those of our own country. They delighted to attack the watch, and to commit every sort of outrage.* Murders were very prevalent: there would have been more had not the police been, for that day, excellent. No one was permitted to have more than one door to his house; if there was more than one it was built up by order of the magistrate. Each house in turn furnished a watchman, who was provided with a bell to raise the city in case of disorder. During certain months of the year each house was compelled to hang a lighted lantern before the door.

The paid guard of the city was formed of old archers to the number of one hundred and fifty, all decorated with the ancient order of the star. Charles VI. added sixty crossbowmen and Charles IX. a hundred arquebussiers. In 1592, and the two following years, Paris was nothing but a walled camp,† in which every house was a tent, every citizen a soldier, and of which the different ranks of the clergy were the officers. During the siege the rich as well as the poor lived upon horses, dogs, cats, and barley bread; towards the close, on roots and herbs gathered even under the fire of the cannons of the besiegers. The

* Mémoires de d'Aubigné.
† Mémoires de Villeroi, discours du siége de Paris, 1690.

streets were filled with dead and dying. Vultures and serpents were found among them.

During a great part of the sixteenth century the ordinary way of recruiting * was for a captain to receive a commission to raise a company: there was no want of candidates for admission. The enlistment was at first only for a month, at the end of which the soldier could retire: each soldier was allowed a servant. At his first enlistment the recruit became, according to the regiment in which he entered, a piquier, an arquebussier or a mousquetaire. The next step was that of lanspassade, broken lance: the name was derived from Piedmont, when, during the French wars the French dismounted cavaliers served with the infantry with that title, which distinguished them from the common run of foot-soldiers. Their pay was a little higher than that of the foot-soldier, and the sergeant had no right to strike one of that grade with his halbert. The next step was corporal, the pay was ten sous per day. Then fourrier, whose duty was to inscribe upon the door of a house where soldiers were billeted the names of those who were lodged there. It was a post of some responsibility and of some danger, for omission to perform the duties of the office was certain to entail flogging; and a fourrier who accepted bribes not to billet soldiers on a particular house was tolerably sure to be hanged. The next step was that of sergeant: the fourrier had charge, amongst other things, of the pay of his men—the sergeant at-

* See Monteil, Hist. des Français, chap. " Pédescaux de Metz."

tended to nothing but their military instruction. The superior grades were, as at present, ensign, lieutenant, and captain. On the march each of these officers was allowed a horse. The lands of an officer were free from tax. The French infantry dated from the time of Francis I. By the ordinance of St. Germain-en-Laye, he instituted seven legions of footmen of six thousand men each. To the legions of Francis I. succeeded the legions of Henry II., under the name of regiments. The number of regiments in the service was never fixed. The four regiments of Piedmont, Champagne, Picardy, and Normandy alone remained unchanged. The others were raised and disbanded as occasion served. The old regiments consisted of twenty companies, the others fifteen.

It was about this time that the change inaugurated by Coligny, the substitution namely of infantry for cavalry as the base of the French army, took deep root in France. Henceforward the infantry formed the bulk of the national force, but the gendarmerie was still a magnificent corps. This was entirely composed of gentlemen, magnificently clothed and equipped; but their arms, consisting of pistol and lance, were hardly so deadly as the heavy cuirass and strong sword of the German reitres. The captain of gendarmes was ordered by the regulations to keep sixteen horses, the lieutenant eight, the cornet six, the sergeant-major five, the trooper three. The expense, however, caused the gendarmerie to fall into disuse. They were replaced by regiments corresponding to the carbineers, lancers, dragoons, and light horse of the present day. The inventor of dragoons was the Count de Cossé-Brissac. They acted sometimes on foot and sometimes on horseback. In the reign of Louis XIII. recruiting was reduced to a system. In most towns some old officer was stationed, a great giver of dinners and suppers, great in anecdote and conversation. Captains who had commissions to raise troops were in the habit of applying to the recruiting agent,* and of placing the levy of the troops in his hands. Some of these officials were little better than crimps, others resorted only to the legal attractions of high bounty, and the *argumentum ad hominem* conveyed to the hungry and the idle, of partridges, loaves of bread, cakes, and other delicacies spitted on the drawn swords of the recruiting party. These were the materials of a feast of which the recruits partook at the end of the day. The classes most commonly attracted by the recruiting parties were, as in other countries, apprentices, idle students of the universities, lazy villagers, mechanics out of work, and servants out of place. It never was very diffi-

* Le tambour parcourait la ville et après avoir battu les trois bans, il portait la main au chapeau et disait, suivant la formule ordinaire : " De par le Roi ! on fait savoir à tout homme, de quelle qualité et condition qu'il soit, âgé de seize ans, qui désirerait prendre parti dans le régiment de Thianges, infanterie, qu'on lui donnera quinze francs, vingt francs selon l'homme qu'il sera, et un bon congé au bout de trois ans. Argent comptant sur la caisse ! On ne demande pas de crédit ; ceux qui seront portés de bonne volonté n'ont qu'à venir !" Alors il devait faire sonner une grande bourse de soie, grillée, pleine d'or et d'argent, &c.—Monteil, Hist. des Français, iv. 48, chap. " Gens de Guerre."

cult to induce a sufficient number of recruits to join the army, the strength of which was kept up to three hundred or three hundred and forty thousand men. Married men, foreigners, and men belonging to the town in which the recruiting garrison was quartered —men belonging to the town of St. Etienne, to the Isle de Rhé, to the Isle d'Oléron, and to the province of Boulonnois, were not allowed to enlist: the first was excluded because the number of workmen in the factory of arms, at St. Etienne, would be thereby diminished; the two next, because the islands of de Rhé and d'Oléron required all their population for their own defence. The inhabitants of the Boulonnois were exempt, as they furnished six regiments for the protection of the coasts. The food in garrison consisted each day of twenty-four ounces of brown bread, and each week three pounds of meat; on the march, the same ration of bread, a pound of meat, a pint of wine, cider, or beer. The citizen on whom the soldiers were billeted at night was obliged to furnish fire for cooking victuals, a pot to contain them, and to allow the soldier to share with his family the comforts of his fire and candle.

The dress of the army under Louis XIII. had become more uniform, but less rich than under Charles IX., Henry III., or Henry IV. Regiments were distinguished by the colour and cut of their doublets, and also by the colour and form of their facings. On their buttons, which were made of tin or of copper, were inscribed the name and number of

CHAPTER VII. their regiment. The colours of the various uniforms were arranged according to strict rules of precedence, one colour being considered more honourable than another. Royal regiments wore the royal livery and were dressed in blue; regiments of the queen, the dauphin, and the princes of the blood in bright colours, as red and green; regiments of the marshals and great nobles in grey. In the seventeenth century, flint locks and a short musket replaced the six-foot arquebuss. About the beginning of the seventeenth century, the bayonet, whose inventor and time of invention is uncertain, was adopted in the French army, and for the first time cuirass and breast-plate were entirely laid aside by the infantry.

Military punishments were terribly severe. The strapado, in which the soldier was tied hand and foot, was hoisted to the top of a pole and allowed to drop suddenly to within a short distance of the earth, was one of the most formidable. But the punishment which was called the "honneur du morion," mixed up with most undeniable cruelty a kind of grim humour. The soldier who was condemned to it was obliged to choose from among his comrades a godfather; the godfather disarmed him, and placed his hat on the point of a pike which the victim held. He then placed him in the position in which a schoolboy of the present day still receives the acolade of the head master, and battered him with the wood of his arquebuss. The blows were thus counted:—the victim was asked whether he was a gentleman; he was obliged to answer that he was, being a soldier. He was then informed that a gentleman should have so many pages, valets, dogs, and hawks; for each he received a blow. He was asked how many towers there were on his castle; it was useless to reply that he had none—the house of a gentleman must of necessity have so many towers—and the unfortunate must receive a blow for each. He then got one for each of the princes of the blood, for the marshals of France, and so on, until at the discretion of his captain the punishment was completed. The four last blows were given with the words,

> "Honeur à Dieu,
> Service au Roi,
> Tout pour toi,
> Rien pour moi."

Then the drum beat the "point of war," and the ceremony was over.

A deserter was punished with death. A soldier who enlisted in two companies, who offered violence to a woman, who struck his officer, or the man on whose house he was billeted, or who stole anything from a house in which he was billeted, was punished with death. The prévôts, assisted by the lawyers of the nearest town, formed a military tribunal which could pass a capital sentence. The constable of France had absolute power. The old constable Montmorency used to walk about diligently telling his beads, and without looking up from the ground, order one to be hanged, another to the strapado, and a third to run the gauntlet. " Dieu nous garde des pâtenôtres de Monsieur le Connétable," was a proverb long in use in the French army.

In the succeeding century most of the military punishments had been done away with. There remained only the stick or the strap for slight offences; the wooden horse and the picket, both of them instruments of intense suffering, for more serious matters.

The prisons were badly built, badly ventilated, and badly lighted. Until the time of the edict of Orleans, in 1560, the great nobles considered themselves entitled to throw their villagers into the dungeons of their castles. These were generally caves hollowed out at the bottom of the towers; but after the edict mentioned above, the nobles were forced to build their prisons above the level of the ground, and to separate them from their castles. A second edict prevented the use of chains in the prisons of the nobles. In the towns, old fortresses and strong places and old towers in the town walls were used as prisons. They were loathsome dens; and it was almost always to their vaults that the plague and other epidemics might be traced. The prisoner was fed at the expense of the accuser if a civilian, but at that of the king in other cases. A prisoner, at the discretion of the gaoler, might be placed in the black hole or in irons. Any one furnishing instruments by which a prisoner could effect his escape was punished as if he himself had been the prisoner; but a prisoner endeavouring to make his escape received no increase of punishment. If a prisoner escaped by the negligence of the gaoler, the latter took his place. Like all other departments of state the prisons were farmed.

As in England, the use of torture disgraced judicial interrogatories. The rack to stretch the limbs of the accused, the fire to scorch the soles of his feet, the boots to smash his knees, and water to distend his chest, were used in a manner sufficiently scientific to satisfy even our James the Second.

At the time of the peace of Vervins, France had drunk the cup of bitterness almost to the dregs. The state was torn by faction. The crown was encumbered with debts and pensions, the nobles were turbulent. A long term of rebellion and disorder had made them almost forget all traditions of allegiance. While in Spain loyalty was pushed to the extreme verge of superstition, in France the king, apart from his influence as a man, received little reverence, and no submission. The royal prerogative had been invaded so often, and the temper of the last weak princes had allowed it to be done so often with absolute impunity, that it had become a mere name. The country was barren and desolated by war. The misery of the country was pitiable. The towns were full of beggars, the high roads swarmed with its disbanded soldiers. Heavy taxes were imposed upon the people; and, until the genius of Sully had found a way to escape from the dilemma, the national resources of France seemed almost completely bankrupt. The plague made periodical ravages in Paris and the other great towns.

CHAPTER VII.

Sully himself gives a dismal description of the condition of the soldiers even so late as 1604.* "It is hard to conceive that, in a nation which from its first establishment has been engaged in war, and has indeed pursued no other trade than that of arms, no care should have been hitherto taken to form and methodize them. Whatever related to the soldiery of France was offensive and disgusting. The foot soldiers were enlisted by violence, and made to march by a cudgel; their pay was unjustly withheld, they heard of nothing but a prison, and had nothing before their eyes but a gibbet. This treatment drove them into all methods of desertion, which was prevented only by the prévôts, who kept them in their camps like men besieged : the officers themselves being ill-paid, had some kind of right to violence and plunder. Henry would often say—and he spoke according to his own experience—that the public could never be well served till the troops were put into another state."

Nevertheless, the genius of Sully began to overcome even these difficulties. He commenced to pay off the crown debts. The nobles were forbidden to make fresh fortifications. The seigneurs, who levied tolls upon the roads and rivers, on condition of keeping them in repair, were compelled to fulfil their engagements or to forfeit their privileges. Commerce revived, and, as it always does, followed facilities of access. The forests and streams were for the

* Mémoires de Sully, book xix.

first time protected. War was made on the footpads and highwaymen who infested the forests and roads. Agriculture was encouraged; silk manufacturers, cloth-workers, glass-workers, established themselves under the fostering care of the king. Sully discouraged the plantation of colonies; but the king, faithful to the traditions of his great and good friend Coligny, considered that a brave and unruly people wanted some safety-valve, and departed in this instance from the advice of his minister.

The Italians and Spaniards, as well as the Dutch and French, were all far in advance of England in the arts which constitute civilization. Our island was a country of fogs and mists: the drainage hardly in a better condition than that in which it had been left by the Romans. Manufactures hardly existed. Our navy was in its infancy; our internal police a farce; our roads the worst in Europe. The disbanded soldiers of Elizabeth wandered as sturdy beggars and "masterless men" over the country. The officers took service with foreign princes, or bid "Stand and deliver" on the king's highway. Mr. Smiles, in his "Lives of Eminent Engineers," says that Chief Justice Popham had been "on the road" in his youth. Our fisheries were so unproductive that the Dutch sold us herrings which they caught on our own coasts. We supplied Europe with wool as America till lately supplied us with cotton. England was but the storehouse of raw material. Though we had abundance of wool, we had no woollen manufactures. Even the small quantity of the latter that was made was sent to be finished by the dyers of Holland.

In the time of James the industry of cloth-workers, silk-weavers, and lace-makers had just begun to take root among us. These trades were, however, confined to foreigners, as exclusively as the banking trade had been in the hands of the Lombards. French and Flemish refugees had brought the skill of Yypres, Bruges, Ghent, and Arras to our shores, but the arts they taught were not yet naturalized among us.

In the preceding century, Danes and Genoese had been our shipbuilders. Owing to the encouragement of Elizabeth, and to the development of maritime enterprise, we had ceased to be dependent upon the foreigner for the building of our ships. Nevertheless, almost every other branch of mechanical science was unknown. A Dutchman was employed to erect a forcing-pump for supplying London with water. We were indebted to Holland for windmills, watermills, and pumping-engines; at a later day we borrowed from them the science of canal-making. The art of bridge-making had fallen so low that we were obliged to call in a Swiss engineer to build Westminster Bridge.*

The contemporary history of Scotland was a record of treachery, fanaticism, witchcraft, and assassination. The king himself entered with zest into the two latter subjects. He was fortunate enough to discover—and to give the world the benefit of the

* Smiles.

discovery—"why the devil did worke more with aunciont women than with others." Witch-finders laid traps, possessed at least of the merit of simplicity, on the public highways. A pinch of salt on a page of the Bible, or a couple of straws in the form of a cross, were considered as of unfailing virtue.

Ever since the dissolution of the monasteries under Henry VIII., even the small amount of drainage which had once existed had been allowed to fall into decay. The churchmen alone had paid any attention to the subject: now that their power was at an end, embankments were neglected, rivers silted up. The extensive fen-lands of the eastern counties were abandoned to the field-fowl and the fishes.* Large tracts of country in Cambridgeshire, Lincolnshire, and Norfolk presented the appearance of desolate and hideous morasses. For miles nothing could be seen in winter but a dismal lake, broken here and there by islets on which a few huts were erected by an ague-stricken population. In summer, ooze and mud replaced the waters of winter, and deadly miasmata arose. The fen-men—fen-slodgers, or yellow-bellies, as they were called—were described as a "barbarous, lazy, and beggarly people." They picked up a scanty subsistence by grazing, fishing, and fowling. But in their case flocks were represented by flocks of geese, which waded about in the shallows, while their herdsmen, if one may so call them, stalked after them on stilts.

* Bloomfield, Hist. of Norfolk.

CHAPTER VII.

The eastern counties were not alone in their misery: agriculture was everywhere grievously neglected. Occasionally, in the forests, which still covered a great part of the land, the traveller might come upon a hermitage in which some heartbroken recluse, or perhaps some gallant soldier, tired of war's alarms, had withdrawn himself from the world : John Smith, the future founder of Virginia was one of these unquiet spirits. In the narrative of his "True Travels and Adventures" you may read that "within a short time, being glutted with too much company, wherein he took small delight, he retired himselfe into a little woodie pasture, a good way from any towne, invironed with many hundred acres of other woods. Here, by a faire brook, he built a pavillion of boughes, where only in his cloaths he lay. His studie was Machiavill's Art of Warre, and Marcus Aurelius; his exercise, a good horse with his lance and ring : his food was thought to be more of venison than anything else : what he wanted his man brought him."*

The picture of an active-minded man and gallant soldier (of whom we shall see more anon), amusing himself with Marcus Aurelius, and riding a-tilt with lance and ring all alone in a forest, gives a curious glimpse of the state of society.

The Scottish border was unquiet. Maxwells and Johnsons fought savagely on the marches; and, if report speaks true, there were many border freebooters as savage as Geordie Bourne, who confessed

* Smith, True Travels, Adventures, and Observations. London, 1629.

before his execution that he had violated forty men's wives, besides committing numerous murders in cold blood. The nobility maintained enormous retinues,* which were constantly quarrelling among themselves. They generally had foreign masters of dancing, fencing, and riding among their retainers. John Smith tells us that his friends, wishing to draw him from the hermitage, " persuaded one Seignor Theodora Polalogra, rider to Henry, Earle of Lincoln, an excellent horseman, and a noble Italian gentleman, to insinuate into his wooddish acquaintances, whose languages and good discourse, and exercise of riding, drew him to stay with him at Tattersall."

King James in vain endeavoured to persuade the country gentlemen to leave the city and to retire to their country seats. The attractions of London were too great for them to resist. London was indeed a very different place from what it is in our day. The magistrates used once a year to go in solemn state to the head of the conduit, now Conduit Street, to inspect the works, and join in a solemn hunt. I have read a description of one of these hunts. They met somewhere in the neighbourhood of Grafton Street; killed a hare in the morning, and after partaking of an excellent dinner provided by the city chamberlain, killed a fox in the afternoon. An examination of the map of London of the time of James II. would enable any curious Nimrod of the present day to follow the run in imagination. He might picture to

* Lord Bacon.

himself how they found a fox in Berkeley Square—how they ran him up Davies Street and across Brook Street—how they dwelt for a moment in the little spinney near the Regent's Circus—how he was headed by a countryman near Cavendish Square, and turning sharp to the right, made for the earths near the British Museum—how Sir Walter Raleigh was mounted on a horse which he had bought for five hundred crowns* from his friend the Duc de Sully—how Sir Hugh Myddelton, who had smoked his morning pipe at Raleigh's suburban villa in the Strand, got a fall while scrambling in and out of the new road which he had lately helped to build from Paddington to the Bank—how a still more august figure mounted upon a roan jennet,† and securely trussed in a high demipique saddle, came ambling carefully along, followed, at a respectful distance, by courtiers who knew the royal weakness too well to press upon him closely.‡

The roads were unsafe: the carriers or packmen, who conveyed goods from place to place with their horse trains, kept generally to the high grounds, to avoid the morasses which lay in the valleys. It was only near great towns that there were regular high-

* Mémoires de Sully.

† Letter from Sir Thos. Howard to Lord Harrington in Letitia Aiken's Memoirs of the Reign of James I., "Above all things fail not to praise the roan jennet whereon the king doth daily ride."

‡ "The king was so tired with multitudes, especially in his hunting, that he caused an inhibition to be published to restrain the people from hunting *him*." Wilson's Life of James I. in the Complete History of England. Folio, London, 1719.

ways, and these were only passable for coaches under favourable circumstances. Indeed, coaches were by no means in general use. Queen Elizabeth's Dutch coachman had presented her with a vehicle of foreign construction, but it had no springs. She was dreadfully jolted while going into the city; and afterwards, bemoaning herself on the subject to the French ambassador, she was careful to indicate what part of her royal person had suffered most from the roughness of the road.*

The queen had always preferred riding into the city on a pillion behind the lord chancellor. Every one who was able to do so, travelled on horseback. The judges rode their circuits—briefless barristers went afoot. Highwaymen haunted the roads near the great towns, and plied their trade without the slightest molestation from the police. If a traveller was robbed, the hundred in which the robbery was committed had to make reparation.

Much light is thrown on the condition and practice of the "knights of the road" by one John Clavell, a highwayman, who, in 1625 or 1626, lay under sentence of death, and who, from his "lonelie, sad, and unfrequented chamber in the King's Bench," issued a poetical account of the profession of "Highway Law," which moved the royal pedant to mercy. The somewhat prolix title of the book is given below.†

---

* La Motte Fénélon's Despatches.
† A Recantation of an ill-ledde Life; or, a Discoverie of the High-way Law, with Vehement Diswasions to all (in that kinde) Offenders. As also Many cautelous Admonitions and full Instructions how to know, shun, and

CHAPTER VII.

The "gentlemen" who formed the rank and file of the early Virginian expeditions belonged chiefly to the unruly class, who only emigrated to avoid worse destinies at home.* The manners of the class from which the adventurers were recruited will not, therefore, be uninteresting.

John Clavell begins his work, after the fashion of that day, with a separate dedication to each estate and condition of men. The king, the queen, "the duchesses, marchionesses, countesses, with the rest of the most noble and most worthy ladies of the court," to whose intercession he presumes he owes his pardon, the privy council, the nobility, the judges, doctors of divinity, justices of the peace, the lawyers, his uncle, Sir John Clavell, his mother, and the reader, are each addressed in a separate and elaborate preface. The style of the book shows considerable education, and some powers of versification. We are favoured with the author's instructions how to know a thief when you see him, "how to ride, when to ride, where to ride."

---

apprehend a Theefe. Most necessarie for all honest Travellers to peruse, observe, and practise. Written by John Clavell, Gent.

Nunquam sera est, ad bonos mores via,
Quantum mutatus ab illo?

Approved by the King's most Excellent Majestie, and published by his expresse command. The second edition. With additions, corrected likewise and amended by the Authour.

London : Printed by B. A. and T. F., for Rich. Meighen, at the signe of the Legge (neere Arundell house in the Strand), and in St. Dunstane's Churchyard, in Fleet-street, 1628.

* Smith, i. 235.

We gather that the knights of the road go forth disguised with vizards and false beards,* that they keep a pebble in their mouth to disguise their voice.

We rode, says Clavell, chiefly by day. It would be too dangerous, and not worth while, to lie in wait by night. The thief could neither watch his opportunity, nor seize on an advantage; he could not see whether the traveller carried pistols, or was a likely man. Clavell speaks with characteristic contempt of "base padding rascalls," who would condescend to rob on foot; an honest horseman would scorn to make himself acquainted with the tricks of such a scurvy trade. Sunday, he declares, is the most dangerous day to ride. No one would travel upon that day unless his affairs are urgent; for urgent affairs "great store of coyne" is necessary. Associate with none who are not willing rather to lose than to have your company. If the horseman who joins you on the road "muffle with his cloake," or rears "a cipresse" over his nose and mouth, mistrust

---

* "Now, you licencious rebels, that doe make
Profession of this wicked course, and take
A pride therein, and would be termed by me
Knights of the Rodes, or else at leastwise be
Stil'd High-way Lawyers; No I doe defie
You, and your actions, I will tell you why;
But first plucke off your visards, hoods, disguise,
Masks, muzles, mufflers, patches from your eyes,
Those beards, those heads of haire, and that great wen,
Which is not naturall, that I may ken
Your faces as they are, and rightly know
If you will blush at what I speake or no."

him. Beware of those that wear a hood, of those that whisper, and that are inquisitive. Beware of a seeming countryman, clothed in russet or a leathern slop, with waistcoat buttoned with a hawthorn peg, haybands about his legs, and hob-nailed shoes, steeple hat, with greasy brim inch-wide. His silly answers and country phrase are but traps to lure you into carelessness, and seize you unawares.

The highwayman never chooses a cross road, he watches always upon the great highway, where he can pick and choose among the passers-by. Ride, then, along the open; keep to the high ground. If you are in company, do not huddle together on the road; keep at least a butt's length distance between each horseman; thieves never attack a scattered company for fear of rescue. Finally, if you do fall among thieves, put a bold face on the matter: an honest man is more than a match for a rogue.

Such is the testimony of John Clavell. He is evidently of opinion that the clergy are a favourite object of attack. "Most inveterate," he says, in his preface to the Doctors of Divinity, " is the malice of the Robbers on the Highway (the children of Beliall, through his instigation) towards you the chosen ministers of God, and great is their advantage, you Riding armed (for the most part) inwardly onely, not with the Sword outwardly; and hence it commeth that men of your coate and Holy function are so often surprised, and suffer injurie by the High-way side."

But it is in his instructions to innkeepers how they may recognize a highwayman that John's honest efforts for the good of society are more especially developed. I subjoin a few lines, as a specimen of his verse and of his instructions, which are curious in themselves.*

> * " I thinke it fitting now for me to show
> Vnto the Inne-keeper, how he shall know
> Such guests from other men, my Host take heed,
> To winke at such faults were a fault indeed.
>   *   *   *   *   *
> Your Ostler must obserue, and he shall see
> About their horses they will curious be;
> They must be strangely drest, as strangely fed
> With mashes, prouender, and Christian's bread.
> If this be wondred, they cannot hold
> Their goodly qualities they must vnfold ;
> Crying, they doe deserue it, and that they,
> By their good seruice, will their cost repay
> With ouerplus, or some words more or lesse,
> By which relation he may shrewdly guesse.
> And then they will be asking, who is he
> That ownes that horse? and whose those horses be
> That stand beyond him? what their masters are?
> What kind of men? whither they ride? how farre?
> And when? So by his answers they surmise
> Which of them all will be their likeliest prise.
> Next of their Cloak-baggs let him notice take,
> They only carry them for fashion's sake;
> For they are empty ones in pollicy,
> Because their horses should not laden be.
> Your Chamberlaine shall find, when as they come
> Vsher'd vp by him to their lodging-roome,
> He shall be sent away, let him giue eare
> And not to taile, he shall be sure to heare
> The gingling of their mony, let him pry
> Behind some secret Cranies priuily,
> And he shall see them share what they have got,
> And every one to take what is his lot.   [This

CHAPTER VII.

The great towns were in disorder. The sunshine of peace upon the slime of war, as Wilson quaintly says, produced riotous demeanours among the evil-disposed portion of the town population. The king cared for nothing but his sports. One of his favourite amusements was lion-baiting in the Tower.* He hated the long pageants in which Elizabeth used to take so much delight. Posies and masques were his aversion; he swore at the crowds which assembled to see him when he rode abroad.† His despotic temper led him to attempt the substitution of royal proclamations for acts of parliament. "Indeed in all this king's reign, from the beginning to the end, you shall find proclamations current coyne, and the people took them for good payment a great while, till the multitude of them lessened their valuation."

The City was in extreme disorder. "The sword and buckler trade was out of date," but "roaring boys," "roysterers," and "bravadoes" swaggered

---

This they by no meanes will deferre, for feare,
Who has the purse should cheat them in the share.
* * * * *
At supper-time let some one hastily
Knocke at your gate as with authority,
You shall obserue a sodaine fearfull start,
Mark then their lookes (the Index of the heart),
And you shall find them troubled, looke you sad,
And aske if yonder Constable be mad?
Bid them say quickly what their danger is,
Then promise no authority of his
Shall enter there if they command it so.

* Wilson, 667.
† Ibid. 668. He dispersed them with frowns that we may not say with curses.

about the streets. Bloody quarrels took place at every corner. In the country, disputes between the gentry and commonalty about enclosure swelled in many cases to the limits of a petty rebellion. " Some were so insolent as to quip and jear the English nobilitie. But then comes a proclamation, like a strong pill, and carries away the grossest of these humours."*

The book which gives most information about the man who conducted the Virginian emigration, and who may therefore be considered as the political ancestors of the Southern Americans, is the account before mentioned of the travels and adventures of John Smith. This man was the central figure, the head and life of the Virginian emigration.

Smith himself had been a soldier from his youth up,—had fought for the independence of the Batavian republic. Indeed, so valiant and so strong a champion was he—so remarkable too, as the real founder of English colonization in America—that it may not be out of place to give a sketch of him.

" The true Travels, Adventures and Observations of Captaine John Smith, in Europe, Asia, Africke, and America," printed in London in 1629, gives a most graphic picture of manners of that day. The man himself, that is his " portraicteur," strong-limbed, broad-chested, big-bearded, good looking, and cruel, stands before us with his hand on his good sword-hilt on the title-page. Then comes a dozen pages of ter-

* Wilson, 674.

ribly bad poetry; the best by Richard Meade, who, alluding to some remarkable exploits detailed in the body of the work, writes thus:—

> "To combat with three Turkes in a single du'le
> Before two armies, who the like hath done?
> Slaine thy great ialer; found a common weal
> In faire America, where thou hast wounc
> No less renoune among their Savage Kings
> Than Turkish warres, that thus thy honor sings."

This, with many other quaint conceits and panegyrical addresses after the fashion of Queen Elizabeth's time, honest John Smith sets forth with pride and satisfaction. Sir Robert Cotton, as appears by the epistle dedicatory, "requested me to fix the whole course of my passages in a booke by itself, whose noble desire I could not but in part satisfie; the rather because they have acted my fatal Tragedies upon the Stage, and racked my Relations at their pleasure." So that even in his own hard-handed times, our Captain found more than one *vates sacer*.

Smith writes his history, like Cæsar, in the third person. It is "venit vidit vicit" both in love and war, all through the chapter. His father dying when he was thirteen years old, and leaving him a competency, "which not being able to manage, he little regarded, his mind being even then set upon brave adventures," Smith "sould his sachell, bookes, and all that he had," and ran away to sea. Fell in with Lord Willoughby's two sons at Orleans, then "little youths under tutorage," who afterwards, when great men—one of them Lord Great Chamberlain of England—stood kindly by Smith and backed him up nobly. His money being at an end, Smith quitted France and took service as a soldier in the Low Countries, his English friends giving him ("but out of his own estate," says he, in a parenthesis) "ten shillings and three pence to be rid of him." After a time, spent principally in giving and taking hard knocks, the ship in which he had taken passage for Italy was driven by stress of weather to anchor near Nice. "Here the inhuman Provincialls with a rabble of Pilgrimes of divers nations going to Rome, hourely cursing him not only for a *Hugonoit* but his nation they swore were all Pyrats, and so vilely railed on his dread soveraigne Queene Elizabeth, and that they never should have faire weather so long as hee was aboord them: their disputations grew to that passion that they threw him overboard; yet God brought him to a little isle where was no inhabitants but a few kine and goats." Picked up and kindly refreshed by "a noble Britaine, Captain La Roche, of St. Malo," who appears to have been in reality what the "Pilgrimes" accused the British of being, to wit, a pirate. For with the next fair wind they ran down to Scandaroone, "rather to view what ships was in the Roade than anything else," and finally fell in with an argosie of Venice. "Whereupon the Britaine presently gave them the broad side, then his sterne, and his other broad side also, and continued the chase with his chase pieces,"—a very easily-handled pirate—accustomed, doubtless, to swift gyrations, and rapid sea-evolutions, astonishing to peaceful argosies.

"The silkes, velvets, cloth of gold, and tissue, pyasters, chicqueenes, and sultanies, which is gold and silver, they unloaded in foure and twentie houres, was wonderful." At Antibo, in "Peamon,"—meaning Piedmont—the Britaine "set Smith on shore with five hundred chicqueenes and a little box," which, he mysteriously asserts, "God sent him." In Tuscany he found "his deare friends the two Honorable Brethren the Lord Willoughby and his brother, cruelly wounded in a desperate fray—yet to their exceeding great honour," as he takes care to add.

Afterwards at Rome, Smith beheld Clement VIII.; saw him "creepe up the holy stayres which they say are those our Saviour Christ went up to Pontius Pilate;" then took service at Vienne in Austria; and in the fourth chapter of his memoir, you may read "the siege of Olumpagh, an excellent statagem by Smith. Also another not much worse" on which we need not dwell.

Hasten we to record "the unhappie siege of Caniza," and the three single combats in which Smith, before the two armies, cut off three Turks' heads, and acquired from Sigismundus, Prince of Transylvania, "three Turkes' heads in a shield for his armes, his picture in goulde, and three hundred ducatts yeerely for a pension."

It appears that the Christians had sat down before

the strong city of Regall, and that their delay in bringing their artillery to bear upon it caused the Turks to deride them, and to say that "their ordnance were at pawne, and that they grew fat for want of exercise."

Finally, a challenge comes to any captain of the army, "To delight the ladies, who did long to see some court-like passtime, the Lord Turbashaw did defy any captaine that had the command of a companie who durst combat with him for his head."

Up sprang Smith and girded on his trusty sword. Truce was made. "The rampiers all beset with faire dames, and men in arms. The Christians in battalio. Turbashaw with a noise of Howboyes entred the field well mounted and armed. On his shoulders were fixed a paire of great wings compacted of eagles' feathers within a ridge of silver, richly garnished with golde and precious stones. A Janissary before him bearing his lance, on each side another leading his horse." A noble Turk advancing gaily to his doom, for "Smith with a noise of trumpets, only a page bearing his lance, passing by him with a courteous salute, took his ground with such good success, that at the sound of the charge, he passed the Turk thorow the right of his beaver, face, head and all, that he fell downe dead to the ground, where alighting and unbracing his helmet cut off his head, and the Turkes took his body, and so returned without any hurt at all."

Second combat with Grualgo, vowed friend of

CHAPTER VII.
—

Turbashaw, who "enraged with madnesse rather than choller, directed a particular challenge to the conquerour, to regaine his friend's head or lose his own with his horse and armour for advantage."

"As before, upon the sound of the trumpets, their lances flew in pieces upon a clear passage, but the Turke was neare unhorsed. Their pistolls was the next which marked Smith upon the placard. But the next shott, the Turke was so wounded in his left arm that not being able to rule his horse and defend himself, he was thrown to the ground, and so bruised with the fall that he lost his head, as his friend before him."

The third combat was with an individual, whose beautiful name was Bonny Mulgro. Smith obtained leave "with so many incontradictible perswading reasons" to let the ladies know that he would give up the heads of the Turks already slaine, if any Turk of their rank would come to the place of combat to redeeme them; further, "they should have his own upon like conditions if they could win it."

Pistols were first discharged, but no harm done; "their battle-axes was the next, whose piercing bils made sometime the one, sometime the other to have scarce sense to keepe their saddles; specially the Christian received such a blow that he lost his battle-axe and failed not much to have fallen after it." Whereupon there was a great shout from the rampiers. The Turk defended himself and pressed his advantage as well as he could; but Smith "by his judgment and dexterity in such a businesse, beyond all men's expectation, by God's assistance not onely avoided the Turke's violence, but having drawne his faulchion pierced the Turk so under the cutlets, through back and body, that though he alighted from his horse, he stood not long ere he lost his head as the rest had done."

But the battle is not always to the strong. In a lonely glen in Transylvania a fight took place, which lasted the whole summer's day. Years after the grass grew rank and green on many a patch of ground that was that day encumbered with heaps of slain. Smith, "among the slaughtered dead bodies, and many a gasping soule with toil and wounds, lay groaning among the rest," till the camp followers who went out to pillage the slain, found him, and judging from his rich armour that he would be well ransomed, saved his life. We next find him, sold with other Christian prisoners like a beast in the market-place, where "everie merchant viewing their limbs and wounds, caused other slaves to struggle with them to trie their strength."

He fell to the share of one "Bashaw Bogall," who sent him to his mistress as a slave. Captain Smith appears to have used a phonetic or other abnormal method of spelling, writing down the words as they sounded to his ear, and making dire confusion with his proper names. In his account of the wars of Sigismund and his gallant companions, few indeed are the names noted as other and more learned historians are wont to do. The "noble gentlewoman" to whom Bashaw Bogall sent him figures as "Charatza Tragabigzanda." She was wont to "feigne herself sicke when she should go the Banians or to weep over the graves," in order that she might converse undisturbed with the interesting captive. In the course of these conversations it appeared that the Bashaw had represented Smith as a noble Bohemian overthrown by his, Bogall's, prowess, and held by him to ransom. Smith sturdily averred that he had never seen the Bashaw until he was bought by him in the market of Axopolis. The lady fell in love with the stalwart prisoner. But her mother, short of pin-money, as may be supposed, made arrangements to dispose of the Bashaw's handsome present, and Tragabigzanda in despair sent him to her brother, "a most tyrannicall Turke." "To her unkinde brother this kinde ladie writ so much for his good usage that he halfe suspected as much as shee intended. For shee told him he should but sojourne there to learn the language and what it was to be a Turke, till time made her master of herselfe. But the Tymour, her brother, diverted all this to the worst of crueltie; for within an houre after his arrival, he caused his drubman to strip him naked, and shave his head and beard so bare as his hand; a great ring of iron with a long stalke bowed like a sickle rivitted about his neck, and a coat made of vegries' haire, guarded about with a peece of undressed skinne." Here, with many more Christian slaves and "forsados" of Turkes and Moores, Smith dwelt, feeding on entrails of horse or "ulgries," and labouring in the Tymour's grange, who "tooke occasion so to beat, spurne, and revile him, that foregetting all reason he beat out the Tymour's braines" and fled to Transylvania, thence to the wars in Barbary, and thence, with the earliest emigrants to the distant shores of Virginia.

An idea of the outfit which was required for an intending emigrant to Virginia may be gathered from Smith's account.* Amongst other things are noted a Monmouth cap; three suits of clothes, one of canvas, one of frieze, and one of cloth; four pairs of shoes; "seven ells of canvas to make a bed and boulster to be filled in Virginia, serving for two men." The sea stores comprised meal, pease, oatmeal, aqua-vitæ, oil, and vinegar. It would seem from the estimate that a complete suit of light armour could be obtained for seventeen shillings, "a long peece five foot and a half neere musket bore" for one pound two shillings, a sword for five shillings, a bandileer for eighteenpence, twenty pounds of powder for eighteen shillings.

We must now turn for a moment to the condition of Holland. It has been already stated that as long as the war lasted,† nothing could be more striking than the contrast between the condition of the obedient and disobedient Netherlands.

Among the various branches of commerce which the

* Appendix.   † Till 1609.

CHAPTER VII.

latter provinces carried on, one of the most considerable consisted in carrying from the Baltic nations, to the different ports of Spain and Portugal, large quantities of corn and naval stores. In return they took back the fruit and vines of the South, besides a large portion of the gold and silver treasures of the Spaniards. They also bought and distributed over Northern Europe the productions of the Spice Islands, of which the Portuguese had a monopoly. During the war of independence this commerce was carried on by the Dutch under neutral flags; but when Philip had determined to put a stop altogether to a traffic which he considered beneficial only to his enemies, such foreign ships as lay in Spanish ports were treacherously seized, and their crews sold into slavery. The Dutch, fired with resentment, instantly resolved to pursue a direct trade with the East, and wrest it, if possible, entirely from the hands of the Portuguese. A furious war ensued between the two countries, in the course of which the Dutch got considerably the advantage of their opponents. They, however, found that so great a number of adventurers were attracted to the trade that profits began rapidly to diminish: over-competition ruined many speculators, and rendered the republic too weak to contend against its enemies. To obviate these inconveniences, the States-General, in 1602, determined to unite the several societies of traders into one body under the name of the East India Company.

Upon this company was conferred the exclusive privilege of trading beyond the Cape of Good Hope,

1602

on the one hand, and the Straits of Magellan on the other. They received the power of administering justice, of building forts, of appointing governors, of raising troops, and of making peace and war with the Indian princes. An enormous capital was at once subscribed. The Portuguese were fairly beaten out of their strongholds of monopoly. Captures were made of the Spanish and Portuguese treasure-ships. The fleets of the monarch who still signed himself in his public acts, addressed to the Netherlands, "Yo il Ré," were often blocked up in his own harbours till the time for entering on their voyages was past. The Spanish settlements on the coast were plundered sometimes by the English, sometimes by the Dutch, with impunity. The coasts of Spain itself were insulted. The galleys which had been sent, under the command of Spinosa, to destroy the cod and herring fisheries of the rebellious provinces, were destroyed, or fell into the hands of the Dutch. Signal vengeance had been taken on the privateers of Nieuport and Dunkirk: the crews of these were treated as pirates. Some were hanged; some were drowned. The fleets of the republic rode triumphant from the Baltic to Gibraltar. Their European as well as their Indian trade was in a flourishing condition.

The Spaniards, unable longer to cope with them, signed a truce for twelve years in 1609. Thenceforward they were treated as an independent nation.

After the signature of the truce the republic became almost immediately divided upon a point of theology. Gomar, a professor of Leyden, maintained that the doctrines of Calvin, in respect of grace and predestination, were no whit too severe; while his brother professor, Arminius, did his best to soften and explain them away. Prince Maurice, the Stadtholder, at the head of the great body of the people, took up the Gomar faction. John Van Olden Barneveldt, the most experienced and able politician of the republic, favoured the milder doctrines of Arminius. Grotius, Vossius, and most of the learned men of Holland, supported the views of Barneveldt. Maurice and his Gomarists prevailed—principally, it may be said, by the unanswerable law of the strongest. The truth seems to be that Maurice intended to use the popularity he acquired for the purpose of making himself absolute master of the republic: under a calm and quiet exterior, the Stadtholder had, from his earliest years, concealed the most ambitious views. The independence of Holland had brought with it no elective franchise for the people: the municipal officers were elected as in a close corporation, or were nominated by the prerogative of the Stadtholder. The officers so selected sent members to the provincial assemblies. It was but natural that delegates chosen by such a process should represent the richest and most influential portions of the commercial community. Many members of the provincial assemblies entertained very strong and definite views as to the conduct of affairs, and desired to keep all the power in their own hands. They were, in fact, a highly conservative commercial aristocracy. They sent members to the States-General; but they were by no means desirous of transferring any great share of the power they possessed to that body. The unrepresented portion of the people, on the other hand, were inclined rather to take part with absolutism than with aristocracy. History affords numerous examples of the temper which this disposition indicates. The Romans raised Cæsar to the purple. The Commons of England sustained Henry VII. in his quarrels with the nobility. The Danes conferred hereditary power on Frederic II. The tendency of a democracy may be considered as almost always towards absolutism, and may be counted upon as its ally, if it be opposed by an aristocracy either of wealth or birth.

The doctrines of Gomar, by denying merit to man, and ascribing salvation solely to the mercy of God, was more grateful to the popular mind than the teaching of Arminius, that each man was to be saved by his own conduct and exertions. One was a purely democratic theory, which denied any difference between one man and another; the other was aristocratic, and admitted the theory of individual excellence and superiority. The religious dispute was carried into all matters of politics; and in a short time the Gomarists, with Prince Maurice, the States-General, and the body of the people, found themselves committed to a bitter struggle with the Arminians, under Barneveldt and the provincial assemblies. The former insisted that political power resided in the States-General; the latter, that it belonged exclusively to the provincial assemblies. The one favoured emigration and colonization; the other fearing new collisions, and disliking the democratic character which emigration always assumed, discouraged it in every possible manner. The victory was not long in dispute, and was proclaimed to the world in a rather summary manner—Barneveldt was beheaded. A blunder, no doubt, as well as a crime on the part of Maurice, who, as he well deserved to do, lost a good part of his popularity in consequence. The quarrel, nevertheless, is chiefly remarkable as regards the object of these pages, inasmuch as it enabled Maurice to direct his attention to colonization.

CHAPTER VIII.

FRENCH SETTLEMENT OF ACADIA.

[1604—1648.]

Henry IV. sends De Monts to Acadia—Compagnie des Cent Associés.

IT is now time to turn to the New World, and to examine the first hesitating steps which were taken, during the time I have just described, by the other nations of the West to rival the splendid American establishments of the Spaniards. France, at the beginning of the century, had paused in complete exhaustion from the effects of her civil wars. The Huguenots enjoyed but a small share of political freedom: toleration was all that they ever expected; and this, under the rule of Henry IV., they at last obtained. Henry had always, as far as was compatible with the security of his crown, a secret leaning to the Huguenot party. The Catholics were well aware of this; and, although they had contrived to extract from him a nominal adherence to the doctrines and authority of Rome, they still regarded him as a heretic—indeed their knowledge of his Protestant bias was doubtless the main cause of his murder.

All over Europe, the enthusiasm which had existed for the Protestant cause had grown lukewarm. Protestants were divided among themselves; while the power of Rome was strong and united. Lutherans persecuted Calvinists; and Calvinists, where they had the power, persecuted the Lutherans. The Roman Catholics, agitated by no great internal question, could devote their whole attention to the extirpation of both sects of reformers. A great reaction was taking place, and the old religion was recovering much of the ground which it had lost in the last stormy century. Religion was so interwoven with politics, that it was impossible sometimes to separate spiritual from secular matters. But the excitement of both religious parties was at an end. The revolutions and civil wars which had raged in France, in Holland, in Scotland, and the contest between England and Spain, had been entirely religious in their origin. The Thirty Years' War, however, was, on one side, an attempt at the acquisition of absolute dominion on the part of Austria; on the other, a coalition for national independence. Community of political objects began to be more regarded by governments, in their choice of alliances, than identity of religious belief. " The war of states succeeded to the war of sects."* Gustavus and Richelieu—one, the greatest Protestant soldier of Europe, owed his throne to a Protestant revolution; the other the ablest prince of the Catholic Church, had waged a fierce crusade against the Huguenots—

* Macaulay, Essay on Von Ranke.

combined against the Catholic House of Austria. Even the head of the Roman church looked on rather with the eyes of a temporal than a spiritual prince. He feared the establishment of an universal monarchy more than he desired the temporal prosperity of the church.

The Catholic powers—Spain, Austria, and Rome—began to find that religion and ambition could well coincide, and that universal dominion could be made at once an instrument and a result of the Catholic crusade.

Henry IV. saw this. But he was in a dilemma. On the one side was his compulsory Catholicism ; on the other, his fear of Austria. Catholicism was the support of his throne ; but the ascendency of Catholicism implied the ascendency of the house of Austria ; and if that house were to gain the ascendancy, his throne would not be worth having. There was but one escape—to separate politics from religion. For the first time since the days of Luther alliances were made and wars planned without reference to creed.*

The house of Austria accepted the change of policy, and recognized the change of motive. The pope, too, acquiesced perforce. The ascendency of Austria would have been as disastrous to him as to France.

* " Le différend entre la France et l'Espagne avait perdu tout son caractère religieux pour devenir absolument politique. Il ne s'agissait plus comme au seizième siècle de la grande lutte entre la pensée catholique et la réforme de Luther ; c'était la conquête, la possession territoriale, la balance des Etats, l'influence des uns sur les autres qui formaient le mobile de toutes les négociations, l'objet des traités."—Capefigue, *Richelieu, Mazarin, et la Fronde,* iv.

Henry IV. was murdered before the outbreak of the storm which he had foreseen. Sully was nursing the finances of France, and working reforms in every department of state; but they were not complete ere his master died. A change followed in the policy of France. Mary de Medicis, wife of the murdered king, was appointed regent. Her sympathies were, and had ever been, with Spain. Her favourite Concini and his wife were in favour of the Spanish party. For a time the influence of France was thrown into the Austrian scale.

At the beginning of his reign Henry IV. had sent out a new viceroy to Acadia—a Calvinist, able and honest, by name De Monts. The fortieth to the forty-sixth degree of latitude were the limits imposed upon the sovereignty of De Monts—limits which included all the territory between Philadelphia and Montreal. What we now call Nova Scotia and New Brunswick, together with a considerable part of the New England states, were thus claimed for France. These boundaries showed more knowledge and less vague assumption than the wholesale grant to Roberval and De la Roche. It is probable, from a passage in the Mémoires of the Duc de Sully, that his (Sully's) contemptuous disbelief in the value of any lands north of the fortieth parallel, may have had something to do with the imposition of a northern limit. "The colony," he writes, "which was this year sent to Canada was among the number of things that did not meet my approbation. There was no kind of riches to be expected from those parts of the New World which lie beyond the fortieth degree of latitude."*

The monopoly of the fur trade, the exclusive control of the soil, government, and commerce, and freedom of religion for the Huguenot companions of De Monts, were collateral advantages more important even than the exact limits of a sovereignty which as yet there was none to dispute. But religious differences were not to be abolished by a stroke of the pen. De Monts, though he stipulated for freedom of religion for his own immediate followers, was glad enough to purchase that concession by allowing fathers of the Roman Catholic Church to accompany his expedition, and try to effect the conversion of the natives. Champlain gives us a glimpse of strong differences of opinion which occurred in consequence. "J'ai vu le ministre et notre curé s'entrebattre à coups de poing sur le différend de la religion." Champlain, with all his earnestness in favour of the ancient faith, could not repress his amusement at these violent demonstrations. "Je ne sçais pas," he continues, " qui étoit le plus vaillant, ou qui donnoit le meilleur coup, mais je sçais très bien que le ministre se plaignoit quelquefois au sieur de Monts, d'avoir été battu, et vuidoit en cette façon les points de la controversie."†

The conductors, both of the French and English

* Mémoires de Sully.
† Voyages de la Nouv. France Occidentale.—Champlain, 1632.

expeditions, seem to have entertained little differences of opinion respecting the stamp of men who were considered good enough to form a colony. De Roberval had permission to ransack the prisons, and to take thence thieves and homicides, spendthrifts and fraudulent debtors; the only criminals excepted being who were detained for treason or for counterfeiting money.

Idlers, men without profession, banished men, besides the usual complement of villains, made up De Monts' expedition. When it is remembered that he was additionally favoured with the company of stalwart controversialists, representing the physical as well as the moral force of the Catholics and the Huguenots, his embarrassment may easily be imagined.

Various attempts failed to discover any more convenient place for the establishment of his head-
1605 quarters than Port Royal. There the first French settlement was made.

The comrades of De Monts, reinforced by the arrival of a number of Jesuit missionaries, gradually spread themselves over what is now the State of Maine. Marie de Medicis and the Marquise de Guercheville contributed liberally to the support of the missions. The order of the Jesuits was enriched by the imposition of a tax for their benefit on the fisheries and the fur trade. Thus in Maine and Canada on the one hand, in Florida and Mexico on the other, the Roman Catholic faith was securely established by the French and Spaniards.

Meanwhile the enemies of De Monts were actively endeavouring to obtain a revocation of his patents and privileges. It was pretended that he had thrown impediments in the way of the fisheries; with more reason it was alleged that his exclusive privileges of trade were unjust. The merchants of Dieppe and St. Malo wished for a share of the fur trade, and at last succeeded in overthrowing the monopoly of De Monts. Champlain a few years previously had been intrusted with an expedition which founded Quebec; and in the following year had 1608 joined a party of Hurons and Algonquins against the five nations of Indians who inhabited the northern wilds of New York.

Champlain returned to France in 1609, and was received with great distinction at Fontainebleau. The king listened attentively to the account which he gave of the new colony, which was henceforth called New France. But De Monts, whose patent was already expired, could obtain no aid. After the death of Henry IV., while Marie de Medicis was regent, there was less chance than ever that the Protestants of Acadia would be assisted. The spread of the Roman Catholic religion was, in the regent's eyes, the greatest work which could be performed. For this she was ready to sacrifice her country, by throwing herself and the power of France with her into the scale of Spain. When, therefore, the English attacked Port Royal, little notice was taken of the matter: the settlers at that post were only 1613

CHAPTER VIII. Huguenots, of whose misfortunes no Catholic in France took much account.

In 1625, the viceroyalty of New France was transferred to a religious enthusiast named Henri de Levy. Through his influence, a considerable number of Jesuits proceeded to America. Just a year before, members of this extraordinary company had reached the confines of Thibet and the sources of the Ganges: they now established a mission which was destined to carry the cross from the St. Lawrence to California.

1627   Two years later, Richelieu established a company, which he called the "Compagnie des Cent Associés." He was himself one of the principal promoters. A charter of incorporation was obtained from Louis XIII. The limits of the company's powers embraced specifically the whole basin of the St. Lawrence, and of such other rivers in New France as flowed directly into the sea. They included, moreover, Florida, or the country south of Virginia, a province that was esteemed French in virtue of the unsuccessful efforts of Coligny. But before the company could begin its labours, France became involved in a war with England,* which demanded the whole attention of Richelieu, and left him no leisure for American affairs: it was not till the matters of difference with England were accommodated, and the Huguenots of Rochelle subdued, that the intended expedition could proceed to sea. M. Rameau, in his description of

* See page 324.

Canada, has devoted some ingenuity to guess what effect this war of 1627 had upon the fortunes of New France.

Little attention, he says, is usually paid to the important effect which the earliest emigration exercises over the ultimate fate of a colony. If, in 1650, there had been a thousand more inhabitants in Canada, the fate of that province a century later might have been very different: M. Rameau is of opinion that Canada was conquered by the English in 1759, because the criminal indifference of France left the Canadians so weak in numbers as to be unable to repel attack. It is undeniable that if the views of Richelieu had been carried out in 1627, and a large and well-provided expedition had taken possession of New France, Canada, instead of beginning slowly and painfully to struggle into existence after the peace of St. Germains, would by that time have been in a fair way to prosperity. It is not improbable, when we take into consideration the energy of Richelieu's mind, that he would have felt a paternal fondness for the settlement which he had created, and that he would have fostered and encouraged its development. If that had been done, the fate of both the United States and of Canada itself might have been changed. It would have been difficult for the English to make head against the French power in America, if that power had been materially stronger than they actually found it. The ambitious views of La Galissonière, and other able Frenchmen his contemporaries who served France in America, might have been carried out. France might have become firmly possessed of the valley of the Mississippi and of the country to the west: the broad lands between the Mississippi and the Pacific, which are now settled by an Anglo-Saxon population, might have been in the hands of men of French Roman Catholic descent; or at least, if they had failed permanently to occupy it, years of warfare might have retarded indefinitely the prosperity of the United States, and possibly established several rival communities on the ground which the United States took possession of without question or molestation. But the war of 1627 changed all this. The English sailed up the St. Lawrence and possessed themselves of Quebec. It was restored at the treaty of St. Germains; but everything had then to be begun afresh. If it had not been for the tenacity of Richelieu, who saw clearly the value which Canada, from its strategic position, might ultimately assume, the diplomatists who negotiated the treaty of St. Germains on the part of France, would have been ready without remonstrance to allow New France to remain in the hands of the English.

Richelieu, embarrassed by the network of intrigue which the French nobles were weaving around him, had not time to devote the necessary attention to transatlantic affairs. Champlain was sent back to Canada, with very inadequate resources; soon after he died, leaving his colony in confusion. " A cette époque," says Charlevoix, " le Canada consistait dans le fort de Québec, environné de quelques méchantes maisons, et de quelques baraques, deux ou trois cabanes dans l'île de Montréal, autant peut-être à Tadoussac et en quelques autres endroits sur le Saint-Laurent, pour le commerce des pelleteries et de la pêche ; enfin, un commencement d'habitation à trois Rivières."

Lands were distributed to emigrants in the neighbourhood of Quebec, and immense tracts of country were conceded on seigneurial tenure, to any who seemed able to establish settlers around him. The concessionaries in their turn granted portions of their territory to settlers at a small quit-rent, generally reserving to themselves the "droit de moulinage," the right, that is, of seizing a portion of all corn ground at the mill, the right of fishery, and the right of traffic in furs. A seigneur, as soon as he had acquired a concession, usually proceded to France, where he enlisted emigrants and settled them on his grant : the religious corporations in Canada were particularly distinguished by their success and activity in this method of colonization.

The "Compagnie des Cent Associés," of which Richelieu was himself a member, was shorn of almost all its glories after the peace. Instead of commencing on a grand scale, it was hardly able to carry to New France a couple of hundred emigrants. The death of Richelieu soon after deprived it of its last chance of life, and the enormous nominal powers with which its founder endowed it, fell entirely into disuse.

CHAPTER IX.

EARLY DAYS OF VIRGINIA.

[1606—1625.]

The Puritans—Northern and Southern Companies of Virginia.

CHAPTER IX. RICHELIEU and Mazarin in France; Buckingham and Strafford in England; Olivarez and Lerma in Spain—had each done his best to keep up and to extend the arbitrary power of the master whom he served.

England and Holland alone, of all the European nations, continued to make head against authority. Even in Holland popular liberty was little understood, and popular institutions almost entirely disregarded.

In the first days of the Reformation in England, the power formerly possessed by the pope was transferred almost intact to the king.

The authority of the king and the pope had been often antagonistic; they were now united in a single individual. But the inhabitants of our country had no mind to exchange one servitude for another.

Tyranny was no more tolerable when its edicts came from Windsor than it had been when they came from the Vatican. For a time, the personal character of our monarchs was sufficiently powerful to prevent the expression of discontent. The successors of Henry VIII., whether hated or feared, were at least respected. High-handed justice was dealt out, but at least no act was committed of such importance to the population as to insure their unanimous opposition. Elizabeth knew how to concede with dignity. Before a remonstrance could be forwarded to her, she relieved the nation from the wrong complained of, and promised not in like manner to offend again. They pardoned her tyranny in consideration of her good qualities. But when James I. came to the throne this kindly indulgence ceased. James not only bullied but irritated. His subjects found that he would give way under pressure. But he gave way not with the frank graciousness of Elizabeth, but with ill-temper and threats of future revenge. Though the king considered himself a model of kingcraft, he made the mistake of believing that he could arrest a revolution. He acquiesced in the change which gave the power of the pope to the king, and thought he might there stop short. He did not see that the same impulse which led men to question the power of the pope indisposed them to submit to the power of the crown. The struggle between prerogative and privilege, which commenced in his time, was carried on on both sides of the

Atlantic. When the English parliament demanded freedom of speech from James, as "their ancient and undoubted right derived from their forefathers," the monarch replied that " he could not admit this style of talking of their undoubted rights, but would rather have wished that they would have said that their privileges were derived by the grace and permission of the sovereign." This was the opening of a dispute which occupied the tongues and pens of men for many years. As Catholics had become Protestants, Protestants became Puritans; the Puritans protested against prerogative, as the Catholics had protested against Rome. Both were in turn persecuted; both were consolidated by persecution. Each began as a weak sect and became a powerful party. The history of England from the death of Elizabeth to the execution of Charles is the history of the struggle thus provoked. The period which that contest occupies almost exactly coincides with the establishment of the English colonies. It may be taken as an axiom that every colonist carried with him the degree of popular liberty which he left behind. The colonies, therefore, which went out with the sanction of the king, went out under the implied, if not actually expressed, theory that liberty depended on the will of the king. The colonists who fled from the persecution of the king, and who at their departure were looked upon with no royal favour at all, claimed and exercised complete self-government. It was long before Virginia enjoyed as much freedom as New England.

It has been observed in a former chapter that England had never abandoned the idea of colonizing the fertile lands which lay between the frozen north and the Spanish settlements on the Mexican Gulf: when de Gourgues returned to France, after his signal and romantic vengeance on the Spanish destroyers of Ribault's Protestant colony in Florida, Sir Walter Raleigh was fighting as a volunteer in the army of the great Coligny. He was there in constant communication with men whose ideas were fixed on the New World as a place of escape from religious persecution, especially with Coligny himself, who thought and spoke much upon the subject. The fruits of the lessons thus learned were seen in the seven expeditions which Raleigh sent out after his return to England.

After Sir Richard Grenville's death, attempts at American colonization languished; but on the accession of James I., two companies of merchants successfully petitioned the king for charters of incorporation, and the exclusive rights without which no enterprise was ever at that date undertaken. During the reigns of the arbitrary Tudor princes, the lawyers, who were all more or less under court influence, favoured the opinion that the sale of patents for the sole making, buying, or selling of commodities, was a part of the royal prerogative, and one of the legitimate sources of the revenue of the crown. Under Queen Elizabeth, this abuse was carried to an excessive point. Many new patents were granted.

But it was not until the evil had reached an unbearable height that the power was formally limited.* The common and statute law of England are decidedly opposed to monopolies, and have been so from the earliest times. Lord Coke lays it down as an axiom that trade should be free,† and he even cites Magna Charta to prove that monopolies " are against the liberty and freedom granted by the Great Charter, and divers other Acts of Parliament, which are good commentaries on that Charter." In consequence of the act of James above mentioned, many restrictions on the internal commerce of the country were removed, and many articles of first necessity which had been subject to monopolists were freed. But the act did not extend to foreign commerce or to the privileges of bodies legally incorporated; and long after the accession of James I., monopolies of portions of the colonial trade were freely granted to every applicant who could give a "substantial" reason to the king's treasury in favour of his demand.

The monopoly given to the two companies just mentioned is an instance of the reckless manner in which such transactions were effected. The company which was formed in Bristol and Plymouth were placed in possession of the northern part of what was afterwards called Virginia, and the London company obtained the southern half. But the limits of the southern company were to extend from the thirty-

* 1624. 21 Jac. I. cap. 3.
† Third institute.

fourth to the forty-first parallel of latitude, while the northern company's boundaries were from the thirty-eighth to the forty-fifth parallel. The country lying between the thirty-eighth and forty-first parallel was thus granted to two rival companies by the same grantor at the same time. It appears, however, that the king, though he knew little of geographical boundaries, knew the inflammable nature of the materials of his new colonies, for he made a proviso that they should not plant within one hundred miles of each other.

On the concession of the first charter, the southern company went heartily to work. The expedition started under distinguished auspices; but the absurd vanity of James, who placed the theory of political wisdom in the practice of low cunning, almost marred the expedition before it had well started. His love of mystery, and his petty greed of power, prevented him from declaring, before the adventurers started, who were to be the leaders of the emigration. One of the principal men among them was John Smith, whose romantic history was narrated a few pages back. The expedition sailed under sealed orders, which were only to be opened on their arrival in Virginia. During the voyage, at the very time when a strong hand was required to repress the mutinous spirit of the motley adventurers, no one was in command. They were six weeks detained by contrary winds, within sight of England. The "baser sort" quarrelled with their chaplain, who, however, refused to abandon his post. On their arrival, the jealousy of the men who were placed in the commission with Smith, found a pretext for excluding him from all share of power. He was even kept for thirteen weeks in irons, but very urgent need of his assistance at length compelled his persecutors to release him. Governor Wingfield was condemned to pay him, by way of indemnity, 200*l.*, which, with characteristic generosity, he threw into the general fund.

Newport, the first commander, went home disgusted. Gosnold, his successor, died. Wingfield, the third in order, embezzled stores, and was deposed; then the command devolved on John Smith. The materials at his command were of the strangest. "An hundred dissolute persons" accompanied the expedition, and appear to have formed the greater part of the rank and file of the expedition. Sir Thomas Smith, one of the leading members of the company, found the stores and provisions. He made his fortune out of the contract; but misery, disease, and want came upon the unhappy adventurers who depended upon his catering; and had it not been for the genius of John Smith, the colony would have been utterly destroyed. "Our drink," said one of the adventurers, "was unwholesome water, our lodging, castles in the air. If we had been as free from all sins as from gluttony and drunkenness, we might have been canonized as saints."*

Smith became presently, as I have said, the historian of the exodus, and cut as sharply with

* Smith's Virginia.

his pen as erewhile with his sword. We have among us "poor gentlemen, tradesmen, serving-men, libertines, and such like, ten times more fit to spoil a commonwealth than either to begin or maintain one."* And at a later day, when by his genius and courage he had pulled them through the crisis of the evil case into which they first fell, " the number of felons and vagabonds did bring such evil character on the place, that some did choose to be hanged rather than go there—*and were.*"*

Selfishness, meanness, and plotting for individual gain at the expense of the rest of their companions, distinguished almost every one of the settlers. Scarcely had Smith received the appointment of president, when better order began to be shown in the works and proceedings of the emigrants. Smith worked with the rest, and even harder than any. He, however, bitterly bewails the perversity of the council in their choice of emigrants. Three years after the landing, we find him writing—

"All this time we had but one carpenter in the countrey, and three others that could doe little, but desired to be learners, two blacksmiths, two saylers, and those we write labourers were for the most part footmen, and such as they that were adventurers brought to attend them, or such as they could perswade to goe with them, that neuer did know what a daye's worke was, except the Dutchmen and Poles, and some dozen other."

* Smith's Virginia.

CHAPTER IX.
[1606—1625.]

The council in England interfered constantly and vexatiously in matters the most minute. They sent out supplies with a niggard hand; and threatened that unless returns commensurate to the expenses of the supplies were sent home, the colonists should be left in Virginia as banished men. A lump of gold, a certain passage to the South Sea, or tidings of some member of Sir Walter Raleigh's missing expedition, such were the demands constantly made, as if the transmutation of metals had been one of the secrets learnt by the poor dissolute gentlemen on escaping from London sponging-houses and bagnios.

Smith's answer to this unreasonable demand gives a most graphic account of the state of the colony. He complains bitterly of a letter written by the company, in which they assert that " our minds are so set vpon faction, and idle conceits in diuiding the country without your consents, and that we feed you but with ifs and ands, hopes and some few proofes." He reminds them of their orders to obey the commands brought by Captain Newport, " the charge of whose voyage amounts to neare two thousand pounds, the which if we cannot defray by the Ship's returne, we are alike to remain as banished men." To these particulars, writes Smith, " I humbly intreat your Pardons if I offend you with my rude Answer. For our factions, vnlesse you would have me run away and leave the Country, I cannot prevent them: because I do make many stay that would els fly any whether." He then proceeds to explain that the instructions sent by Captain Newport were of such a nature that to carry them out would have involved the whole colony in ruin. He had nevertheless, at the desire of the council, crowned Powhattan, and sworn Captain Winne and Captain Waldo members of the council in Virginia. "For the charge of this Voyage of two or three thousand pounds, we have not received the value of an hundred pounds. And for the quartred Boat to be borne by the Souldiers over the Falles, Newport had 120 of the best men he could chuse. If he had burnt her to ashes, one might haue carried her in a bag, but as she is, fiue hundred cannot, to a navigable place aboue the Falles. And for him at that time to find in the South Sea, a mine of gold ; or any of them sent by Sir Walter Raleigh : at our Consultation I told them was as likely as the rest. But during this great discovery of thirtie myles, (which might as well haue beene done by one man, and much more, for the value of a pound of Copper at a seasonable tyme,) they had the Pinnace and all the Boats with them, but one that remained with me to serue the Fort." As soon as the exploring parties had started, Smith began to instruct workers of " Pitch and Tarre, Glasse, Sopeashes, Clapboord, whereof some small quantities we haue sent you." But he urges, very sensibly, that although the factors of the company might collect without delay in Russia and Sweden as much of such commodities as would freight all their ships, to make them in Virginia would cost far more than they were worth. He then gives a lamentable picture of the condition of the settlement Most of the men were sick, and nearly famished. Even the miserable stores sent out by the company were embezzled by the sailors, and by the officers at home. " From your Ship we had not provision in victuals worth twenty pound, and we are more then two hundred to liue vpon this : the one halfe sicke, the other little better. For the Saylers (I confesse) they daily make good cheare, but our dyet is a little meale and water, and not sufficient of that. Though there be fish in the Sea, foules in the ayre, and beasts in the woods, their bounds are so large, they so wilde, and we so weake and ignorant, we cannot much trouble them. . . . The Souldiers say many of your officers maintaine their families out of that you sent vs : and that Newport hath an hundred pounds a yeare for carrying newes. For every master you have yet sent can find the way as well as he, so that an hundred pounds might be spared, which is more than we haue all that helps to pay him wages. Cap. Ratcliffe is now called Sicklemore, a poore counterfeited Imposture. I haue sent you him home, lest the company should cut his throat.—What he is, now every one can tell you : if he and Archer returne againe, they are sufficient to keepe vs alwayes in factions. When you send againe I entreat you rather send but thirty Carpenters, husbandmen, gardiners, fisher men, blacksmiths, masons, and diggers vp of tree's roots, well provided, then a thousand of such as we haue : for except wee be able both to lodge them, and feed them, the most will consume with want of necessaries before they can be made good for any thing."

The personal character of the president influenced those under his control. The gentlemen of the expedition were taught the use of the axe, and followed the excellent example of manual labour which he set them. They soon became masters of woodcraft, "making it their delight to heare the trees thunder as they fell; but the axes so oft blistered their tender fingers, that many times every third blow had a loud othe to drowne the echo, for remedie of which sinne the president devised how to haue every man's othes numbered, and at night for every othe to have a cann of water poured downe his sleeve," which discipline had speedily the effect of abolishing the use of strong language.

It was at this moment that the charter of the company was enlarged. Lord Delaware was appointed to the command of a new expedition. Five hundred adventurers joined him. His departure was delayed for a short time, and three commissioners were empowered to assume the reins of government until his arrival.

A storm scattered the ships, and drove that which contained the commissioners far to the southward. The remainder of the emigrants landed in the colony just as Smith had succeeded in getting it into something like working order. The new arrivals threw everything back again into confusion. Smith was superseded, but those who should have succeeded him were not forthcoming. Ever ready in emergencies, Smith resolved to retain his authority until the commissioners' arrival; but an accident disabled him, and obliged him to return to England. It was soon seen how much of the seeming prosperity of the colony was due to the personal character of Smith. No sooner had he left them than dissensions broke out. The Indians, whose friendship was due to his exertions, became hostile. Their stock of food was wasted. His courage, his self-possession, his fertility of resource, his merry smile and cheerful tongue had kept them in heart; when he left them they had none to lead. Famine overtook them. Smith left them four hundred and ninety strong: they were speedily reduced to sixty. Some took to piracy; the remainder, in despair, determined to sail for Newfoundland, and distribute themselves among the ships of the English fishermen who frequented the banks. They had already started when they met Lord Delaware, the new governor, with ample supplies.

The colony wore on with varying success. Sir Thomas Dale, an experienced soldier in the Low Countries, who figures prominently in a long dispute about arrears of pay with the States General,* succeeded Lord Delaware, and established martial law. James I., in establishing the colony, had taken good care to give the colonists no rights of self-government. Vir-

* Holland Documents, New York Col. MSS.

ginia was the only colony in which there ever was an established church. The church, as well as the state, were subjected to martial law; and courts martial, under Sir Thomas Dale, had authority to punish indifference with stripes and infidelity with death.

Sir Thomas Gates, the leader of a new expedition, for a time superseded Dale, who formed a new settlement a little higher up the river. To each man a few acres of land was allotted to plant at leisure for his own use. Private property was thus recognized in the colony.

Now for the first time the plantations of the English in the New World seemed based upon a solid foundation. The settlement on the James River numbered several hundred persons. A neat church was erected, and around it commodious cabins were grouped. The clearings of the settlers extended a considerable distance back into the forest. The governor loudly asserted, in defiance of the pretension of France, the right of England to the whole coast as far as the forty-fifth parallel of latitude; nor was an opportunity long wanting for a practical assertion of the claim. An armed vessel, under the command of a young captain named Argall, cruised for the protection of the fisheries off the coast of Maine: Argall, who was a man of rude and savage temper, heard of the settlement planted by the French near the mouth of the Penobscot, and at once formed the resolution of destroying it. On the arrival of the

Chapter IX.

[1606—1625.]

Jesuit missionaries in Acadia, Marie de Médicis, and the Marquise de Guercheville, had some years before provided funds for the establishment of a settlement within the limits of the Southern Company of Virginia. The Indians between the Kennebec and the Penobscot became the allies of France, and De Saussaye erected some rude fortifications on the eastern side of the island of Mount Desert, where the Jesuit father, Biart, had already founded a village, and established the head-quarters of a mission. Upon this settlement, 1613 Argall made his attack: he cannonaded the fort: he pillaged the village and the ship which was in the harbour. The cross erected by Biart was overthrown; the inhabitants of the infant settlement 1615 scattered. A second expedition burnt Port Royal, and overthrew the fortifications of De Monts on the island of St. Croix.

The attention of the Virginian colony had been directed only to the manufacture of potash, of soap, of tar, and of glass. In these branches of industry they could not compete with the natives of the Baltic. Vineyards now gave place to tobacco plantations. Tobacco was planted in every open space. It grew in the fields, and even in the streets of Jamestown. Tobacco became the staple, and eventually the current coin of the colony.

The company's rule was still marked with mismanagement. The coarse and cruel Argall was appointed governor. He oppressed the colonists and defrauded the company. Complaints against him, that might have been unheeded under other circumstances, were eagerly listened to when they were directed against a public defaulter. Reports of his tyranny reached England, and scared those who intended to emigrate. The council observed that Virginia was rapidly falling into disrepute : life and liberty were alike insecure. The interest of the company and of the colonists for once coincided; Argall was recalled. Drum-head courts-martial were soon afterwards replaced by civil tribunals. Yeardley, a mild and popular man, was made captain-general, and the colonists appointed an assembly to assist the governor, and, if necessary, to control him : thus, out of Argall's stupid tyranny arose popular institutions. The new assembly had, however, no legal existence : its acts required ratification at home. The assent was never accorded ; but the representatives of Virginia were, at a later day, indebted to royal cupidity for their recognition,* as they had been indebted to the cupidity of Argall for their existence.

The character of the emigration gradually changed. Few women had gone out in the early days of the colony : the emigrants had intended to make rapid fortunes and return to Europe : the first settlers were succeeded by men who intended to make their home in the New World. A number of girls of good repute were persuaded to emigrate ; a subscription was raised to defray their expenses : the colonists willingly paid a hundred pounds of tobacco for a wife—

* See page 326.

a very pretty girl went as high as a hundred and fifty pounds. A debt for a wife was looked upon as a debt of honour. Even in a mercantile point of view the company prospered by its venture.

The company soon assumed a degree of importance which attracted the attention of King James. He attempted to interfere in the election of governor, but on every occasion he had the mortification to see his nominees defeated. The courts of the Virginian Company had gradually become schools of debate, like the courts of the East India Company in the time of Warren Hastings. Many of the great parliamentary leaders took a part in their proceedings. Fierce struggles ensued for the control of the company; it was hardly concealed that James was himself the head of one party; Sir Edwin Sandys and the Earl of Southampton led the opposition. Southampton was elected treasurer in opposition to the four candidates nominated by James, and Sir Francis Wyatt was sent to the colony as governor, with orders to establish there a form of government on the model of the English constitution. The company increased till it numbered a thousand proprietors, of whom two or three hundred sometimes appeared at the meetings. The struggles that went on in Parliament against the royal prerogative were renewed in the company's courts. There the Royalists were in a minority; the edicts of the Privy Council on the affairs of Virginia were invariably reversed on the ground of their incompatibility with the terms of the charter. "The Virginia courts," says Gondemar, the Spanish ambassador, in a letter to James, "are but the seminary to a seditious Parliament." In 1622 James once more attempted to dictate to the company; again the royal message was disregarded, and Southampton re-elected treasurer. The king in great indignation resolved to seize the pretext of petition, alleging various grievances against the company, to sequestrate the patent. An order in council appeared announcing that the king reserved to himself the right of nominating the officers of the company, and to negative, at his pleasure, the nomination of officers appointed in the colony. Commissioners were sent to Virginia to investigate the alleged grievances on the spot. They had orders to procure from the colonists a petition in favour of the abrogation of the charter. But it was under the charter that their House of Assembly had been allowed to assemble; the colonists, therefore, steadily refused to sign any petition which might countenance the withdrawal of their political liberties. The commissioners, nevertheless, reported, as might have been expected, in the interest of the king, and the charter was formally withdrawn.

CHAPTER X.

THE SPANISH MONARCHY.

[1620—1625.]

Historical Sketch of the rise of Spanish Power—Its Decline—Proposed Marriage between the Prince of Wales and the Infanta of Spain—His Marriage with Henrietta of France.

CHAPTER X.

1625

ENGLAND, meanwhile, was condemned to playing a contemptible part. The successor of Elizabeth was doing his best to overturn those national liberties, which, in spite of her despotic temper, the great queen had fostered. Two great writers have left us pictures of James, which will live as long as the English language. English readers remember how degrading vices, and equally degrading weaknesses, brought his person and his court into contempt. They recollect the often-repeated account of his ignominious affection for men whose only qualifications were personal good looks; the crimes which his worthless favourites perpetrated with impunity almost in his presence; the shameful debauchery of Whitehall, where ladies of the court reeled with intoxication at the court balls; the king's personal cowardice, his stutter, his pedantry, his unmanly tears, his mingled weakness and ferocity, his garrulity, his buffoonery. If they are recalled here, it is because James I. was the king under whom England took possession of her heritage in America, and because his personal character exercised a very great influence over the fortunes of our countrymen beyond the Atlantic: it was not his fault if the high position which England had achieved abroad under Elizabeth was not completely destroyed.

At the very outset of his reign he signed an ignominious peace with Spain, moved thereto, if we may credit Osborne's "Traditional Memoirs," by counsellors whose advice was bought with Spanish gold.* It could hardly be from dread of Spanish power, for the monarchy of Spain had already passed its zenith. Year by year the causes which were to drag it down to the lowest point of degradation were becoming more and more visible. It still held its immense possessions in America. Rousillon, Artois,

---

* "He held his thoughts so intent upon play and pleasure, that to avoyd all interruption likely to impede any part of the felicity he had possessed his imagination with from the union of these crowns, and to fit an example for his neighbours' imitation, whom he desired to bring into the like resolution, he cast himselfe, as it were, blindfold into a peace with Spaine, farre more destructive to England than a warre. * * * And as this peace was of infinite consequence to the Spaniard, so he spared for no cost to procure it. And, to prevent the inserting any article that might obstruct his recourse to or from the Indies, he presented all, both Scotch and English, with gifts, and those no small ones; for by that, the Earle of Northampton, brother to Suffolke, had, he was alone able to raise and finish the goodly pile he built in the Strand, which yet remaines a monument of his, &c. Nor are there a few other no lesse brave houses, fresh in my memory, that had their foundations, if not their walls and roofes plastered with the same mortar."—*Osborne's Traditional Memoirs of James I.*

CHAPTER X.

Franche Comté were still beneath its sway; but the best and most populous part of the Netherlands had braved Philip II. for nearly a generation, and had at length achieved a *de facto* if not a *de jure* independence.

The causes which had raised it to the foremost place among the nations of Europe may be easily discerned by any one who will recall the events of Spanish history. The reasons of its decline are no less evident.

For ages the Spaniards had been distinguished by two great characteristics—loyalty to their king, and bigotry in their religion. Religious fanaticism had grown with their national growth, and formed the distinguishing mark of their national character. Every circumstance in their history seemed to tend to this object, and to this alone. The English and French both underwent disturbances and persecution, but in their countries the spirit of toleration gradually spread; the State pursued secular as well as spiritual objects, and ultimately separated the two. In Spain no such separation occurred; the power of the Church increased in Spain as rapidly as it diminished in other nations. At last it absorbed all power in itself and ruined the monarchy.

For many centuries after the overthrow of the Roman power, the Spaniards were engaged in religious wars. The Vandals who settled in Spain were Arians; the Franks who overran France were believers in the Trinity: Clovis, Childebert, Clotaire, during the fifth century, successively attacked their heretical neighbours; and thus for nearly a century a war of independence was also a war of opinion. During all this time the war was for the purpose of defending Arian opinions. The Arian priesthood, the expounders of those opinions, obtained great power. In the seventh century, Recaredo and his people abjured Arianism : with the zeal of a new convert, he endeavoured to so increase the power of the new priesthood as to surpass that of the old— another rise in the priestly power : the monarchy of the Goths, says Sempere, was but a theocracy. In the eighth century, the Arabs came over from Barbary and overran Spain; the Christian Goths, penned up behind the mountains of Asturias, relapsed almost into barbarism; the poor were reduced to such distress that they wandered about naked, and lived like wild beasts in the hills and forests : extreme ignorance followed on extreme poverty; extreme superstition waited, as it ever does, on ignorance. At length the Christians began to take heart. They emerged from their mountain passes and attacked the invaders. Then began a struggle which lasted without interruption for near eight hundred years. Again it was a war of independence—Spaniard against Arab ; again a war of religion—Christian against Mahommedan. The same causes which had operated to raise the Arian clergy during the war with Clovis and Childebert, acted with double force in favour of the clergy now. The bishops, in warlike garb, led the Christians to battle: they were amongst the most skilful leaders; soon they began to consider themselves the chosen champions of God. Chests of relics were carried to battle; men believed that they saw saints and angels fighting in the forefront of the battle. Religious fanatics have in all ages been well-nigh invincible; such were the Mahommedans in the early days of Islam; such were Cromwell's warriors in the Puritan times; such were the Gothic Spaniards fighting against the Moors. Painfully the Christians won back Spain from the invaders: it took them near two hundred years to win the line of the Douro: in two centuries more their frontier was on the Tagus: it was not till the eighth century of hard fighting was nearly over, that the Moorish garrison were beaten out of their last strongholds—Malaga and Granada.

Eight centuries of fighting, and all the time one war-cry—the Holy Cross! What wonder if religious fanaticism became not only a part of the Spanish character, but the Spanish character itself? These various causes were aided by the geographical position of Spain, which isolated it, in a great measure, from participation in the events that were going on in the rest of Europe. Spain was less disturbed than other nations by questions which in the sixteenth century shook Europe to its centre. The spirit of inquiry was stifled at once: learning was in the hands of the monks; it was their province rather to inculcate belief than to encourage inquiry. Literature soon assumed, and long retained, the peculiarities of the class who alone possessed it. It became thus from its dogmatism an instrument of barbarism rather than an ally of truth; knowledge was retarded rather than advanced, for the inquiries necessary for dispelling error were prohibited. The Reformation, which weakened the dominion of the church in most countries, strengthened it in Spain, for it showed the church its own power. The two powers, monarchy and the priesthood, became the predominant, and, indeed, the only powers in Spain: unquestioning obedience was thus gradually established as the moving spring of the Spanish character.

The loyalty which distinguished the Spaniards was also of slow growth. When first they broke out of Asturias, they were few and weak. Divided councils would have been ruin, annihilation, loss of national existence. It was necessary to choose a leader; to stick to him through good and evil report; to obey him with unquestioning obedience, and to make that obedience a sacred act of duty and of faith. This, too, became engrained in the national character. As time went on, and the frontier to be defended embraced the whole breadth of Spain, powerful chiefs settled themselves in the principal cities, and established their independent sovereignties; but each was regarded by his followers with the same loyalty as the first; for the same causes were still at work. At length, in 1492, the last Moorish soldiers were driven out of Spain, and the crowns of the great kingdoms of Castile and Arragon were united in the persons of Ferdinand and Isabella. From them sprung a long line of famous princes, to whom the undivided loyalty of the Spanish heart was given. It was carried to such a pitch that the proudest grandee addressed the king kneeling; no man might mount a horse which he had once ridden, or look upon the face of wife or mistress whom he had discarded.

The line of Austrian princes were just the men to claim to the uttermost that devoted loyalty, and, according to Spanish ideas, to deserve it. They were creatures of their time. They carried to the full extent the remorseless fanaticism which their people loved. And because they did so, the church, whose authority they supported, exerted all its influence to uphold the power of the crown. One by one the popular liberties of Spain were curtailed. The Cabildos were abolished, the Cortes insulted and destroyed. But the Spanish kings led the way to one conquest after another, and did their utmost to extirpate heresy root and branch from their dominions. Look at the wide conquest of the Emperor Charles, and at the unsparing endeavours he made to root out heresy from the Netherlands: Ferdinand had already established the Inquisition, and the reformation, which was convulsing Europe, had no chance and no hold in Spain : both Charles V.'s greatest wars were wars of religion—one against the German princes of the Reformation, one against the Turks. Thus the sixteenth century completed eleven hundred years of almost uninterrupted religious warfare waged by Spain; for Philip followed in his father's steps. There is no need to repeat how his viceroys hanged, burned, and buried alive in the Netherlands; how unsparingly the Inquisition was worked in the Indies; how the Great Armada came and went that was to relight the fires of Smithfield. By that time the Spaniard was the finest gentleman, and, physically, the noblest race in Europe. Centuries of toil and strife had produced a people of extraordinary energy and daring; the exigencies of constant danger had made them, by hereditary right, hardy, self-reliant, obedient to authority, true as steel, and proud as Lucifer. A race that has those characteristics is a conquering race, be it Roman, or Goth, or Anglo-Saxon. And the Spaniards did conquer. In the last years of the fifteenth century one prince sat on the throne of Castile, another on that of Arragon, a Mohammedan bore sway in Granada. Before the middle of the sixteenth, one of the Spanish kings was Emperor of Germany; in America his viceroys governed Mexico, Peru, and the Isles of the Ocean; in Europe, he held the Netherlands, Portugal, Navarre, Rousillon, Artois, Franche Comté, the Milanese, Naples, Sicily, Sardinia, the Balearic Islands, and the Canaries; he had numerous possessions in Africa, and rich settlements in Asia. The princes of the Austrian house were absolute, and they had the advantage of succeeding to institutions in some degree liberal. The Cortes and the Justiza Major, while they were free and powerful, had played their part, amid the increasing power of the crown, in forming a nation of warriors and statesmen elsewhere unmatched. It was the misfortune of Charles V., and of his successors, that they found themselves strong enough to strike down this remnant of Spanish independence, and to concentrate in themselves the whole power of the nation.

They threw their cast and lost it. Philip II. had aimed at universal dominion—not so much for himself as for the Church of Rome. The whole power of his empire, the wealth of his western mines, the blood of his gallant soldiers, the intellect of his generals and diplomatists, were spent in the endeavour to place a Catholic on the throne of England, to reduce the Netherlands to obedience, to make the princes of Europe vassals to the most Catholic king. Philip was foiled in his designs against England. He was not more successful with Holland. The little country whose dykes scarcely defended them from the inroads of the sea, and whose land was but the wash and ooze of great rivers which watered happier climes, even threw off his sway. His grandson—an idle and effeminate lounger, a man for whom even Spanish loyalty could hardly affect anything but contempt—watched without a sigh the partition of his empire, and the downfall of his power. In truth, the system of Spanish government was rotten to the core; the whole machine depended upon the ability of the prince: when that broken reed failed, it went to pieces. The finances had been wasted by Charles V., and by Philip II. Philip III. was not content with wasting wealth, he must exterminate those who produced it. He determined to get rid of the whole Moorish race. If anything were wanting to prove the enormous power which the priesthood had acquired in Spain, this fact alone would demonstrate it. Philip III., too indolent to give to affairs that minute and careful supervision which his father and grandfather had given, intrusted his whole authority to the Duke of Lerma. This wholesale abnegation of sovereign authority, among a people so loyal as the Spaniards, greatly weakened the ancient reverence for the person of the sovereign. Lerma, to obtain some reliable support, played into the hands of the clergy. It was at their request that the expulsion of the Nuevos Christianos, or Moriscoes, as they were called, was decided. It was not pretended that they were heretics, but they came of a heretic stock. They had been ordered, as far back as 1566, to learn the Castilian tongue, to leave off the dress and the customs of their forefathers. It was made illegal to speak Arabic, either in public or in private. All deeds and contracts written in Arabic were void. The edict provided that Arabic books should be given up to the president of the *audencia* of Granada. Moorish ceremonies were forbidden at weddings, which were to be conducted solely according to the customs of the church. Even their musical instruments were forbidden, and the

Moorish girls were prohibited from singing the songs of their fatherland. But even these harsh enactments, through rigidly enforced, were not enough. Nothing would suffice but their absolute extirpation. It was debated whether Morisco children under seven years of age might not be excepted from the proscription; but the Archbishop of Toledo could understand no such squeamishness. He would have none of the accursed seed in Spain. A million of the most industrious inhabitants were murdered or expelled.

The financial prosperity of Spain came down with a crash. The manufacture of silk and paper; the cultivation of rice, cotton, and sugar; the general practice of husbandry and irrigation,—had been in the hands of the Nuevos Christianos.* The Spaniards considered such matters beneath their dignity: they confined themselves to war and religion. Whole districts were made desolate. On the map of Spain, the word " Despoblado "† was written in a thousand places. There were no industrious inhabitants to take the place of those who had been expelled. Organized bands of robbers, which to this day have not been entirely extirpated, took possession of the countries from which the industrious inhabitants were thus rudely withdrawn.

In this miserable condition of the Spanish nation, the neutrality of England was almost as valuable to Spain as her active co-operation. Philip IV.,

* Laborde's Spain, ii. 216.
† Circourt, Hist. des Arabes d'Espagne, iii. p. 227.

who had now succeeded to the throne, was willing to make great sacrifices in order to retain it.

A marriage was proposed between the Prince of Wales and the Infanta of Spain. The marriage was exceedingly unpopular in England; but in spite of all opposition, the Prince of Wales and the Duke of Buckingham started off, much against his Majesty's will, for Spain.

Prince Charles and his friend were received with romantic respect. The former had a gold key which admitted him at all hours to the private apartments of the king. His arrival was celebrated with rejoicings similar to those which were accorded to the kings of Spain on their coronation. A large number of the criminals of Madrid were let loose upon society, by a general gaol delivery, in honour of the happy event.

The unbridled temper and imperious arrogance of Buckingham prevented the intended marriage. He treated the grandees with disrespect. He even offered a personal affront to the Duke of Olivarez, a man as ambitious and far more able than himself. The King of Spain, after making concessions which proved to all Europe that the court of Spain was really sincere, and receiving, in return, insults which covered the British king with infamy, broke off the alliance and prepared for war.

A struggle was already raging on the Continent, which owed its origin to the ambition of Olivarez, and had for its object the realization of the often-defeated scheme of universal dominion for Austria. Bohemia was successfully attacked. Spinola conquered the Palatinate. The armies of the Austrian house soon extended their conquests over a great portion of the empire. The Dutch, who were hotly engaged in their Arminian and Gomarist disputes, now thought it high time to unite and make common cause against the common danger. This was rendered the more easy by the victory which had been obtained by the Gomarists. Maurice took the field at the head of such troops as he could collect. He busied himself with some effect in withstanding the progress of Spinola, whom he obliged to raise the siege of Bergen-op-Zoom. The French by this time had passed out of the weak hands of Mary de Medicis and Concini. Louis XIII. was persuaded to take the government into his own hands. On the death of Luynes, his first minister, the direction of affairs fell into the hands of Richelieu. The cardinal dexterously took advantage of the quarrel between England and Spain to further the interests of France. His subtle policy required action in two opposite directions. The internal distractions of France required the reduction of the Huguenots. Her external policy demanded an alliance with the Protestants against the great Catholic powers. He had also a third object—to humble the turbulent French nobility. For the furtherance of these various schemes an alliance with England was indispensable. The Prince of Wales was tempted with the hand of Henrietta, the beautiful sister of Louis: the marriage treaty was pushed eagerly on, and an English army was sent, under Count Mansfeldt, to co-operate with Prince Maurice for the relief of the Palatinate. But the reign of James was disastrous to its close. The enterprise of Mansfeldt came to nothing; and James died in 1625, just in time to avoid the mortification of learning the defeat of the King of Denmark and the death of Prince Maurice.

CHAPTER XI.

THE PURITANS.

[1620—1648.]

Puritan Agreement with the Southern Company of Virginia—Their Settlement of New Plymouth.

CHAPTER XI. WHILE James I. was yet engaged in his disputes with the company of Virginia, and disputing as to the degree of liberty which he would be pleased to allow it, a small band of Puritans escaped from his grasp and founded a settlement at New Plymouth, in what 1620 is now the State of Maine. The Puritan expedition was conducted on a footing quite distinct from the adventure of Smith. Its objects differed as widely from the Spanish goldseekers of the south, as from the French traders and state-founders of the north.

1625 James quarrelled with the Puritans, as in the earlier part of his reign he quarrelled with the Catholics. He hated them with even more than the hatred of Elizabeth. Her dislike had been political; the hatred of James was personal. They troubled him in Scotland, where he was weak; he determined to revenge himself in England, where he was powerful. They had been originally but a harmless sect; persecution changed them into a malignant faction. There was nothing in the religious opinions of the Puritans that need have made them antagonistic to the monarchy, until penal laws made them so. It is true, no doubt, that a church consisting of a hierarchy of many grades, each different in rank and emolument, and connected by many ties with the state, will be more in harmony with monarchical institutions than a church formed on the Calvinistic model. It is no less true that any church is disaffected when it is the object of persecution, and actively loyal in proportion as it is warmly favoured and protected.

As regards the Puritans, persecution stirred up to active hatred, to opposition vehement and inflexible, a body of men who had originally differed from the government about matters in themselves puerile and unimportant. The surplice and the square cap, which moved the indignation of the Puritan leaders, were but the symbols of discontent. They were quite unconnected with government or with the real interests of religion. An opposition, which, if let alone, might have proved trifling, was fanned into a flame. The petty tyranny of James irritated rather than subdued it, and left to his son a legacy of smouldering discontent, which was destined to overthrow the monarchy. Charles sternly contended for the royal prerogative, the people with still firmer determination claimed the right to think and to pray like freemen.

CHAPTER XI.

[1620—1648.

From the time of the Tudors down to the end of the stormy period which comprises the Protectorate, the Restoration, and the Revolution, the English Church was subjected to assaults similar in character to the mighty revolutions which had agitated Catholicism. In a former chapter we have noted the principal features of that contest, and the manner in which the power of Rome alternately advanced or receded. It was attacked by the Albigenses in the thirteenth century; by the Lollards in the fourteenth; by the Lutherans in the sixteenth: and after every assault there followed a reaction in its favour. From the first two attacks the papacy easily and completely rallied. The last and most important was never entirely overcome. There was a time when the political alliances of kings were dictated by their theological predilections; and the pretexts of national enmities were religious. But at length political ambition resumed its place. Both churches, by the separation of politics from religion, gained in purity, though they lost in grandeur. Rivalry is now confined to purely spiritual topics; and each party depends for success with its proselytes on appeals to reason and weight of argument.

A similar history may be traced in the Church of England. From the beginning, both her doctrine and ritual were a compromise: her doctrine was elaborated by men who were sincerely desirous, if it were possible, to remain in communion with Rome; who wished to correct corruptions which had crept into the teaching of the Roman Church, but not to assert any doctrine at variance with her fundamental dogmas. The ritual of the English Church was composed by Cranmer, whose first and strongest desire was to stand well with Catholics and Protestants alike. Lord Macaulay, in one of those sparkling sentences which flow so readily from his pen, says that the plan of the framers of the Liturgy was "to transfer the cup of sorceries from the Babylonian Enchantress to the other side, spilling as little as possible by the way." Whatever may have been the motive which actuated the English reformers, it was desirable that they should change as little as was possible; if it was necessary to mutilate the venerable fabric which had been reared during so many centuries of toil, it was surely necessary that the demolition should be undertaken in a spirit not of spoliation, but of respect: the framers of the English ritual felt this truth and acted upon it; but the partial character thus given to the English Reformation at once arrayed against it two classes of persons—those who considered that it went too far, and those who considered that it did not go half far enough. Some could perceive no sufficient reason for resigning communion with a church in which their fathers had lived and died: there was but little difference between the religion held orthodox by the English king, and that taught by the pope; one issued his orders from Windsor, the other dated his bulls from the Vatican, but both seemed equally arbitrary and unreasonable. Others, again, thought that compromise was in itself evil, and detested all half-measures as an abomination. These last were the most important and the most pertinacious enemies of the English Church. Thus, as the Church of Rome was attacked by Lutheran and Calvinistic schismatics, the Church of England was attacked by Puritan schismatics.

Puritanism was at first regarded with some dislike and some contempt: it was long before it acquired sufficient importance to be actively hated or oppressed. While Elizabeth was confronted with the deadly enmity of Spain, the greater danger entirely absorbed the less. The queen disliked the Puritans: she was not personally disinclined to the gorgeous ceremonies, and even the distinguishing doctrines, of the Roman church. Not only was the extreme simplicity which the Puritans imposed distasteful to her; she wanted all the strength at her command to cope with Philip, and regarded with disfavour noisy fanatics who distracted her attention from the great game. But at that time no active disloyalty entered into the views of the Puritans; they were at least as anxious as anybody else for the final triumph of Protestantism, and were willing to give such aid as was in their power to the state. It was reserved for the grinding bigotry of James, and the shameless bad faith of his son, to convert a body of mere dissentients into a faction, dark, active, brave, skilful, daringly energetic, and absolutely uncompromising. A time came when

Puritanism grew to such a power that it overthrew the priesthood, the peerage, and the monarchy. Then followed the reaction; each power had expended its utmost strength, and had been unable to annihilate the other; they agreed to compromise—to divide their empire over the minds of men.

But one thing was wanting to make the parallel between the European reformation and the Puritan schism complete: and it was not absent. Religion and politics had once been mixed up together: but though the language in which the quarrel was carried on had been religious, the mainspring of action had always, with the majority, been political: doctrinal disputes were handed over to the minority, to whom such matters were in themselves interesting. The great body of the people pursued the old struggle, but the contest was avowedly between prerogative and the growing spirit of republicanism.

In consequence of the disputes with the Catholics, in which King James became involved soon after his accession, he considered it prudent at first to temporise with the Puritans. It, however, soon became evident that the truce could not be of long duration. They were anxious for a clear understanding upon the subject of toleration, and expressed a desire for "a more clear reformation." This the bishops opposed as trenching too much upon their powers. The king was likewise averse to it, regarding it as an attack on his prerogative. "The bishops," says Wilson, "instilled the maxim into the king—no bishop, no monarch." A conference was held at Hampton Court in which the Puritan champions presented their demands. They desired, reasonably enough, as far as words went, " that the doctrine of the church might be preserved in purity ; that good and faithful pastors might be planted in all churches; that church government might be sincerely administered ; that the Book of Common Prayer might be fitted to more increase of godliness." In the course of the conference it appeared that they claimed for every minister the power of confirmation in his own parish. They revived the old objection against the cross in baptism, the ring in marriage, the surplice, the oath ex-officio. The king himself answered most of these demands, " sometimes gently, applying lenitives, where he found ingenuity (for he was learned and eloquent), other times corrosives, telling them these oppositions proceeded more from stubbornness in opinion than tenderness of conscience ; and so betwixt his arguments and kingly authority, menaced them to a conformity, which proved a way of silencing them for the present." *

" You are aiming," he exclaimed, " at a Scots presbytery, which agrees with monarchy as do God and the devil. Then shall Jack, and Tom, and Will, and Dick meet, and at their pleasures censure me, and my council, and all my proceedings. Then Will shall stand up and say it must be thus ; then Dick shall reply and say, Nay, marry, but we will have it

* Wilson, Complete History.

thus; and therefore here I must once more reiterate my former speech, and say Le roi s'avisera."

"Was there ever such a king since Christ's time!" exclaimed Bishop Bancroft, who was one of the audience.

"Your majesty speaks by the special power of God," added the aged Whitgift.

James expressed his own opinion, that he had "soundly peppered the Puritans."

The bishops having thus got the upper hand, turned the opportunity to their advantage. The Puritan ministers were silenced, imprisoned, and exiled. At length, after two unsuccessful attempts at escape, a large company assembled on the seashore near the mouth of the Humber, and set sail for Holland. They established themselves first at Amsterdam, and then at Leyden, where they were joined by brethren in misfortune. Their company became very numerous. Poverty compelled even their ministers to work hard for bare subsistence. Brewster, who had formerly been a diplomatist, confined himself to preaching. Others learned mechanical trades: Bradford became a dyer. The safety in which they lived acted, in the opinion at least of their leaders, unfavourably on their minds. Their zeal languished for want of opposition. The more active spirits among them grew tired of indolent security—they longed for room to expand, for influence, for power, for liberty to regulate their own affairs uncontrolled by any superior, or by any law except their own. The ministers, too, began to fancy that the example of the Dutch soldiers, who were fighting under Prince Maurice, and who were anything but rigid moralists, exercised a sinister influence over the younger portion of their flock. They turned their eyes to Virginia.

Application was made to the Plymouth or Northern Company of Virginia. The territories of the company had remained unoccupied ever since the grant of James in 1606. Several expeditions which had been sent out had failed, and the grant itself was almost in abeyance. They obtained their land upon ruinous terms: the labour of each emigrant was to be considered equivalent to a capital sum of 10*l*., and to be thrown into a common stock; at the end of seven years the profits were to be divided. This arrangement gave rise to the idea that in possessing all things in common they were imitating the primitive Christians. So says Robertson.* But though their conduct was in many points marked by the spirit of the early Christians, they never imitated them in money matters when they could help it. In this instance their arrangement with the Plymouth merchants left them no alternative, and they reverted to the more ordinary rules of private property as soon as they could. The enforced system of community of goods was immediately and inevitably productive of inconvenience; it was, of course, the interest of no one in particular

* Hist. America, book x.

to be industrious, so that it was found necessary to introduce the most arbitrary regulations into the code of laws which they drew up on landing: activity and diligence were secured on pain of whipping.

Cold and famine terribly thinned their numbers: at one time the living were scarcely numerous enough to bury the dead; but amidst their sufferings the Puritan emigrants remembered with thankfulness that at least they were free from religious persecution. They were, as had been stated in the memorial of Robinson and Brewster, "weaned from the delicate milk of their mother-country, and knit together in a strict and sacred band whom small things could not discourage, nor small discontents cause to wish themselves home again." James I. did as much as he could by severe usage to drive all those who in any way stood forward as the champions of civil and religious liberty into the ranks of the Puritan party. Many men of talent, especially among the ministry, sought in America that freedom which they were every day less able to enjoy at home. John Cotton, the most esteemed of all the Puritan ministers, was among the refugees: he was threatened with the censure of the king's ecclesiastical commissioners, which his secession had long invited, but which his personal character and popularity had hitherto averted: he took with him several of the same views as himself. But if he had emigrated for conscience' sake, he found in America many whose consciences were even more tender than his own. The red cross on the English banner was a stumbling-block to some; the presence of ladies when he said grace scandalized others. The latter seems a strange rock of offence, but is reported by credible historians. Mrs. Hutchinson, the wife of the governor of Massachusetts, and her ladies, treated him very flippantly. They sent him a present of candles as a hint that he wanted more spiritual light.

After a few years the limits of the colony began to spread. They were joined by other parties of Puritan emigrants, who rapidly pushed forward in all directions from the original settlement at Plymouth. They had gone out without any sanction from the king, their form of government had therefore not been decided for them. They looked for no protection; but they counted on being free from interference. They made their own laws, appointed their own government, and, in fact, became completely independent. They hesitated at first about inflicting capital punishment, but they had no scruples about whipping, branding, or the pillory. They soon got rid of their qualms respecting the infliction of the punishment of death, and hanged their criminals with easy consciences. Their political position was much more agreeable than that of their neighbours in the royal colony of Virginia. There the king was perpetually meddling; he appointed the governors, he tried to control all the proceedings of the company to whom he had delegated his authority, but no one dreamed of molesting the New Englanders. They went on their own path in peace. Flying from monarchical tyranny in the Old World, it was natural that they should bring democratic notions to the New. Many of them had lived in Holland, and had gazed with admiration on the republican institutions which the Dutch had established with so much courage and patriotism. Their first care was to declare that the laws which they framed should be governed on the strictest principles of democracy. The only restraint by which they were hampered was the bargain by which they held their land : it has been already stated that the company received payment in labour, not in money. At length the settlers were able to scrape together enough money to pay off the proprietors: from that time their advance was rapid.

After the death of James I. they obtained a confirmation of the concession made to them by the Plymouth company, by a charter from King Charles. The king's supremacy is so carefully asserted in this document that some historians have expressed surprise that Puritans should have emigrated with such confidence of immunity from persecution ; but it is evident that there was a general and full understanding, that though no formal stipulation existed, ample latitude was to be allowed. The king's supremacy was never the point on which they were uneasy, for the utmost loyalty prevailed ; and it is also presumable that the king would make some concessions in order to obtain the settlement of his distant dominions, especially as very considerable reluctance had been displayed to going there. The new colony proved so attractive that Charles became alarmed, and published a proclamation " to restrain the disorderly transportation of his Majesty's subjects, because of the many idle and refractory humours whose only end is to live beyond the reach of authority." Lord Nugent thinks * that John Hampden and his cousin Oliver Cromwell were in one of the ships which were stopped at the moment of sailing in accordance with the king's proclamation. Hampden bought an extensive tract of land in Virginia,† no doubt under the impression that political events might take such a turn as to make it useful to him at some future day; but it does not appear that he did more than send out an agent to take possession, and subsequently "sold the land in 1636," says Miss Aikin. If the story be true, Charles I. must often have regretted his opposition to the voyage of Cromwell and Hampden. They could have done little against him in America; but in England they could measure intellects with him—swords, too, if necessary, in a manner which should prove to all men that the weapon of the red-nosed brewer was the sharper of the two.

* Life of Hampden, vol. i. p. 254. † Miss Aikin, Life of Charles I.

CHAPTER XII.

DUTCH SETTLEMENTS AT MANHATTAN AND IN BRAZIL.
NEW SWEDEN.

[1614—1648.]

Hudson's Voyage—Assembly of XIX.—Swedish Emigration—Cession of the Dutch Settlement.

IN 1613, when Argall returned from his expedition against the French settlement at Port Royal, he found a few hovels on the island of Manhattan, which had been erected during his absence by the Dutch.

A few years before, Hudson, an English navigator who had been twice engaged by London adventurers in a search for the north-west passage, took service with the Dutch. Under their directions he went to America, where he coasted along the shores of Virginia. Accident caused him to round the narrow spit of land called Sandy Hook. He thus found himself in the magnificent bay of New York, whence, after a short delay, he proceeded to explore the river which now bears his name. Holland had scarcely attained independent existence as a state, when she thus founded an offshoot in America. The truce

CHAPTER XII.

with Spain was signed in April; and in September Hudson landed at New York.

The union of the United Provinces was in its very nature commercial. Zealand and Holland are both so surrounded by the ocean that their industry naturally takes a maritime direction. Their plains are with difficulty kept from the sea; their population from earliest youth are accustomed to be afloat. Before their emancipation they had hardly money to keep their dykes in repair. In a few years they found themselves raised to opulence, and possessed of the maritime supremacy of the world. That supremacy was only to be kept and increased by perseverance in enterprise. They possessed no forest; yet they built more ships than any other nation. They had not a field of flax; yet they had large linen manufactures. They had no flocks; but they were the centre of the woollen trade. They had no corn land; but they had the best-stocked granaries in the world. They were the connecting link of the scattered ends of the world—the commercial centre and emporium. This was the secret of the Dutch emigration. Their religion was free at home. They had just won its freedom through a bloody revolution and dire persecution. Theirs was no flight for conscience' sake, as the English Puritan emigration was a few years later. Nor was it of a romantic or adventurous kind, like the Virginian emigration which had just begun. It was an expedition purely mercantile. Profit and loss shrewdly calculated — no anticipations of gold and silver mines—no desire for showy conquest. The merchants who fitted out the expedition were men of intensely practical views; and they carried out their ideas after a fashion delightfully quaint and matter-of-fact.

The first explorers who followed Hudson on the part of the Dutch, received from the States-General a monopoly of the trade of the country they had discovered for four years. They, however, did not form a corporation; nor had they, till 1614, any establishment, and then only a small trading post near Albany. There was no colony; not a single family had emigrated; a few commercial agents were alone to be found there: and as yet the Dutch made no claim to the country, which was within the limits of the English colony of Virginia. During the long suspension of hostilities, the United Provinces had increased with unexampled rapidity in commerce and in power. They had taken a position as a maritime nation second only to England. They had consequently obtained a considerable influence in Europe. In 1620, when the twelve years' truce with Spain was on the point of expiring, the States-General encouraged the formation of a mercantile association under the name of the Dutch West India Company. An East India Company already existed, which possessed the exclusive trade, so far as the Dutch were concerned, of the Indian and Chinese Seas, and of the Pacific shores of America. The West India Company was incorporated for twenty-four years; and among other privileges had the exclusive right of trade between Holland and the whole eastern coast of America from Newfoundland and the Straits of Magellan.* Subscription to the joint stock was open to men of every nation; and the States-General presented to the company half a million of guilders, besides becoming stockholders to the amount of another half million. The States-General did not guarantee any possessions which the company might acquire. In case of war they were to be known only as its allies and patrons. There were seventy-four directors, who were divided into five chambers, one for each principal city of the republic. Eighteen members formed a central board, to which the States-General sent one in addition: this body, which became almost absolute, figures prominently in Dutch colonial history as the Assembly of XIX.

It was not strange that a company which treated with its own government on terms of absolute equality should acquire vast political power: we find it repeatedly interfering in matters of the highest state policy, and expressing its opinion, not unsuccessfully, on questions of peace and war.

Colonization was neither the real nor the avowed object of the company: no provision was thought of for securing civil rights to any colonists that might emigrate under its auspices. A large part of its resources consisted of plunder wrested by its armed cruisers from Spanish merchantmen. Its settlement

* La Richesse de Hollande, tom. i., 62.

on the Hudson was for many years but an inconsiderable trading station, whence a few bundles of peltries were annually brought. It was not till a later day, when circumstances had conferred on its possessions at Manhattan some increase of value, that the company thought of asserting territorial jurisdiction. Spanish prizes were far more remunerative than honest trade : privateering was carried on with such success that on one occasion alone the booty of the company amounted to eighty times the value of their whole American trade for the four previous years.*

The early authorities recorded their transactions with great care, but none of the records, either of Director Minuit's or of Director Von Twiller's administration are forthcoming. The archives of the Netherlands constitute one of the richest depositories of historical information in Europe, commencing at the period of the union of Utrecht, and continuing down to the French Revolution. But valuable as is the information which may there be gleaned, the papers of the Dutch West India Company, which had the entire direction and supervision of the colony of New Netherlands, would be of still greater interest for our immediate purpose if only they could be discovered. In 1841 the legislature of the State of New York sent an agent to Europe to collect documents to illustrate the history of America : it was supposed, until the researches of the American agent proved the

* Bancroft, Hist. United States, 299.

reverse, that these records, commencing from the formation of the company in 1621, were preserved complete at Amsterdam. It was mortifying to discover that all documents belonging either to the East or to the West India Companies, of a date prior to 1700, had been sold by auction at the desire of the government of the Netherlands.

Papers, however, which remain in the archives of the Netherlands throw a very curious light on the intentions and views of the United Provinces in establishing their West India Company, and of the political status of the company itself. From the first it was not concealed that the company was looked upon principally in the light of an effective scourge of the Spaniards. No people ever acted upon the maxim of making war pay for war more thoroughly than the Dutch. Their commercial prosperity ever increased most rapidly in times of commotion. The West India Company, as long as their privateers were permitted to prey upon Spanish commerce, saved the States-General the expense of a fleet. It had, besides, a merit which a fleet could not have. If its energetic prosecution of the war should involve more than ordinary diplomatic difficulty, its actions could be disowned. It is curious to remark, as one may do in the "New York MSS.," how rapidly the political authority of the Assembly of XIX. increased. At first they meddled only indirectly in affairs of state, and acted under the sanction of the States-General; but a few years later we find them interfering with the States-General themselves, even on questions of peace or war, and interfering successfully. In 1624 the ambassadors of the States-General in England wrote a secret despatch,* informing their high mightinesses, that the day before, the Prince of Wales had sent to them the first lord of his bedchamber, to

* Holland Documents in New York, Col. MSS., p. 33:—

"*4th June*, 1624.—My lord, the Prince of Wales, sent Mr. Caer, first lord of his bedchamber, some days ago to us, and requested us, through him, that we would believe that Sir Ferdinand Georges, Governor of Portsmouth, is an honest and honourable gentleman, and that we should so consider him, in whatever he had to transact with us, without the above-named Caer knowing anything of what the above-mentioned Sir Ferdinand had to do with us, or the purport of the aforesaid accommodation.

"*4th June.*—The aforesaid Sir Ferdinand Georges came to us, and made known that he and his being disposed to annoy the Spaniard, one of his sons, who is in New England, proposes some notable enterprises in the West Indies. And inasmuch as he, seeing the uncertainty of the resolutions in England, was afraid that his son, having performed the exploit and coming home, may be complained of in consequence to the king; he prayed that in case the King of Great Britain remained in friendship with the King of Spain, his son may be guaranteed by your High Mightinesses, and commission granted him to annoy the King of Spain in your name. We praised his good disposition, and said that the exploit, when achieved, could be best avowed. That otherwise, when naval commissions were issued by your High Mightinesses, they were formerly maintained. He said he made no difficulty as to that; and, afterwards, put his request in writing, which we have brought over to your High Mightinesses.†

" We have heard, &c.
                        " (Signed)   FRANCOYS VAN AERSSEN.
" Thus done and communicated by us, undersigned,
                                     " ALB. JOACHIM."

† Extract from the Journal of the Dutch Ambassadors in England.
(From the original in the Royal Archives, at the Hague.)
Extract of the Journal or Report of the Messrs. Francis van Aerssen, Lord of Sommelodyk, &c., and Albert Joachim, Lord at Ostend in Oudekenskercken, Ambassadors from the States-General of the United Netherlands, near the King of Great Britain, from February to July, 1624.

present to them Sir Ferdinand Georges, Governor of Portsmouth, as an honest and honourable gentleman, and to request that they would so consider him in whatever he had to transact with them. Also, that Sir Ferdinand Georges had made known to them "that he being disposed to annoy the Spaniard, one of his sons, who is in New England, proposes some notable enterprises in the West Indies," and he therefore begged that in case the King of Great Britain remained in friendship with the King of Spain, his son might have a commission from their high mightinesses to annoy the Spaniard. "We praised his good disposition," add the ambassadors, "and said that the exploit, when achieved, could be best avowed." Great Britain was then at peace with Spain; and it is somewhat curious to find the Prince of Wales and a prominent official of England conspiring with one ally to levy war upon another. It must be remembered in explanation, if not in extenuation, of the Prince of Wales's conduct towards a nation from whose king he had just received the most cordial and generous reception, that he was at that moment meditating the rupture of his marriage engagement with the Infanta of Spain, and he well knew that any conduct tending to humiliate the Spaniards would be extremely popular in England. A few years later, the company argue and act like a body fully confident of their position, and well aware of the great extent of their power. They put forward the warfare waged by the company on the Spaniards in the conviction that it would be considered as good service done to the state; they evidently believe that the position they occupy fully entitles them to treat on equal terms with the supreme authority of the state.

A renewal of the truce with Spain had been proposed by the States-General,* and it appeared at one moment likely that the project would be carried to a conclusion. It was time for the West India Company to step in: they urge, that though their company was principally established to increase trade and commerce, "without which the great multitude of seamen bestowed by God on this country cannot be employed," it was equally important to keep a check upon the King of Spain. They assert that the lands yet remaining undiscovered in America are not sufficiently rich or productive to afford remunerative employment to their merchants; that the Spaniards possess the richest portion of the country; that, in plain terms, it is easier to plunder the Spaniards than to maintain honest industry: if, therefore, say the Assembly of XIX., you make a truce with the Spaniards, whom shall we plunder, how shall we live? They proceed to give at considerable length ten excellent reasons against the truce, which may be thus epitomized: " First, It was a difficult matter to get up the company, and it

---

* It will be remembered that a truce for twelve years was made between Holland and Spain in 1609. At the expiry of the truce, hostilities were punctually recommenced in 1621.

would be a pity to let so much labour and expense be thrown away. Secondly, You, high mightinesses, are large shareholders—a million of guilders! so if we suffer, you share our misfortunes. Thirdly, The capital is all paid up, and we earnestly desire the spread of the reformed religion. [The connection between these two reasons is not very apparent.] Fourth, We employ many ships, which would otherwise be idle. Fifth, We have improved the build of ships. Sixth, We have over a hundred vessels of large tonnage, all fitted for war. Seventh, We have fifteen thousand sailors. Eighth, We have victualled and fitted the ships before mentioned with warlike stores for eighteen months. Ninth [gradually coming to a climax]. We have provided all our ships with heavy guns, over four hundred metal pieces, and two thousand swivels, besides 'pedereros' more than six hundred. Finally, One hundred thousand pounds of powder! We have imported vast wealth. We say nothing of elephants' teeth and the like, but 'the capture of the fleet from Spain amounted to so great a treasure, that never did any fleet bring such a prize to this or to any other country.' We have now, 'during some consecutive years, plundered the enemy and enriched the country,' with indigo, sugar, 'the handsomest lot of cochineal ever brought into this country,' and other matters; and we have 'captured some even of the King of Spain's galleons, hitherto considered invincible.'"

Certainly a very convincing document. It is pleasant to remember that their high mightinesses did not make truce. On the contrary, they kept up the war till it was five-and-twenty years old, with great glory, and not a little profit in the matter of prize-money, Stadtholders Maurice and Henry Frederick showing well in front all the time, and developing great military talents, as all historians agree.

The American head-quarters of a company so warlike in its operations could not fail to acquire some importance. It is true, as the company once stated to the States-General,* that colonization was difficult for the Dutch, " not so much through lack of population—with which our provinces abound—as from the fact that all who are inclined to do any sort of work here, procure enough to eat without any trouble, and are therefore unwilling to go so far from home on an uncertainty." It is stated, in the same memorial, that the people transported to America by the company " have not been any profit, but a drawback to the company."

Nevertheless, around the block-house on Manhattan the cottages of New Amsterdam began to cluster. The country assumed the form of a colony; and Peter Minuits, the commercial agent of the Dutch West India Company, held for six years the office of governor.†

The colony was quaint and rude in its beginnings;

* Holland Documents in New York Col. MSS., i. 33.
† Bancroft, Hist. United States, 298.

[1614—1648.]

CHAPTER XII.

it was composed chiefly of hunters and Indian traders. The vessels of the Dutch penetrated every inlet and navigated every river in search of fur-bearing animals. In the little settlement the straw roofs and the windmills of Holland were reproduced with fond minuteness. Feudal institutions were introduced. The emigrant who would within six years undertake to plant a colony of forty-eight souls, became a patroon or lord of the manor, with absolute power over the territories he might colonize. It was not to be expected that the Dutch, who were ruled by an oligarchy in Holland, would take much pains to introduce political institutions of a democratic character into America. There was no popular legislature. The power of the governor was absolute, and the patroons stood to him in the same relation as the great French seigneurs to the monarchy. The monopolizing spirit which every European nation of that day considered it necessary to exhibit towards its colonies was soon in active operation. Manufactures were strictly protected. No emigrant might make any woollen, linen, or cotton fabric, on pain of exile.

It is tolerably easy to make such institutions—to confer rights and privileges—but not always so easy to keep the privileged person in order. The patroons soon came into constant collision with the Assembly of XIX.

1634   In 1634 the disputes between these two parties came to a crisis, and had to be referred to the States-General for arbitration. The patroons conducted their argument in a very lengthy and rather an incoherent manner, which may be read at length in the "Holland Documents."* The company, as might be expected from a powerful corporation, behaved haughtily and disdainfully: causing the patroons to exclaim, "Alas! your high mightinesses will remark what damage the change of persons and the unsteadiness of humours have brought on this praiseworthy company and the good patroons."† Their principal and not unreasonable cause of complaint was, that the company gave them large privileges, encouraged them to spend a great deal of money, and then entirely duped them. Their freedoms, they say, were undermined. The patroons were commanded to do things which experience taught them were impracticable. "Yea, all their exemptions were drawn into dispute;" and the absolute power granted to them proved to be absolutely without value ; for the company asserted the right of exclusive trade in peltries—exclusive right of importing goods—exclusive right of doing anything by which a profit could be made. It seems evident that the company in the endeavour to encourage emigration, and at the same time to keep the trade of the colony in their own hands, had outwitted themselves. It was impossible for men residing in Europe to maintain local privileges against men living in America. Their own agents appropriated the best lands and defied their distant power. No result followed the reference to the States-General, except a

* Holland Documents in New York MSS., i. 85.
† Ibid.

new project of extended freedom which was never put into execution.

Meanwhile the English emigrants, before so friendly, began to establish themselves all round the little Dutch settlements, and the English merchants could by no means be brought to understand that the trade of the Hudson River with his Majesty's plantation of Virginia was not open to his Majesty's ships. The Massachusetts men, with their enthusiasm and zeal for popular liberty, quite overpowered the more phlegmatic Dutchmen. The neighbours quarrelled a great deal; but on the whole the position of affairs was not for a considerable time materially disturbed. The New York MSS. narrate many of these disputes. On one occasion a testy English master mariner demanding compensation of the States-General, stirred up a diplomatic flurry between London and Amsterdam. The Spanish ambassador's hand is visible in the squabble, too, and the Dutch factors behave with grotesque impertinence. It is the first of the quarrels which arose between England and Holland, and which terminated in the cession of New Netherlands.

Ambassador Joachim writes thus to the States-General:—

"Messrs. William Cloberry, &c., merchants here in London, having fitted out a ship to trade on Hudson's River as they call it, have been prevented to traffic there and in that vicinity by the Dutch West India Company. Deeming themselves injured thereby, they pretend to demand reparation for their damages. Previous, however, to submitting their complaints to the king or the lords of his Majesty's council, they concluded to speak to me and place the information in my hands, to see if they could obtain satisfaction voluntarily for what they claim. Copy of the aforesaid information accompanies this. I have also sent a like copy to the directors of the aforesaid company. Parties have given me the name of a person who offered them a good sum of money for the claim, in order, as they say, that these complaints may be added to the other grievances. For the Spanish ambassador gathers together all that can be collected against your high mightinesses and your subjects with a view to provoke and foster misunderstandings among this nation against your high mightinesses and the inhabitants of the United Netherlands.

" To this they seem to attach altogether too much credit. Some months ago, disputes broke out here in presence of the king and his Majesty's council between those who have the king's charter for Virginia and those who sail to colonize New England. A noble lord, who regrets to perceive that there is any misunderstanding between the English and Dutch nations, has informed me that the aforesaid disputes did not arise because the parties above-mentioned were suffering any injury the one from the other, but in order to pick a quarrel with the Dutch about the possession of New Netherlands. The aforesaid lord was of opinion that the disputes above mentioned were forged in the Spanish forge. He asked if the Dutch could not be disposed to pay the king some acknowledgment for what they occupy there. I cut him off from all hope of that. The intrigues of the Spaniards are many and palpable. They have great advantage, because your high mightinesses' power at sea is looked on with great jealousy here. I humbly crave your high mightinesses to make such an order that I may know by the first opportunity how I am to act further in this matter. The right way would be to leave these people to the law. But I fear that this case would not be allowed to be tried in the ordinary manner, inasmuch as the question of the king's jurisdiction is mixed up in it, &c., &c.

"*London, 27th May,* 1634."

There seems no reason to doubt that Joachim was in the right, and that the Spanish ambassador fomented the quarrel to which he refers. The occasion of dispute was that a certain vessel "The William," of London, was fitted with divers goods to be transported to Hudson's Bay adjoining unto Virginia, within his Majesty's dominions, there to be trucked and bartered away for beaver skins, &c. That the ship reached the Hudson River (on her voyage to Hudson's Bay !) and was stopped by the Dutch factors, and with many indignities forced to return. "The governor," (the Dutch factor, director Van Twiller, who was there at that time,) " did bid them to bee gone—and the governor and others of his companie came into the said shalloppe and did sticke greene bowes about her and carried a trumpetter with them . . . and by the way the said trumpett was sounded — (sounded," says another witness, "in a triumphing manner, in despite of ye Englishe), and the Dutch drancke a bottle of strong waters of three or fower pints, and were very merrie." Gross injustice coupled with derisive gestures would have been annoying enough, even if they had been unaccompanied by more solid inconvenience. But in this instance the expulsion cost the unfortunate master "four thousand pounds sterling at the very least, beside what they might have got in trade with the natives." The quarrel was referred by the Council of XIX. to the States-General in a very temperate paper, in which they urge the propriety of a proper boundary being drawn between the King of England's dominions and those of the States-General. But the latter had all along declared that they would not be answerable for the protection of the company's lands, for which, as they plainly declare, the company's own fleet should suffice. The quarrel was thus narrowed, much to the advantage of the English, to a dispute with a trading corporation only, and not with the States-General. As a natural consequence, the victory remained with the parties most in earnest, viz., the New Englanders. These and such-like quarrels soon proved that the English were by no means content to allow the Dutch to settle uninterrupted on the Hudson. Sir Dudley Carlton, ambassador from England to the Hague, had several years before sent in the following peremptory notice to the States-General :—

"Several of his English subjects, lords and other persons of station and quality having a long time ago taken possession of all the precincts of Virginia, and planted their settlements in certain parts of the northern quarter of said country, which takes its name (Nova Anglia) therefrom — his Majesty, desiring the successful issue of so sacred and useful an enterprise, which tends to the advancement of the Christian religion and the increase of trade, granted several years ago, as is notorious to every one, by his letters patent, quiet and full possession of the whole of the said country to several private individuals. Notwithstanding which he is informed that some Hollanders have last year landed in some parts of said country, and there planted a colony, altering the names of the ports and harbours, and baptizing them anew after their fashion, intending to send thither other ships for the continuance of said plantation, and that, in fact, they have now six or eight vessels all ready to sail thither.

"Now, H. M. having incontestably the right to the said country (jure primæ occupationis), has commanded me to represent to you the state of said affair, and to request you, in his name, not only that the ships already equipped for said voyage may, by your authority, be stopped, but also that the ulterior prosecution of said plantation may be expressly forbidden.

"Which, gentlemen, you will take, if you please, into prompt deliberation, communicating to me, at the earliest, the answer which I am to make his Majesty on your part."* It was therefore evident that so many causes of quarrel must eventually produce a rupture of friendly relations.

Though, for many years, the Dutch forts remained in the hands of the company, they soon became surrounded by English settlements. Hartford was the first to fall into the hands of the encroaching settlers; and, as these became more numerous, they invaded New Netherlands. If Englishmen could urge any shadow of claim to Hartford, they could at least advance none to Manhattan: but the States-General looked on with apathy, and saw, without a remonstrance, the arms of Holland thrown down from the great standard post on Long Island, where they had remained since the time of Hudson, and replaced by some grimly humorous Massachusetts men, with the effigy of a fool's head with cap and bells.

A short time after the New England invasion the colony was almost annihilated by the Indians. The Dutch at last confided their defence against their savage assailants to one of the reckless Indian fighters of New England, whose manner, tinctured with the licentiousness as well as the bravery of the soldiers of his day, had procured his banishment from

* Sir Dudley Carleton's Memorial to the States-General. State Paper Office, Holland, 9th February, 1622.

Massachusetts. He was placed at the head of an army of 120 men; and the Dutch burghers made their bargains in peace. New Netherlands, like all young colonies, demanded for its development perfect freedom of trade; this the Assembly of XIX. were not willing to grant: it had borne all the expenses of the foundation of the colony: it would tolerate no interloper. But it was not easy to establish a supervision over such distant possessions—the monopoly could not be enforced: it was replaced by export duties. Meanwhile the settlers from New England continued their encroachments on the Dutch; Stuyvesant, the governor, knowing that the States would under no circumstances incur a war to save their colony, went himself to Hartford to do what he could by negotiation; but he could only postpone for a time the inevitable evil.

The operations of the Dutch West India Company were not confined to the shores of the Hudson, nor, indeed, was the settlement at Manhattan, which had already been several years in existence when the company was formed, the principal object to which they directed their attention. The Dutch remembered that when they had resolved to sail into the East Indies, they had succeeded, notwithstanding the enmity of the "Portingales," who "then inhabited and had strong forts therein, and far surpassed their power for quantity of ships." The trade of the East had become so enormously valuable that in 1608 it was estimated at forty-three millions of guilders. It

was also computed that it had "yielded to the customs, in the space of seven years, no less than thirty-five tons of gold, and the proceeds of the succeeding seven years were still greater."* They determined to invade the as yet untouched monopoly of the Spaniards and Portuguese in America, and trade directly with Brazil and the Spanish Main. With characteristic caution, they at first sent out a few ships only, laden with the goods of neutral powers. They then began to trade for hides to Cuba and Hispaniola, where the buccaneers offered a ready market. By degrees they insinuated themselves into other branches of the West India trade,—sugar, rare woods, ginger, and cochineal. But in 1624 a fleet went out on a less peaceful mission. They seized San Salvador in Brazil, whither, in the following year, they sent a garrison of 1300 men from Holland. In 1628 they succeeded in capturing the Spanish plate fleet on its homeward voyage, and rifled the settlements in Cuba. Fifty per cent. was declared upon the paid-up capital of the West India Company that year.†
Two years later they seized St. Eustache and Curaçoa, and undertook the invasion of Brazil.

A sketch of the Portuguese government of Brazil, up to the time of Thomé de Souza, the first governor-general, has already been given. De Souza was recalled, at his own request, in 1557; he was succeeded by Duarte de Costa, who established a great

* McCullagh, Industrial History of Free Nations, vol. ii. p. 324.
† Ibid., p. 328.

Jesuit college on the beautiful plains of Piratininga, whence they rapidly extended their missions over the interior, and particularly along the banks of the many navigable rivers with which Brazil abounds. Da Costa was, in his turn, succeeded by the celebrated Mem da Sa, under whose government Coligny's colony was established by Villegagnon.* After the expulsion of the French, the Portuguese settlements, which extended in a narrow fringe along the sea-coast, were so harassed by the Indians, that had it not been for the influence which the Jesuits had acquired over the natives, they must have been completely destroyed. Mem da Sa ruled for fourteen years. On one occasion a successor was sent out to supersede him; but Spanish or Portuguese ships steering for the coasts of South America were always compelled to run the gauntlet of the buccaneer cruisers of the English and French. Luiz de Vasconcellos, the governor elect, was killed in action off Terceira, on his way to take possession of his viceroyalty, and the company of Jesuits, which, as a matter of course, accompanied a new governor, were all massacred by a French pirate. At the death of Mem da Sa, the command was intrusted to Luiz de Almeida. The year 1579 was disastrous to the Portuguese; for King Sebastian, with the chief of his nobility, was cut off during an expedition against the Moors, and Philip II., sending Alva with an army of Spaniards into Portugal, defeated Antonio,

* *Ante*, p. 127.

the reigning king, and annexed his crown to that of Spain. The Portuguese colonies became by this means involved in the quarrels of the Catholic League. The Spaniards took little interest in possessions so far inferior to their own in mineral resources. Neither gold nor pearls, silver nor emeralds, were to be found there: they neglected the defence of Brazil just at the time when the freebooters of Elizabeth had discovered that it was worth plundering and unable to resist attack. Cavendish infested the coast with his pirate ship in 1591, and sailed up the Thames, after one of his successful forays, with topsails made of cloth of gold. Two years later, Sir James Lancaster took Pernambuco. Lancaster had been bred up among the Portuguese, had served with them as a soldier, and dwelt among them as a merchant; he turned his acquaintance with the place to base advantage by seizing the city, which he sacked, and loading his fleet with treasure, sailed home to England. From this time the progress of the Spanish and Portuguese colonists was only interrupted by occasional skirmishes with the natives, until in 1630 a Dutch fleet of forty-six sail arrived at Pernambuco, landed 3000 troops, who assaulted and took the city of Olinda, and subjugated the whole *capitania* of Pernambuco. In a few years the captaincies of Hamaraca, Paraiba, and Rio Grande were added to the Dutch possessions. John Maurice, Count of Nassau, a near relation of the stadtholder, was appointed to the command, with the high-sounding title of Governor of Brazil and South America. He brought with him sufficient troops to maintain his ground against the utmost efforts of the Portuguese. In 1640 a fleet of ninety ships was sent from Spain, with orders to drive the Dutch from the coast. They were met by a small squadron, under the Dutch admiral Loos, who beat off his assailants, but was himself killed in the action. His successor, Admiral Huyghens, fought the Spaniards for three successive days, and on the last drove them with much loss on the rocky shallows near the coast. Many died of hunger and thirst, some perished by drowning. Of all the great armada, only five crippled vessels crept back to Spain.

1640 was the year in which Portugal successfully asserted her independence. It was not probable that the Portuguese and Dutch who had, in their common hatred of the Spaniards, such a bond of union, would remain long at enmity. The Count of Nassau, forseeing the probability of a peace between his country and Portugal, and the impediment which would thereby oppose itself to his further aggression in Brazil, determined to get as much Portuguese territory as possible into his hands, during the short war time that remained. He recovered the captainship of Sergippa, and in the following year the island and the whole of the rich captainship of Maranham. In June, 1641, peace was signed between Portugal and the States-General. The Assembly of XIX. by this time exercised the same unwise interference with their Brazilian possessions as had produced so much discontent on the Hudson. A large number of the inhabitants of the Dutch provinces, especially those engaged in the cultivation of sugar, were Portuguese. When, therefore, the Assembly of XIX. began to press heavily upon them for large contributions, not only in sugar and Brazil wood, but in money, the wishes of the Portuguese peasantry turned to their own countrymen, who were not more tyrannical than their new masters, and had at least the advantage of not being alien in race. Count Maurice represented in vain the impolicy of the demands made by the company, and at length returned home in disgust, taking with him thirteen ships of war and the greater part of his forces. The government of Dutch Brazil was then intrusted to a commission, consisting of a merchant of Amsterdam, a goldsmith of Haarlem, and a carpenter of Middleburg—men who were as unfit to undertake the government of a great and turbulent province as Prince Maurice would have been to build a house or make an emerald locket. They endeavoured to perform their duty by punctually executing the orders of their employers. So successful were their exactions, that a revolt was organized under the advice and countenance of the Portuguese viceroy. The leader of the insurgents, John Fernandez Veira, had been originally a butcher's apprentice in Portugal, then a page to one of the merchants of Olinda, and, after its capture, the factor of one of the Dutch sugar plantations. This man led the malcontents with extraordinary skill and good fortune. For some time a war was carried on between Holland and Portugal. Several fleets were sent to Brazil with reinforcements; but in spite of all exertions the Dutch were eventually compelled to abandon the last of the possessions which they had acquired in Brazil.

In the mean time a new power claimed a share of Northern America. While the New Englanders encroached on the Dutch in the east of New Netherlands, the Swedes sent a colony to Delaware Bay. In 1629 Gustavus of Sweden had found himself at the head of the league which was to protect the princes and states of the empire against the encroachments of Austria; success at home induced him to follow the example of Holland, and to endeavour to extend his dominions to the west. An adventurer named Wsslinx was the prime adviser of the king in this matter; he was a Netherlander, and had long been devoted to the study of colonization. The scheme which he proposed bore the impress of the practical Dutch character. The English always pretended, in their charters, that one of their principal objects was the spread of Christianity among the natives; Wsslinx, after the fashion of the Dutch, regarded the settlement of new countries merely as an advantageous speculation. Political questions which might arise in the affairs of the colony were reserved for the decision of a royal council, on the ground that such matters did not concern merchants, and were beyond their province.* It was urged that slave-labour was admitted in the colonies of other nations, and that still those colonies prospered; but it was not considered advisable to introduce it into New Sweden. This unwillingness proceeded not from motives of humanity, but from economical considerations: "Slaves," say the framers of the charter, "cost a great deal, labour with reluctance, and soon perish from hard usage; the Swedish nation is laborious and diligent: surely we shall gain more by a free people with wives and children."†

Gustavus took a wider view of the matter than that presented by Wsslinx and his fellow-workmen. He saw that troublous times were coming. The power of the pope was beginning to revive. It seemed almost as if the insurrection, which had been carried on at such cost against intellectual servitude, was likely to be at length suppressed. Gustavus was himself loudly called upon to contribute his strength and genius to the defence of the Protestant cause. It was natural that he should look at his project of establishing a colony in the light of a security to those who had become fugitives for religion; a benefit to the whole Protestant world. Before Gustavus could carry out his intentions, the danger of Europe became so imminent, that he was forced to suspend his project, and place himself at the head of the Protestant forces. In alliance with France, he made a de-

* Argonautica Gustaviana. † Ibid. 11.

scent on Germany; and, in little more than two years and a half, a great part of it submitted to his arms. The Battle of Lutzen was glorious for the Protestant cause; but the victory was won at the expense of the life of its champion — Gustavus perished on the field, after having made dispositions which insured the victory to his soldiers.

Oxenstiern, the chancellor and friend of Gustavus, carried out the views of his master. Minuits, who had been disgraced by the Dutch, and deprived of his government of New Amsterdam, offered his services to Sweden: they were accepted; and, though various delays opposed themselves to the carrying out of the design, it was accomplished in the year 1638. The spot selected for the Swedish colony was on the beautiful banks of the Delaware: land was purchased from the natives; a fort was erected, and called Christina, after the young Queen of Sweden.

Although the great Gustavus was dead, and his sceptre held by the weak hand of a young girl, the work which he had begun in Europe was still carried on successfully. A new war had been undertaken against Denmark, which terminated gloriously for Sweden at the peace of Bromsbro'. The States-General were therefore deterred, by the success of Swedish arms in Europe, from offering more than a mild protest against the invasion of their transatlantic territories, although the new settlement was within the limits claimed by their West India Company. They adhered firmly to their often-expressed maxim, that the Council of XIX. must look after their own foreign possessions, and that they must expect no help from the parent State. In the mean time Swedish emigration had largely increased. The ships were so crowded that many families were unable to obtain a passage to the New World. By 1640, the banks of the Delaware, from the ocean to the falls, were known as New Sweden. The Dutch and the Swedes continued, although regarding each other with jealousy, at peace till 1656, when the Dutch governor, marching against them with an army of six hundred men, compelled them to acknowledge Dutch supremacy.

The Dutch, though they could outnumber and conquer the Swedes, could not maintain an independent existence. They were jealously watched from home: they enjoyed only a mockery of liberty: their neighbours in New England and in Maryland were free, and enjoyed all the advantages of independent states: many of the Dutch and Swedish settlers went over to the English provinces and became absorbed in the population of those happier lands. The very soldiers deserted. While New England increased rapidly in population, the streets of New Amsterdam became a solitude.

In New England and in Virginia pauperism was unknown, for the people governed and worked for themselves. In New Netherlands the poor were so numerous that it was almost impossible to provide for their assistance. In New England schools were kept up for the education of youth; in New Netherlands there were no schools at all. When danger threatened New England, every able-bodied man turned out for its defence; in New Netherlands the inhabitants alleged that it was the duty of the States-General to protect them. The company would not risk its dividends in defence of its subjects; the subjects would not risk their lives in defence of tyrannical masters. Out of such a dilemma there could be but one escape: the Dutch colony was ceded to the English, and the Hollanders, retaining only some island at that time insignificant in the Spanish main, thenceforth disappear both in the north and the south from the history of American colonization.

CHAPTER XIII.

MANNERS AND MODE OF LIFE IN THE COLONIES AT THE
TIME OF CROMWELL.

[1625—1660.]

Quarrels between Charles I. and the Parliament—Virginian Legislature recognized—Charles quarrels with the Scotch—Cromwell—Execution of Charles—The Commonwealth—Social Condition of Virginia—Of New Plymouth—Of the French Colonies.

CHARLES I. began his reign under evil auspices. In breaking off the Spanish marriage to please himself he had acted in accordance with the views of the popular party: the applause which had rewarded his renunciation of an alliancee which was distasteful to the nation, induced him to believe that he was very much beloved: he hastened to meet his Parliament. War had been declared by Spain immediately after the unworthy insults of Buckingham and Charles. England could not meet her assailants without funds, but Charles imagined that he should obtain ample subsidies without trouble: he was soon undeceived. The Commons insisted that their grievances should be inquired into before they proceeded to supply. Even James had never set the dangerous precedent of raising money without the consent of Parliament;

CHAPTER XIII.

1626

1627

but the new king's indignation at the opposition he encountered was so great, that he attempted to raise money by letters under his privy seal, without the assent of the two other estates of the realm. He called another Parliament; it impeached Buckingham: the king threw the movers of the impeachment into prison, and endeavoured to raise a forced loan. The troops which had returned from a fruitless expedition to Cadiz were billeted in private houses; the gentry who refused to contribute to the loan were imprisoned; the peasantry were impressed into the navy or the army. The tyranny of the king was of a character which affected not only political rights, but personal liberty: while the servile priesthood preached passive resistance, the soldiers committed outrages on the families upon whom they were quartered. As if all this was not enough, the king added to his crimes a blunder: he engaged in a war with France.

One of the chief articles of impeachment against Buckingham was that he had assisted Richelieu against the Huguenots: the matter on which the Commons most strongly insisted was relief for the Puritans at home, and aid for the Huguenots abroad. Buckingham imagined that if he could effect a diversion in favour of the Huguenots by bringing about a war with France, the feeling of the English people would turn in his favour. An expedition was undertaken to relieve Rochelle: it was led by Buckingham in person, and failed ridiculously. While he was engaged in forming a second expedition with the same object, he was assassinated by Felton.

The king was by this time in extreme want of money. Forced loans were again resorted to, and soldiers again billeted on private persons. But the supplies obtained by these illegal means were totally inadequate to supply the king's necessities. As a last resource, a Parliament was assembled which proved as intractable as their predecessors. They made a bargain with the king: they voted him five subsidies on condition that he would solemnly engage never again to resort to forced loans, benevolences, taxes without the consent of the people, arbitrary imprisonment, the billeting of soldiers in private houses, or martial law. The king acceded to the terms proposed. He accepted the five subsidies, and declared, with tears in his eyes, that he was entirely reconciled to his Parliament. No experience had any effect upon the king: within six months all was again in confusion: the house met after the recess to exclaim in terms of indignation against his perfidy. Taxes had again been illegally raised, troops again billeted on the people: after one of the most stormy scenes recorded in parliamentary history, a resolution was carried condemnatory of the royal proceedings. The speaker declared that the king had forbidden any such question to be proposed. He was held down by force in his chair: the doors were locked, and the resolution carried, while the king's messenger knocked in vain to summon them to the bar of the Lords.

CHAPTER XIII.

1629

For ten years Charles governed without the aid of Parliament. The Petition of Right was disregarded in every particular. Every kind of illegal impost was levied. The Puritans were fined, mutilated, imprisoned, branded, hunted to death. Many fled to America—at first in small numbers, but afterwards in very considerable companies. It has been mentioned in a former chapter that James I. had died just as he was preparing to despoil Virginia of its charter: his son found other means to put his transatlantic subjects to account. Though profoundly ignorant on colonial affairs, he fully understood the pecuniary value of monopolies. He conceded the sole supply of the British tobacco market to the Virginians, and sent an intimation that he was prepared to become through his agents the sole factor of the company. This happened at the time of his expedition to Rochelle, the time of the murder of Buckingham, and the presentation of the Petition of Right. Charles's frantic efforts to dispense with Parliament altogether in the Old World, curiously enough inaugurated representative institutions in America. He desired that an assembly might be summoned to consider his proposal: the assembly met: it protested against the proposed monopoly; but it had assembled by the king's command, and had received the royal sanction to its deliberations. Thenceforward it could plead the royal instructions in justification of its right to assemble.

In the years which followed, the colony increased in numbers and in civil freedom. One by one the old oppressive statutes were repealed : and at length, partly owing to the exertions of the House of Burgesses, and partly to the apathetic indifference of the English authorities, who never interfered except when it appeared possible to screw out of Virginia a little money for the exhausted treasury, the Virginians were left at liberty to manage their own affairs as they pleased.

The colony, planted by Royalists and replenished almost exclusively by Royalist emigrants, was strongly attached to church and state. While their liberties were in abeyance they could be radical enough: when these were established they stopped short and showed great dislike to further political change. At first they entertained no desire to persecute the Puritans, who were invited to quit the inhospitable land of the North, and join the Virginian colony. Puritan merchants established themselves on the James River. Even the obnoxious Brownists received the offer of an asylum. " Neither surplice nor subscription is talked of," said Whitaker. But the political revolution in England changed this state of things. The Parliament was in arms against the king : to tolerate Puritanism was to encourage a republican party : a Puritan was not only a religious sectarian, he was a levelling politician. None of the evil effects of Charles's tyranny had fallen upon the colonists; they enjoyed nearly all the liberties which a monarch could concede without losing his supremacy. There was a small party in the colony for the

Parliament, but the main body was stanch for the king. Intercourse between the Virginians and New England became less frequent. Puritan ministers were forbidden to preach; Nonconformists were banished; " Virginia was whole for monarchy,"* and Charles, long after he was a fugitive among the Scots, was still, in the minds of the colonists, sovereign of Virginia. In 1648 the number of the colonists exceeded twenty thousand. Twelve English ships, twelve Hollanders, and seven from New England, were trading to the James River. They possessed all the advantages of political independence. They had a teeming soil, they were governed by laws themselves had made. Little agitated by the storms which agitated the mother-land, they were free, contented, and happy.

Charles was not more fortunate with his Scotch than with his English subjects: he resolved to introduce episcopacy into Scotland: the reading of the Liturgy in the cathedral church of St. Giles was the signal for an outbreak. The people looked upon the surplice and the book of the primate as marks of popery; the bishop escaped with difficulty out of the hands of the mob, and the civil power was called in to turn the rioters out of the church. The Scots rose in rebellion. Charles was unprepared with means to support his measures with a high hand: he hesitated and temporized: the Scots appointed a provisional government: they then raised an army

* Hamond.

and summoned a general assembly of the kirk. The new government was eagerly obeyed, and its manifesto, the celebrated "Covenant," welcomed with acclamations. Negotiations were attempted and failed: the Scots adhered to their covenant and prepared for war. There was a short and indecisive campaign. The king's treasury was exhausted: if he had found it difficult to levy ship-money and poundage before, it was impossible to do so now that a large part of the kingdom was in armed rebellion. He summoned a Parliament, which met in April, 1640. Considering the outrages which had been heaped upon the nation, and the shameless way in which the royal word had been broken, the moderation of that assembly was remarkable. But like all their predecessors they refused to enter upon the question of supply till they had received some satisfaction for the past and guarantees for the future. Oliver St. John brought up the minutes of the proceedings against Hampden, and a committee reported that it was a matter of grievance. The king recognized the inflexible character of the men with whom he had to deal and hastily dismissed them. Several members were thrown into prison: ship-money was exacted with even more severity than before: no expedient which sore need could contrive was omitted. At length the king scraped together a sufficient sum to move his army northward. The Scots acting, as was believed, on the advice of the English opposition, moved forward to meet him. His general, Conway, was defeated at Newburn-upon-Tyne. The royal soldiers fled to Berwick: even here they did not consider themselves safe, but continued their flight to York. Charles soon found that he had disaffection to deal with in his army, as well as at Westminster: the beaten warriors mutinied for pay: the people clamoured for redress of grievances. No resource remained: on the third of November the most famous of our English Parliaments assembled. The king began with fair promises; he would do nothing without the consent of men in whose talent and character the people could confide: he would govern in harmony with the Commons: he would call Falkland, Hyde, and Colepepper to his councils. The nation was delighted: they supposed that the king had at last seen the necessity of a complete change of system. They were willing to forgive the past and to look hopefully at the future: but they were grievously disappointed. Only a few days after he had promised to do nothing without the consent of the Commons, he sent the attorney-general to impeach the leaders of the opposition. He himself, accompanied by soldiers, went down to the house to seize them within the walls of Parliament. During the night that followed this foolish outrage the capital was in a ferment. The mob surrounded the king's coach, and followed him with shouts and curses even to the gates of Whitehall. The disorder was so great that the king's servants, fearing for his personal safety, persuaded him to quit London. From his retreat at Oxford, he attempted to treat with the House of Commons. But it was too late. The men who but lately would have been contented to see him surrounded by all the insignia of royalty, and exercising all the powers that had ever belonged to our kings, were now so exasperated by his systematic duplicity, that they would hardly consent to leave him the shreds or vestiges of his former authority. Neither party would yield: and at length the sword was drawn. For a time the Cavaliers were successful. But among the ranks of the Commons was one whose genius and energy were equal to any emergency, and whose name will ever be revered as one of our best and wisest rulers. Oliver Cromwell, though nominally second in command, was in reality the soul of the Parliamentary army. He was busily occupied in forming out of the unpromising materials at his command an army such as had never before been seen. Fortune, which in the first skirmishes of the civil war had been on the side of the crown, now veered completely round. In one battle after another the royal troops were routed. The king fell into the hands of the Puritans. By that time the fierce army which Cromwell had created, slipped from the leash in which he had held it. He could no longer lead it; he had gone too far to draw back. In an evil hour for his fame he consented to the murder of the king. Nor could he stop even there. The king being dead, the Parliament was the supreme power in the state.

CHAPTER XIII.

Cromwell trod on the Parliament as he had trodden on the monarchy. He became dictator armed with absolute power.

The execution of Charles did not make any immediate effect on the plantations.

The Puritans, republican at heart, hailed with satisfaction the triumph of their own party. They rejoiced that Charles, the man of blood, had been resisted even to the death, with a joy not inferior to that of the stern regicides themselves. The Commonwealth was at once acknowledged.

Virginia, "whole for the king," resisted. All communication between Virginia and Massachusetts was forbidden by the Puritan assembly. The prohibition, however, interfered with trade, and was at once repealed, though the old dominion still held for the king. But Cromwell was not a man to be trifled with. He had no intention of oppressing the colonies: he did not wish to interfere with their internal government. He offered that if Virginia would adhere to the Commonwealth she should be the mistress of her own destinies. But he added a stern reminder, that refusal would be followed by war. The iron-handed Protector was not to be denied: the Virginians had reflected and wept over the execution of Charles; but the very magnitude of the crime struck them with reluctant admiration. They heard that the English commonwealth had been recognized by the King of Spain, by the republic of Holland, by the republic of Venice, by the regency of France. If the craft of Mazarin and the pride of Philip were unable to withhold their recognition of the great Englishman, could they—a little colony on the Chesapeake who four years before had been in danger of annihilation from an Indian massacre—withstand him?

An English frigate appeared off James Town; and Virginia submitted to the Protector.

Ten years ensued, during which England rose to a height of power which she had not reached since the days of Elizabeth. If Cromwell was a tyrant, he at least suffered no one to insult his country but himself; the growing power of the Dutch, and their rapidly increasing naval preponderance, excited his jealousy: he ordered his fleet, with Blake* and Monk at their head, to sweep their commerce from the sea. They obtained at first some slight success: Blake was defeated, and Van Tromp sailed up the Thames with a broom at his masthead; but the insult was soon avenged: two decisive victories obliged them to sue for peace, and extorted from them engagements, not only that their cruisers should lower their topsails to our flag, but that no prince of the house of Orange should ever again be stadtholder. They also undertook finally to separate themselves from the cause of the Stuarts. Nor were Cromwell's victories only by sea; it has been the opinion of some historians that his true policy would have been to throw

* Blake had stood for a fellowship at Oxford, but lost it from lowness of stature.—Brit. Emp. iv. 317: Brodie.

CHAPTER XIII.

the weight of England into the scale of Spain, and to espouse the cause of Philip IV. against the French; but such was not the course he pursued. Charles II. held his dreary court at St. Germains. There the English Royalists and malecontents crowded around him: if the armaments of France had been at his command, the reactionary movement, which the utmost efforts of the Protector could only just restrain, would at once have broken out in England. The danger of aggrandizing France by bringing the house of Austria to her feet was a remote contingency, to be dealt with hereafter; alliance with France was an immediate gain: Cromwell entered into alliance with Mazarin. He stipulated for ample pay. Dunkirk, Mardyke, and Gravelines were to be recovered from the enemy and placed in his hands. The English would then have the command of the harbours of the Spanish Netherlands. The engagement was promptly fulfilled. A joint English and French armament appeared by sea and land off Dunkirk. Twenty thousand of Cromwell's veterans marched under the leadership of Turenne; and twenty English ships attacked the harbour. In vain Condé and Don John of Austria threw their whole forces against the besiegers. The military genius of Cromwell had raised a force which crushed everything that ever was opposed to it. The fortifications had just been pronounced impregnable. But the English drove back the Spaniards in headlong rout, and carried the works by storm. Dunkirk was handed over to the English. The Spanish plate-ships were seized at Cadiz. The Spanish fleet was cut out from Vera Cruz. An attack on Hispaniola failed; but Jamaica surrendered. The den of the Barbary pirates was destroyed. An insult to England was avenged on Tuscany. The influence of the Protector reached even to the retreat of Charles at St. Germains, and closed France against the fugitive. The battle of Dunbar delivered Cromwell's enemies into his hands; Barebones' Parliament sat, proved intractable, and were dissolved: France, torn to pieces by absurd disputes of royal princes, churchmen, and high-born courtesans, who quarrelled round the throne of the boy-king Louis XIV., was in no mood to be anything but a dutiful ally. England was great, and respected in all lands. To Cromwell, rather than to the weak prince of whom the words were spoken, did Shakespeare's splendid prophecy apply. He seemed to be indeed the successor of Elizabeth—

> "Who from the sacred ashes of her honour
> Shall star-like rise, as great in fame as she was,
> And so stand fixed. Peace, plenty, love, truth, terror,
> That were the servants to this chosen infant,
> Shall then be his, and like a vine grow to him.
> Wherever the bright sun of heaven shall shine,
> His honour, and the greatness of his name,
> Shall shine, and make new nations: he shall flourish,
> And like a mountain cedar spread his branches
> To all the plains around him."

But at the height of his power Cromwell died. As the great Elizabeth was succeeded by a weak and

CHAPTER XIII. foolish heir, so the iron sceptre of the great Protector descended to the nerveless hands of his son.

It is now necessary to inquire what was the temper of the English colonies during the period which witnessed these stirring scenes.

The settled part of British America was a narrow slip along the eastern sea-coast. From the Mississippi to the Pacific was a vast debatable land, claimed by France and England alike. The English charters purported to convey to each grantee a belt of land right across the continent from the Atlantic to the Pacific: the French affected to consider the possessions of the British as confined to the actual plot of ground occupied by their planters, and claimed the whole land behind the English plantations. Few of the English stretched back far from the shore, except where a planter took up his position in some spot favoured by nature on the banks of an inland stream. The back country was unknown and unexplored. A few wandering trappers hunted peltries and traded with the Indians as far west as the Rocky Mountains. But these men of the woods from the first became a race apart. They intermarried with the Indians, and adopted their customs and habits of life. "Coureurs des bois,"—"voyageurs," —"bois brûlés," were their names among the Canadians—Indian pedlers and fur-hunters among the English settlers. In the course of the wars which took place in after years between the French and English colonies, these men became on both sides

EXODUS OF THE WESTERN NATIONS. 337
1625—1660.]
scouts, guides, and leaders of the Indian contin- CHAPTER XIII.
gents.

Virginia contained perhaps thirty thousand inhabitants. They were settled thickly on the shores of the James River and in "the city" of James Town. But the farms of rich planters and the huts of poorer settlers might be found scattered about the wilderness. No town except the capital had yet been founded. Farmers were not uncommon who had as much as two thousand acres under cultivation. No churches existed except at James Town; and clergymen were so scarce that a bounty was offered for their importation.* Lawyers were more abundant and less welcome. An Act was passed by the Assembly " for the total ejection of mercenary attorneys."†

To James Town the farmers brought in their crops and grain. Thither, on market-days, their wives rode gaily on their pillions, and chaffered over their eggs and garden produce. The town itself straggled along the banks of the river. The houses were mostly of wood, with large awnings and verandahs as a protection from the sun. Wooden piers afforded accommodation to the vessels which brought manufactured goods from England and took back their return cargo of tobacco. Tobacco was everywhere. It grew in every field, in every clearing; even in the main street of James Town. The good wife paid for her knitting-needles, the good man his score at the

* Heming, i. 14. † Ibid. i. 275.

VOL. I. Z

alehouse, the merchant the bill of his English correspondent, in tobacco. Tobacco was the currency, the mainstay, the subject of conversation of the colony. Vessels from London, from Bristol, from the Dutch republic, and from New England lay in the river. The war between the English and Dutch hardly disturbed the commercial relations of the colony either with the republic or with Manhattan. In the very midst of the troubles, while Blake and De Ruyter were pounding at each other in the narrow seas, Virginia and New Netherlands were arranging terms of mutual free trade.*

At the farms and country-houses of the planters might be seen, besides the original emigrants themselves and their descendants, a large number of the loyal nobility and gentry who had fled in horror after the execution of the king. They brought over the amusements and vices, as well as the political principles of the old country. The enforced recognition of the protectorate by the loyal colony changed neither pursuits nor principles. Cock-fighting and racing occupied the wild young gentlemen who were debarred from pursuing those occupations in their ancestral domains. The well-stocked forests of the New World made some amends for the loss of English trout-streams and hunting-fields. Hard drinking and dice-playing required little fostering in such a congenial atmosphere; and a duel with sword and pistol was a not unfrequent termination to a riotous debauch.

* In 1656.

The forests were full of game. Unlike the woods of the North there was here no undergrowth, and the sportsman could pursue, at what was proverbially known as "planters' speed," the wild pigs which roved about in droves among the trees. The soil teemed with fertility. Everywhere could be seen new and strange animals and luxuriant vegetation. Wild fowl swarmed in the morasses and streams, quail and wild turkeys abounded in the woods, oysters in the creeks, fish in the rivers. Land was cheap, labour dear. The poor man could easily buy the one or dispose of the other.

In the summer evenings the little army which protected the colony strolled out by twos and threes to the parade, where their stout captain put them through the arquebuss drill, and examined into the serviceable state of buff jerkin and head-piece. Groups of smokers collected under the spreading verandahs of the alehouses that opened on the road; and the sound of skittles, which had been brought over by the Hollanders, might be heard in the bowling alleys at the rear. Among the loungers might be observed some Dutch skipper who had just brought over a cargo of negroes from Africa, and who came to smoke his pipe and chat gravely with his consignees after seeing his black cargo properly handcuffed for the night in the common prison. Next him, perhaps, with cropped hair and steeple hat, the captain of a New England sloop. Indians, plumed and painted, stalked along the streets, or on the road leading to

CHAPTER XIII.

the great wooden house among the trees, where good old Governor Berkeley engaged in many a deep carouse with royalist comrades from beyond the sea. Down that road Governor Berkeley's great lumbering coach rolled heavily on great occasions; and the honest cavalier was not without hope that King Charles II. himself would one day travel along it, to take refuge with him from the unrelenting rebels who had killed his father.*

Yonder old man at the tavern door can remember the foundation of the colony—the building of the first hut in James Town, the first dreary winter of famine and disease which carried off so many of the adventurers. A bystander might probably hear him discourse somewhat after the following fashion :—

" Yes, comrades; I well remember Captain Smith and the other members of the council. A brave gentleman and an honest was the captain, which was more than Gosnoll and some of the others were. Such a fellow to laugh was he, always ready with his joke, and a merry smile for every one even when we were well nigh dead in the first horrible winter. I recollect once when we were fighting with the savages—that was before we made friends with Powhattan, and before Mr. Rolf had married the lady Pocahontas—the captain captured a savage and tied him to his arm, and so used him as a buckler against the arrows that were shot by the

* Clarendon, b. xiii. ; iii. 466.

Indians. You may see a picture of it as natural as ever was life, in a book writ by the captain himself, who was a great scholar as well as a soldier. Many is the can of water I have had poured down my sleeve for swearing * when we were cutting down the trees. We had no tobacco then, nor horses either for that matter ;† we got our living by making potash and tar. Ay, Virginia was a terrible place at first.

" Why did I come? sayest thou. Why, because I could not help it. I was a serving-man in my lord the Earl of Essex's family, in good Queen Elizabeth's time, and I had the misfortune to kill a man in a quarrel. I fled to the Low Countries, where I joined the captain. Faith, though, I was a lamb to some of those that came after me, was I not, gossip? Don't be ashamed, man : lift up thy sleeve, and let us see what sort of a mark the hangman has branded on thy shoulder. Some of those that came after us had their choice between being hanged and coming out here. Some of them preferred being hanged.

" Shall I tell you, friends, what happened to us in our first voyage ?

" When at length, after near a year's delay, we set sail from Blackwall, we had one ship of 100 tons, another of 40, and a pinnace of 20. We tossed about

---

* Captain Smith resorted to this quaint mode of punishment to abolish swearing.
† Kine and horses were sent by Lord Delaware, 1611.—Bancroft, i. 109·

CHAPTER XIII. so long in the Downs that many tried to throw our parson overboard, believing, as sailors do, that a parson brings ill luck to a ship. The wind changed, and we sailed to the Canaries. There, with a loathesome beast like a crocodile called a gwayn, tortoises, pelicans, parrots, and fishes, we daily feasted.* It was five months before we reached Virginia, and the ships were only victualled for two. Little ye think who see James Town now what the country was when we first landed. Many of our fine gentlemen were of such tender education that they were frightened because they found not English cities, nor fair houses, nor any of their accustomed dainties, with feather beds and down pillows. They expected to find taverns and alehouses in every breathing place, and plenty of gold and silver and dissolute liberty. Little they cared for but to pamper their bellies, to fly away with our pinnaces, or to procure means for their return to England. The country was to them a ruin and a hell.† When the ships went away, mutiny and sickness together left us in sorry plight. Our president‡ engrossed to himself oatmeal and sack and aquavitæ, and beef and eggs; but we, the common adventurers, had each day but half a pint of wheat, and as much barley boiled in water to every man each day. The barley, too, had as many worms in it as grains.§ We lived on sturgeon and land

---

* Proceedings and Accidents of the English Colony in Virginia. By William Simons, Doctour of Divinitie.
† Smith's Virginia, ii. 145. ‡ Kendall; Gosnoll was dead.
§ Thomas Studley's Narrative in Simons.

crabs; and between May and September fifty poor fellows died away out of their misery.

"Our new president had but little judgment in dangers, and still less industry in peace. Smith had the ordering of all the work. Some he set to mow; others to bind thatch; some to build houses, others to thatch them,—himself always bearing the greatest task for his own share. After that, a party shipped with the captain in the shallop to search the country for trade. We saw deer and turkeys, but we got little for our pains but hard knocks from the savages; and when we got back, our discontented spirits had stolen the pinnace, and were off for England. We were just in time. We had a sharp bout with the mutineers; and we had to sink their vessel in the river before we could compel them to stay.

"Many times we tried to find the source of the Chicahamania river, as we called it then; and many times did we return to the settlement; but at last we got so far with a party of about six or seven, that we had to cut a passage for our barge through the trees. When we could get no further, the captain took a canoe, with two savages that had spoken friendly to us, and with me and one other moved higher up the river. Poor George Cassen! that was our comrade's name. He was a great favourite with the captain, and, indeed, with all of us. He was one of the few labourers that came out with us.* The captain often wished we had a few more such men, instead of the

* Dr. Simons' list of names of the first planters.

CHAPTER XIII.

idle crew he had.* When the canoe could go no further, the captain left me and George, and went ashore to kill wild fowl for our supper, and he charged us not to stir from the canoe till he came again.† But nought would serve George but that we too should go ashore. We had hardly landed, when, from an ambuscade in the woods the savages rushed out upon us. I called to George to run, and ere I got to the canoe I had a dozen of their devilish arrows sticking in my skin; but poor George was taken and bound. I saw him led away to the woods, the savages jumping and dancing around him, with hideous noise. I paddled down to the barge, and long we waited for the captain; but night fell and he came not. William Cassen, George's brother, was of the party,‡ and much he prayed us to return to find his brother; but the captain was away, and we dared not stir without orders. Long after we heard what had become of Cassen. They tied him to a tree, and with mussel shells and reeds the executioner cut off his joints, one after another, ever casting what he cut off into the fire. Then did he case the skin from his head and face, and ripped his belly, and so burned him tree and all.§

" But we knew not what would be done to him when we were then waiting all night for the captain; and we knew not till after how he himself had fallen into their hands. He being got to the marshes at

* Smith. † Studley's Narrative in Dr. Simons.
‡ Simons' " list."
§ " Thus themselves reported they executed George Cassen."—Smith's Virginia, ii. 144.

the river's head, twenty miles in the desert, found himself beset with two hundred savages, two of whom he slew, still defending himself with the aid of a savage, his guide, whom he bound, as I told you before, with his garters, using him as a buckler. Yet he was shot in the thigh a little, and had many arrows that stuck in his clothes, but no great hurt. Thinking to return thus to his boat, and regarding them as he marched more than his way, he slipped up to the middle in an oozy creek, and his savage with him. Yet dare not the savages come to him till, being near dead with cold, he threw away his arms.* You all know how, after that, the Lady Pocahontas saved him when the king Powhattan would have beat out his brains, and how they entertained him with most strange and fearful conjurations: you may read it all in Master Thomas Studley his book. Master Studley writ some poetry about it. I remember two verses:—

"'But his waking mind in hydeous dreams did oft see wondrous shapes
Of bodies strange and huge in growth, and of stupendious makes.'"†

The next colony to the north was the settlement of Manhattan. I have already narrated the circumstances which distinguished the colony, and as, to avoid the necessity of recurring to the subject, I mentioned the cession of their establishment to the English in 1664, I need only remark that at the time of which I now speak Manhattan still exhibited considerable commercial activity. The Dutch imported

* Thomas Studley's Narrative. † Ibid., chap. ii.

negroes and exported furs. In dress and national characteristics they differed both from the Virginians and from the Puritans. All religions were tolerated; they had learned this much from their ancestors' long contest against Spain. They carried with them to the New World both the keenness in money-making which had so rapidly raised their country to the position of a great maritime power, and the sedate and rather phlegmatic disposition which produced so many statesmen and jurists. Their dress consisted of the short broad breeches such as those our sportsmen now wear under the name of "knickerbockers," together with the buff coats and broad hats which we see in the pictures of Teniers and Rembrandt, both of whom were then in the zenith of their reputation.

Still further to the north was the Puritan colony of New England. The indefatigable John Smith, who made a voyage there in 1624, a year or two after the Puritan emigration, gives an account of its appearance at that time, of which the following is an extract:—

"At New Plimoth there is about 180 persons, some cattell and goats, but many swine and poultry, 32 dwelling-houses, whereof 7 were burnt the last winter, and the value of five hundred pounds, in other goods; the towne is impailed about halfe a mile compasse. In the towne vpon a high mount they have a fort well built with wood, lome, and stone, where is planted their ordnance; also a faire watch-tower, partly framed for the sentinell: the place it seems is healthfull, for in these last three yeeres, notwithstanding their great want of most necessaries, there hath not one died of the first planters. They have made a saltworke, and with that salt preserve the fish they take, and this yeere hath fraughted a ship of 180 tunnes.

"The gouernour is one Mr. William Bradford, their captain Miles Standish, a bred souldier in Holland; the chiefe men for their assistance is Master Isaak Aldenton, and divers others as occasion serueth; their preachers are Master William Bruster and Master John Layford.

"The most of them liue together as one family or houshold, yet euery man followeth his trade and profession both by sea and land, and all for a generall stocke, out of which they haue all their maintenance, vntill there be a diuident betwixt the planters and the aduenturers.

"Those planters are not seruants to the aduenturers here, but haue onely counsells of directions from them, but no instructions or command, and all the masters of families are pastures in land or whatsoeuer, setting their labours against the stocke, till certaine yeeres be expired for the diuision; they haue young men and boies for their apprentises and seruants, and some of them speciall families, as ship-carpenters, salt-makers, fish-masters, yet as seruants vpon great wages. The aduenturers which raised the stocke to begin and supply this plantation were about 70. Some gentlemen, some merchants, some handy-craftsmen, some aduenturing great summes, some small, as their estates and affection serued.

"The generall stocke already emploied is about 7000*l.*, by reason of which charge and many crosses, many of them would aduenture no more; but others that knowes so great a designe cannot bee effected without both charge, losse, and crosses, are resolued to goe forward with it to their power; which deserue no small commendations and encouragement. These dwell most about London; they are not a corporation, but knit together by voluntary combination in a society without constraint or penalty, aiming to doe good and to plant religion : they have a president and treasurer, every yeere newly chosen by the most voices, who ordereth the affaires of their courts and meetings, and with the assent of most of them vndertaketh all ordinary businesses, but in more weighty affaires, the assent of the whole company is required. There hath beene a fishing this yeere vpon the coast about 50 English ships; and by Cape Anne, there is a plantation a beginning by the Dorchester men, which they hold of those of New Plimoth, who also by them haue set vp a fishing-worke. Some talke there is some other pretended plantations, and all whose good proceedings the eternal God protect and preserue ; and these haue beene the true proceedings and accidents in those plantations." Smith ends his account with the following words : "Though I promise no mines of gold, yet the warlike Hollanders let us imitate but not hate, whose wealth and strength are good testimonies of their treasury gotten by fishing; and New-England hath yielded already by generall computation one hundred thousand pounds at the least. Therefore honorable and worthy countrymen let not the meannesse of the word fish distaste you, for it will afford as good gold as the mines of Guinea or Potassie,* with lesse hazard and charge, and more certainty and facility."

The worthy captain's advice was followed: fishing fleets went every year to pursue their calling on the coasts; and at every renewal of persecution in England the victims fled to swell the population of Massachusetts. From the first the inhabitants gave themselves up to the wildest religious fanaticism. Far from extending to others the toleration which they had left home and country to obtain for themselves, they punished the slightest departure from their peculiar tenets with torture, fine, and imprisonment.

It is evident to any one who has no special leaning to Puritanism, however much he may admire and respect the self-devotion of men who for the sake of their religion left all that made life endurable, so far as this world is concerned, that the founders of New England made the place a most undesirable residence.

Every hardship was to be encountered, death in every shape was to be braved. Men, and women too, who had been delicately nurtured, committed themselves with scanty supplies to the wilderness.

* Query—Potosi ?

They faced death by famine, by fever, by exposure. They met their fate without a murmur, and with a martyr's joy. But even in the midst of pestilence and famine the survivors set to work at once on penal laws directed against those who should presume to differ with them. Their first act was to send home the brothers Browne, who persisted in using the Book of Common Prayer. Reinforcements came: during the long summer voyage "three sermons a day beguiled their weariness."

Among the new arrivals was a man who, perhaps more than any other, has influenced the national character of the New England men—I mean Roger Williams. He was a Puritan, and, as such, a mark for persecution in England. But nothing can well be imagined more distasteful to the intolerant New Englanders than the doctrines he enunciated. He boldly announced the doctrine of the sanctity of conscience; he denied that any man can impose his own religion on another; he asserted the right of the civil magistrate to restrain crime, but not to punish opinion. Like Pascal and Descartes, he followed his own proposition to its logical conclusion, and deduced from his simple proposition results that made his Puritan friends thrill with horror. They had passed a law inflicting whipping for the crime of "indifference," and death for that of infidelity. Williams declared that the statute against nonconformity ought to be repealed—in which they agreed with him; and that the law compelling attendance on divine worship was contrary to God's word—for which they were ready to inflict on him the punishment due to indifference. They banished men who used the formularies of the English church: Williams asserted that the civil government should afford equal protection to all. They called the pillory and the scourge to the aid of the minister: Williams proclaimed the right of every man to consult his own conscience alone.

Principles such as these brought Williams into perpetual conflict with the clergy and government of Massachusetts. He added to his other delinquencies one that probably shocked the good pastors fully as much as all the rest. He asserted that no one should be bound to assist in maintaining public worship against his own consent. "What!" exclaimed the clergy, "is not the labourer worthy of his hire?"—"Yes," retorted Roger Williams, "from those who hire him, but not from others." Another point, still more inconvenient, upon which Williams strongly insisted, was this:— That the government of the king had no power to grant to the colonists lands belonging to the savages. It was equally difficult to deny or to admit this proposition; there was nothing for it but to banish a man so inconveniently candid, so stubbornly pertinacious. Williams received orders to quit Massachusetts. Yet before he went he contrived to stir up a storm of fanatic hatred against the red cross in the banner of St. George. Half the trained bands would not march with the cross, the other half refused to stir without it. One of the soldiers cut out the cross and trampled it under foot as an idolatrous emblem. Williams was expelled, and retired to the Indian town of Mooshausick, where he founded the colony of Rhode Island.

Williams had hardly been disposed of when the Antinomian heresy raised its head in the colony. Calvinists, as were the ministers of Massachusetts, strongly as they reprobated the Romish doctrine of salvation by works, they could not admit that reformation of heart and life were absolutely of no account. Mrs. Hutchinson, who was principally instrumental in introducing this strange doctrine into the colony, asserted that to demand any rule of life and manners was to sin against the Holy Ghost. The whole colony was soon divided between the covenant of works and the covenant of grace. The ladies, especially, followed the new doctrine. It was not till Mrs. Hutchinson was banished to Manhattan that even the extreme rigour of Puritan ecclesiastical law could in any degree prevail against the alarming heresy.

Sir Harry Vane, the governor, was a follower of Mrs. Hutchinson, and lost his place at the next election in consequence. Though he had left his "father, his mother, his country, and that fortune which his father would have left him here," and had " abstained two years from taking the sacrament in England, because he could get no one to administer it to him standing,"* he had not brought his mind to conform in all things to the Puritan fashions. It was considered essential that a good Puritan's hair should be cropped quite short; Vane could not persuade himself at first to part with his love-locks. Mr. Endicott, the next governor, and the members of the fraternity who had "bound themselves with him to resist long hair to the last extremity," were too powerful for Vane, whom we presently find congratulated on having "glorified God by cutting his hair." The next disturbance in the colony was about the Quakers. Fearless, illogical, intolerant, that singular sect, whose great founder had been moved by the Lord not to take off his hat to any, high or low, and to say thee and thou to all alike, without respect to rich or poor—who had been impelled to go on the morning of a first day to the steeple-house of Nottingham and cry against the idol—who catechized Pope Innocent XI.—whose apostles made their way to Rome, to Jerusalem, and to Egypt, and even went to Japan in search of the unknown land of Prester John—this sect sent its emissaries into New England. The Quakers had in the Old World opposed passive resistance to stripes, to the stocks, to the pillory; they braved even death itself: every member of the community emulated in his own person the constancy and enthusiasm of the great man in leather breeches himself. In the New World they found a persecution as relentless, nay, even more

* Strafford's Letters, Sept. 1635.

cruel than in the old. Their ears were cut off, their tongues bored with hot irons; they sat in the stocks, they stood in the pillory; many were put to death; and only the strict order of King Charles stopped the colonists from putting into operation a law which pronounced sentence of death on every Quaker.

In a society so devoted to ecclesiastical controversy the lighter arts were not likely to flourish. There was not among the New Englanders, as among the Virginian emigrants, an idle class who had leisure for hunting and fowling. If any backslider had wished to indulge in gambling or debauchery the attempt would have been summarily repressed, and the offender either banished or imprisoned. Taking the complete civil and religious liberty of the Virginians into consideration, and balancing that advantage against the iron-handed religious despotism of the New Englanders, it can hardly be doubted which was the most desirable residence of the two.

Yet, though one not connected with the Puritans by the ties of descent may be excused for giving due weight to the peculiarities which interfered with happiness under their jurisdiction, it would be wrong not to render justice to the purity of mind which their severity was intended to render habitual. The faults of the Puritans were the faults of the rude and heavy-handed age in which they lived: their virtues were protests against such of those faults as they did not adopt. They were cruel, but they had been taught cruelty by years of persecution. Revenge was looked upon by all Europe as a virtue; it was dear to the persecuted Puritan, but he called it zeal for the Lord. He considered that the doctrines of the New Testament had been corrupted and perverted by priest and people. He turned to the Old Testament, and among the records of that people whom God had chosen to execute his judgments upon idolatrous Canaan, he found commands given by God himself to smite and spare not. He did not pause to consider that the new commandment had abrogated the old. He read the divine message through the spectacles of semi-barbarism. He mistook the *sæva indignatio* of his heart for the impulse of Divine will. He mingled the ferocity of the soldier with the fervour of the saint. He performed cruelties when he got the opportunity that would have gladdened the heart of Alva, and taught Pietro de Verona a lesson. But it is fair to add that he practised strict purity of life and morals, and tolerated no weakness save the pride which he mistook for strength. In the New England society, toleration was looked upon as the worst of crimes. " Polypiety," said Ward, " is the worst impiety in the world." The other elders acquiesced in his opinion. The American historian, Bancroft, himself a descendant from the Puritans, endeavours to excuse their excesses. He says that their severities were practised in self-defence : his argument is this ; the people did not attempt to convert others, but to protect themselves : they never punished opinion as such : they never attempted to torture or terrify men into orthodoxy: the Puritans established a government in America such as the laws of natural justice warranted, and such as the statutes and common law of England did not warrant: the Episcopalians had declared themselves the enemies of their sect, and waged against it a war of extermination; Puritanism therefore excluded Episcopalians from its asylum : the Anabaptist was regarded as a foe; he, too, was expelled: the Quakers denounced the worship of New England as an abomination, and its government as treason; Quakers were therefore excluded on pain of death. It is not possible to assent to such a view of the case. Philip II., when he ordered the remorseless persecutions which decimated his subjects in the Low Countries; the Guises, when they planned the massacre of St. Bartholomew; Elizabeth, when she persecuted the Catholics; her sister, when she burned Ridley and Latimer,—might all urge, with quite as much show of reason, that they were acting against men who wished to subvert established authority. We may admit the plea, but do we hold that it justifies the crime? Surely not. It is more merciful and more just to the New England fanatics to acknowledge that they had possessed liberty too short a time to be able yet to know how to use it, and to pass on as soon as possible to a more worthy part of their history.

Prosperity followed almost immediately after the horrors of their first years. The emigrants struck deep roots in the soil. Cromwell invited them to re-emigrate to Ireland, which he had just conquered: but they refused the invitation. Drunkenness was unknown; profane oaths were never heard. There was not a beggar in the settlement: in 1660 there were about twenty-two thousand inhabitants.

The French colonies were hardly yet of sufficient importance to require more than passing notice. The first settlers of Acadia were sailors and fishermen, who remained there only during the winter. Wandering merchants, artisans, and cultivators of the soil were brought over by the different adventurers who succeeded to the privileges of De Monts. In process of time, an agricultural population, poor and laborious, had been formed at Port Royal. The colony encountered many vicissitudes of fortune. They were plundered by Argall. Their town was taken; and their fortifications destroyed. The inhabitants soon mended their log huts; but during many years the unhappy colony was devastated by war. Sometimes they were disturbed by their English neighbours, sometimes by their own internal dissensions. The country had been divided into seigneuries, and the feudal struggles of Europe were reproduced in miniature in the northern wilds. The home government appeared not to care in any way for its luckless dependency: nor did it ever interfere, except for the purpose of giving titles and patents, which often contradicted each other, and always had the effect of envenoming the local disputes. Each petty chief constructed for himself a little citadel, and compelled his retainers to cultivate a little land in the immediate neighbourhood. In the long intervals of labour, he devoted his attention to the destruction of such property as had been amassed by his neighbours. The country went to ruin. Trade could not be said to exist. Establishments were made on this principle at Cape Breton, on the Gut of Canso, at Cap de Sable, and on the River St. John. The continual state of hostilities in which the settlers lived fostered a martial spirit among the population. They were always at war among themselves, and not unfrequently with the English colonies. In summer their shores were frequented by a nomade population of fishermen, who added to their peaceful calling the more exciting occupations of smugglers and pirates. The Acadians intermarried with the Indians belonging to the tribe of the Abenaquis, and before long became a generation of half-breeds. Such was the settlement of which the Protector, in a season of profound peace between England and France, took possession: no persuasion could induce him to restore it,* and it remained in the possession of England till 1667.

Canada was little more than a collection of trading posts. It resembled a French canton transported across the seas. The population consisted of peasants, peaceful, laborious, regularly organized under their seigneurs, with the aid and encouragement of the government. Establishments had been formed

* Haliburton, i. 61.

for the prosecution of the fur trade at Quebec,* at Three Rivers, and at the Saguenay: there was a fort and town at Montreal: the Jesuit missionaries, who came into the country in great numbers, were animated with the spirit of crusaders. They ventured alone among the savages, and laboured with single-hearted zeal at their conversion. Generally beloved, they yet carried their lives in their hands, for whenever a quarrel arose between their French countrymen and their fierce catechumens, whenever a tribe at war with the French fell in with a tribe in alliance with them, the life of the missionary was always the first to be sacrificed; and his martyrdom, according to the savage customs of the Indians, was generally accompanied by the utmost refinements of torture.

In the forts were usually detachments of soldiers from the veteran regiments of France. One of them, the regiment of De Carignan Salières, which had greatly distinguished itself in the war against the Turks, became notorious in the new field, against an enemy not less savage.

The company "Des Cent Associés," raised by Richelieu under such brilliant auspices, and formed of elements the most powerful, with respect to the number, the rank, and the accorded privileges of its members, was about to fall. It had grievously mismanaged its territory: it had failed to establish a colony: it was involved in discreditable squabbles with invaders of its monopoly: its agents had set

* Founded by a company of merchants from Dieppe and St. Malo, 1608.

the fatal example of selling ardent spirits and firearms to the Indians. The settlers were blockaded in their forts: many proposed that the settlements should be abandoned, and that they should return to Europe. Supplies ceased to come from France. The governor was obliged to sue for peace, and to consent to an exchange of prisoners with the Indians. The whole of New France taken together only numbered from eight thousand to ten thousand scattered inhabitants. Such was the condition of the French colonies at the time of the English restoration.

CHAPTER XIV.

[1660-1698.]

REFUGES.

Maryland—The English Church—European Rulers—Emigration of Covenanters: of Cavaliers: of Rebels: of Huguenots—The French on the Mississippi.

VIRGINIA and New England were the two original divisions of British America. Parcels of land were measured off from the limits of one or other of them, as often as new proprietors obtained a patent for establishing a plantation, or some religious sect required a haven to which it might fly from persecution.

In the reign of Charles the First, while Prynne was standing in the pillory with his "Histriomastix" about his neck, and Mr. Oliver Cromwell, not yet famous, was denouncing Arminianism in the House of Commons, far-sighted Catholics discerned the evil times that were coming for the old faith, and obtained a settlement within the limits of Virginia. Lord Baltimore, an Irish peer, was the first patentee. He was succeeded by his sons, the younger of whom went out with emigrants, and established Maryland. The colonists were mostly men of good

1633

CHAPTER XIV.

Catholic families. During the infancy of the settlement they received ample supplies from the proprietors: the rule established by them was in every respect mild and beneficent: every denomination of Christian was welcomed: even in times when the spirit of intolerance was unrestrained in the other colonies, no one was persecuted in Maryland. Puritans were invited from New England; and a home 1666 was not refused even to the Quakers.

The original limits of the old colonies were now 1663 still further curtailed. North and South Carolina were divided off from Virginia; and New England 1670 was broken up, principally in consequence of quarrels brought about by the arbitrary temper of the Puritan inhabitants, into six divisions, which are now the Yankee, or New England States.

The reasons which caused this rapid extension of settlement are to be looked for in the contemporary annals of England. The events of those stirring years which preceded the great Revolution are so familiar to Englishmen, that a reader who will look at the date of any particular emigration, and take the trouble to recall the particular phase which at that moment the quarrel between crown and people had assumed in England, would in most cases be able to pronounce without further information to which political party the emigrants belonged, and to what part of America they directed their steps.

After every fight the victor persecuted the vanquished according to his power, and drove some of them to America; the indomitable spirit of every colony was thus kept alive by a succession of victims. All these men would in their own country have been persecutors if they had got the opportunity, and if the fortune of war had been different; in the colonies they did get the opportunity, and used it unsparingly. At first, as a general rule, loyalists fled to Virginia, and republicans to New England; but in after times it was found that these territorial landmarks could not be preserved, and loyalty settled down side by side with republicanism. Nevertheless Virginia and Massachusetts each preserved somewhat of its individuality. To the very last "the old dominion" was enthusiastically loyal, and Massachusetts intensely puritanical. But as the surrounding country became settled, the importance of Virginia and Massachusetts diminished. Eight or ten neighbouring states hemmed them in, whose inhabitants, recruited from both parties, felt little inclined to keep up a perpetual feud on matters which possessed no significance for any but those in the immediate neighbourhood of the seat of war. As long as the quarrel was really as well as nominally religious, the colonists continued to feel strongly interested. They had themselves been victims of persecution. The vicissitudes of the strife determined the character of the successive batches of emigrants: each new comer who settled among them gave an accession of strength to one or other of their religious parties. But when the issue became political their interest ceased. Their country was the *corpus vile* upon which English statesmen were to try their theories, their nostrums, their panaceas. The colonial policy of the mother-country was henceforward the object of their individual attention; and they left squabbles in which they were no longer interested to those who were affected by them.

It was not to be expected that a cluster of young nations, four thousand miles away, would follow with any eagerness the details of party warfare from which they had escaped. They had fled for liberty, they had got it; they were fully resolved to keep it. They soon discovered that one English party succeeded another without affecting their interests in any great degree. In peaceful times the strife of parties is mostly a strife for places, men, and names; principles are very rarely disturbed; never, indeed, except in times of revolution, for the disturbance of a great principle is, in fact, a revolution. The maxim which regulated colonial policy was this —a colony is a market which the mother-country may control and work for her own advantage; it shall be left free to regulate its own police, its own municipal affairs, its own religion; it shall be protected from foreign aggression; it shall enjoy the advantage of sharing the glory and the liberty of a great empire. In return, it shall open its ports to the goods of the mother-country, and, when called upon, consign its commodities to her markets. This was the fundamental doctrine of both the great parties who alternately directed English politics. Both acted upon it consistently; neither party questioned it, until the colonies had resolved to sever their connection with England by force. Then, indeed, one of the great parties came to the conclusion that the system had been wrong all along; but the conclusion came too late: the views which animated the colonies were equally simple, and were held with even still greater tenacity; they determined to keep up the ties which connected them with the mother-country just as long as their safety rendered it absolutely necessary, and to throw it off at once, and for ever, at the earliest possible opportunity; to take advantage of such protection as should be extended to them; to mix themselves up as little as possible in the quarrels of England; to obey as little as possible; and to give as little as possible in return for such advantages as, till better times, they might consent to accept. There was no question of gratitude, not even much of affection, on either side.

It seems strange that Great Britain should have attached such importance to the retention of societies who, from the beginning, were mutinous and disaffected; who increased neither her trade, her wealth, nor her greatness; who, presuming upon the exaggerated value placed upon them by the mother-country, refused, from the very beginning, to bear any share even of the burdens necessary for their own defence.

CHAPTER XIV.

But that mistake was one which England shared with all other nations who possessed colonies. It was the common opinion of Europe* that colonies added importance and wealth to their metropolis. It was also the common opinion that colonies ought to be so handled as to become a source of profit to the mother-country. But no other country ever treated its colonies with such consideration and generosity as England; none was repaid by more systematic ingratitude and dislike. From the beginning there was no love lost between the two. England looked upon their formation with indifference, supported them with her power during their nonage, and did not oppress them half as much as other nations oppressed their colonies during the time of their dependence. The colonies clung to British protection till they were strong enough to walk alone; treated England with systematic disregard, refused assistance even for their own defence, and took up arms against her as soon as the fall of Canada relieved them from the danger of falling under the sway of France.

No doubt the navigation laws at last bore heavily upon the increasing trade of the plantations. But those laws were equally obnoxious to European nations, and must not be considered as engines of oppression invented for the benefit of our colonies. It is natural that colonies should desire independence, and history has proved that as soon as they are

* See Adam Smith, B. iv., 276.

strong enough for independence they will obtain it. It is no doubt much to be regretted that when America was ripe for separation we did not permit her to go without fruitless bloodshed. But we look in vain for evidences of the senseless tyranny which, as we have always been taught to believe, goaded America into rebellion. It does not exist. It never did exist. When the supreme authority over a large extent of country is vested in a power which resides at a long distance, it is natural that some mistakes should be committed. American grievances were exaggerated on one side and neglected on the other, till both sides became exasperated. But in sober truth the grievances were small. They were but the excuse for a separation which other things had made desirable. In essentials the Americans, even before the revolution, were as free, nay, more free, than any other nation on earth. They made their own laws, they appointed their own assemblies, they claimed for those assemblies authority "equal to that of the Imperial Parliament." Their defence was provided for by England, but not at their expense. When they were in danger, England went to war on their behalf. The war which broke out in 1739 was principally a colony quarrel; and in making up the balance sheet of profit and loss between England and her colonies, its expenses ought to be charged against the colonies. The war of 1754 was exclusively a colony quarrel; and because they were asked to pay a small portion of the expenditure incurred for their

CHAPTER XIV.

protection they rebelled. The choice of a pretext showed great cleverness on the part of the American patriots. It put them in the right. The abstract proposition for which they fought was undeniable. No nation ought to be taxed against its own consent; England has passed through many a year of civil war in defence of the proposition. But it was never before denied that a nation of free men should provide for their own defence. There can be no doubt that the tax would have been adopted by the colonial assemblies, and voted with enthusiasm, if the French had still been in Canada; if, in fact, they had not been determined in any case to set up independently for themselves. As regards the restrictions on colonial trade, of which so much has been said, can it for a moment be supposed that any nation would incur the expenses which were incurred by England on behalf of her colonies, without seeking recompense in some form or other? Nations must be judged by the degree of enlightenment which prevailed at the time : we cannot bring them to the bar of public opinion and try them by a standard of right and wrong which did not then exist. Political science was cultivated to so limited an extent, that the navigation laws and the enforced monopoly of the colony trade enjoyed by the mother-country were considered additions to her wealth. England looked to the advantages obtained from them as a reward for her sacrifices and a return for her lavish expenditure. The monopoly was, in reality, quite the reverse of profitable,* and every one now admits that it would have been better policy to let the colonies go at once than to fight them feebly first and let them go after all.

But to resume the immediate subject of this chapter. A few years back statesmen had looked with dismay at the excessive power of Austria. The Austrian house was now no longer to be feared: but France had become the object of general dread. It was doubtful whether she would not succeed in completely overthrowing the European balance of power. She had extricated herself from the factions and internal dissensions which had so long paralyzed her vigour. Mazarin and Colbert had devoted their vast abilities to the task of placing unlimited finances at the command of Louis XIV., a prince who was disposed to use every weapon for the furtherance of military ambition.

From the beginning of his reign, Louis XIV. aimed at nothing less than a revival of the power of Charlemagne. At one time it seemed almost probable that his dream would be realized. It was difficult to see whence an adequate opponent could arise. Never before had France seen such a crowd of able negotiators and soldiers: never had her finances been in a state of greater prosperity. Spain, weakened by a long period of misgovernment and exhausted by wars, was in no condition to resist; Charles II. was but a child : Maria of Austria, the queen-regent,

CHAPTER XIV.

Circ. 1665

* Adam Smith's Wealth of Nations, B. iv. *passim*.

was completely under the influence of Nithard, her confessor—a German Jesuit whom she had appointed grand inquisitor. The weakness and ignorance of this man were to be equalled only by his arrogance and vanity: while he trifled over matters of the most puerile ambition, the frontiers were left unguarded, and the Low-Country fortresses ungarrisoned. Nor was there any reason for Louis to apprehend serious opposition from the Dutch. They had long been in alliance with France. Even had it been otherwise, they were not a military power. Their strength lay mainly in their navy. Their recent quarrels with the English and Spaniards had all been fought out upon the sea. The frontier fortresses, which had formerly stood them in good stead, had fallen into decay. Their small army was ill-disciplined, and worse commanded. The old officers, who were for the most part devoted to the house of Orange, had been dismissed during the triumph of the republicans: the burgomasters of that party had replaced them with raw youths who paid little attention to their military duties. William of Orange was still little better than a state prisoner, and though he had already shown to the discerning eye of his great rival, De Witt, signs of the commanding genius which afterwards made him the arbiter of Europe, he was but a youth and untried.

Men's eyes turned in vain to England. The king upon the throne was a lounging fop, with the instinct but not the energy of a tyrant—a puppet whose strings were pulled by harlots in the pay of Louis. The interval of reason which had produced the triple alliance had been succeeded by apathy. The king alternately indulged in an outburst of despotic temper, and pusillanimously retreated before the storm he had created. When he was neither in a paroxysm of fear or a paroxysm of rage, the King of England sank into a state of fatuous sloth that was more disastrous to himself and his people than either.

Tidings came in rapid succession of events which almost seemed to show that the poets and orators of Versailles took an accurate view of the genius and destiny of Louis. Twenty years before the English revolution, it appeared as if nothing could set any limit to the success of that boundless ambition. The English king was a pensioner on his bounty, and was forced at his order to make unnatural alliance with him against Holland. Louis could, whenever he pleased, conquer a separate truce with one of his opponents, while he devoted his whole attention to the annihilation of another: sometimes he was able to defy the united efforts of them all. But as William III. attained to manhood the case seemed to become less desperate; the country which had shaken off the iron yoke of the Emperor Charles V. and of his son Philip II. was not likely patiently to submit to the power of Louis: after the murder of De Witt, William became stadtholder, and the French monarch found that he had to do with a man of different temper from the easy foes he had heretofore engaged.

Attacked by France and England together, the stadtholder opened the dykes and flooded the country, and then from his island fortresses made preparations for transferring his whole republic to the eastern seas. Offers of alliances, of gold, of friendship, were made to him in vain ; William coldly rejected them, and from his boyhood till his death fought sternly and resolutely with such weapons as came to his hand, and such alliances as from time to time he could command in the cause of liberty against arbitrary power.

The settlements of Virginia and Massachusetts just before the English restoration have already been described. Within fifty years of that time Puritans, Cavaliers, followers of the unhappy Monmouth, and Calvinists flying from the dragonnades of Louis XIV., had taken refuge among them. Carolina was settled by a very heterogeneous population. Lord Clarendon, the Duke of Albemarle, Lord Ashley Cooper, afterwards Earl of Shaftesbury, Sir J. Colleton, and others of King Charles's friends, had received the first grant : some of them, Monk especially, had just at that time been mainly instrumental in bringing the king back from his eighteen years of exile : his Majesty was still full of gratitude, the nation still wild with enthusiasm. The first settlers were naturally very loyal. Their characters might not bear examination : it was the old story—London sponging-houses and rookeries, even London gaols, furnished forth food good enough for "the plantations." Locke, the greatest philosopher of the age, made the laws, and produced a new constitution, unlike anything ever seen before, and if one may venture to say the word, supremely absurd. Some of the loyal gentlemen figured in the new constitution as landgraves; some even as caçiques; but one may gather that the derision of the vulgar deprived the new titles of their value, for the caçiques soon dropped their dignities, and reverted to plain master and esquire. A sufficient number of emigrants could not be assembled at short notice for the first colonization; their numbers were increased from Virginia, and from Barbadoes: a few years later, South Carolina was cut off from the northern province, and plentifully supplied with negro slaves from the West Indies: many of the Dutch, who were then quarrelling at Manhattan with the New England men, took the opportunity of settling afresh in a less turbulent neighbourhood. Next year King Charles departed from his usual plan of letting the colonies shift entirely for themselves; and sent out to Carolina, at his own expense, two ships full of foreign Protestants who had taken refuge in England. In 1680, the year of the defeat of the Exclusion Bill and the execution of Stafford, came an emigration of impoverished cavaliers. A year later a congregation of Somersetshire dissenters, led by Joseph Blake, brother of the gallant admiral, who, looking to the

CHAPTER XIV.

professed Catholicism of the Duke of York, anticipated evil times for the dissenters. Blake devoted to this emigration the fortune he had inherited from his brother: thus the plunder of the Spanish galleons contributed to establish a Protestant colony. Next came an Irish emigration under a man named Fergusson; and then, after Monmouth's rebellion, many of those who were lucky enough to escape the rack and the gibbet, came out under the leadership of Lord Cardross. Thus almost every turn of fortune sent a waif to the shores of America.

1686

1678 The evident bias of King Charles in favour of the Roman Catholic religion, had so roused the temper of the English, that they were prepared for an outbreak at the first opportunity; even the fictions of Oates were not too monstrous to receive a ready belief: a persecution burst out against the Catholics, in which many innocent victims were sacrificed. Encouraged by the evidently Puritan bias of the nation, the
1679 Covenanters in Scotland, after murdering Archbishop Sharpe near St. Andrews, broke into open rebellion: the troops quartered in the western counties were ordered to disperse conventicles, wherever they should be found. Some temporary successes emboldened the Covenanters to set forth a declaration against Episcopacy, and publicly to burn the Acts of Parliament which had ordained that form of religion in Scotland: they took possession of Glasgow, and formed a camp in the neighbourhood: thence they issued proclamations declaring that they fought, not against the

king's person, but against his supremacy in religious matters, against popery, prelacy, and a popish successor to the crown.

The rebellion was easily quelled; and, as was usual in all the religious persecutions of that time, a bloody revenge was taken. A large body of the unhappy Cameronians fled to America, where they settled in New England.

While these events occurred in Scotland, a new Parliament met in London. Now, for the first time, the two parties which divided the state assumed the names of Whigs and Tories. The Whigs were mainly composed of those who distrusted, and wished to curtail, the growing power of the king; the Tories comprised the Catholics, and such of the old cavaliers as the faults of Charles had not yet alienated. The House of Commons manifested a very violent spirit: they passed a bill excluding the Duke of York from the succession; it was, however, thrown out in the Lords. Enraged at their non-success, the majority impeached the judges; they attacked the friends of the Duke of York; they tried and executed Stafford: 1680 it was now the turn of the Cavaliers to seek a refuge in America: a considerable body of the Cavaliers settled in Carolina.

In the year 1685 the Protestants received the 1685 severest blow that had fallen upon them since the days of the Bartholomew massacre: it fell both in France and in England at once. King Charles II. died: and the Duke of York, who succeeded his brother, was an avowed Catholic. His accession had been regarded with dismay by a large portion of the population : the old advocates of the Exclusion Bill were willing to snatch at any proposal which might have the effect of keeping a Roman Catholic from the throne : the old story of Charles's marriage with Lucy Walters had been often disproved; Charles himself had denied it in the most formal manner, but it was again revived. It was announced that the rightful heir was going to claim his own, and to call on all friends of the Protestant succession to support him by force of arms : the Earl of Argyle declared for the Pretender, and landed in Scotland, where he soon found himself at the head of a couple of thousand men. But the king's authority was too firmly established to be shaken by such a force : the Marquis of Athol pressed Argyle in one direction, Lord Charles Murray in another : he was at length hemmed in between the Duke of Gordon and the Earl of Dumbarton : having tried in vain to effect a junction with the Covenanters in the Low Country, the unfortunate earl crossed the Clyde : his army melted away: he was taken prisoner and hanged. The pretender Monmouth himself was equally unfortunate: he landed in the west of England, and was received with extraordinary marks of affection at Taunton. In many other towns of the west he was saluted as king. But he had not the talents necessary to support the high part he had undertaken to play : he was defeated and beheaded. His rebellion evoked a horrible vengeance. The arbitrary temper of James seized with avidity the opportunity for a judicial massacre. Colonel Kirke was first intrusted with the task of punishment: but that officer's military executions, barbarous and lawless as they were, were yet too mild for the savage spirit of the king. James despatched the infamous Judge Jeffreys to the spot, with special commission to hang, to banish, to mutilate, and to torture. Both Kirke and Jeffreys enjoy the unenviable reputation of being venal as well as cruel: a moderate bribe could purchase from either of them leave to reach unmolested some seaport whence the fugitive could sail for America. The New England ships were so crowded with fugitives from Sedgemoor that there was a great danger lest the water and provisions should fail: those who were lucky enough to escape hanging, and were too poor to purchase their freedom, were sold as slaves to the traders of Barbadoes at fifteen pounds a head.

The same year was even more disastrous to the Calvinists in France. Their political power had been crushed by Richelieu: they had become distinguished only as among the most orderly and industrious of the French population: the Edict of Nantes had bestowed upon them liberty of conscience, and had left them at leisure to devote themselves to useful and ornamental trades. The silk manufactories, the art of weaving, were in their hands; they alone knew the secret of making hats, of which the French had hitherto enjoyed the monopoly. They were not prevented from writing and speaking in defence of their own doctrines. Some of them held high commands in the armies of France; some took a prominent part in the civil administration. Their disloyalty had naturally ceased with the cessation of persecution. It would have been politic not to meddle with a sect which had ceased to be formidable, and which had long merged the heretic in the Frenchman. But from boyhood Louis XIV. had hated the Protestants. One by one the privileges they had enjoyed were withdrawn. The ministers were forbidden to preach, the churches were shut up. Huguenots in the civil or military service of the king were dismissed. Persecution had its usual effect: the old spirit which had successfully contended in former generations against the whole power of the crown was re-aroused. Some feeble opposition was offered to the royal will. Then the storm burst—the Edict of Nantes was formally repealed. Dragoons were quartered on the Huguenots, and permitted to adopt every rude mode of conversion which might occur to the military intellect. The preachers were banished, and their flocks prevented by force from following them. The frontiers were strictly guarded. But in spite of all precautions a vast emigration took place. It was said that 50,000 of the most industrious inhabitants of France fled in a few months from the cruelty of Louis. Some joined their co-religionists in Holland. Some carried into England the secret of various trades hitherto unknown there; some planted vineyards at the Cape of Good Hope; some joined the English colonies on the Chesapeake: such were the early settlers of the South.

The North was broken up into more divisions, but the emigrants came from less diverse stocks: with the exception of Pennsylvania all were settled by Puritans. Rhode Island was planted, as I mentioned in a former chapter, by Roger Williams, when his doctrines were considered "unsavoury" by the stern planters of Maine. Massachusetts, Connecticut, and New Hampshire were all settled by Puritans between 1625 and 1640: Pennsylvania was granted to William Penn by the king, in satisfaction of a debt due by his Majesty to Penn's father.

The French colonies, meanwhile, progressed but slowly.

It was not till the downfall of Richelieu's Compagnie des Cent Associés that New France began to improve or its population to increase. The company had been formed under most brilliant auspices; many of the most powerful names in France were among its proprietors: it had possessed exclusive power for thirty-four years; it was now obliged to resign its charter into the hands of the king. The company had administered a government more paternal than legal. No courts of justice existed; no council assisted the governor—from his sentences there was no appeal. He usually first attempted to arbitrate: if he failed in arbitration, he proceeded to deliver judgment. The result naturally was that almost all suits were decided by arbitration. Charlevoix says that the inhabitants of Canada were so little litigious—" qu'ils aimoient mieux pour l'ordinaire céder quelque chose de leur bon droit, que de perdre le tems à plaider." He goes on to say that nothing in the colony was kept under lock and key, and that there was no instance of the confidence thus shown being misplaced. This patriarchal simplicity did not long continue. A royal governor was sent out, and a council appointed. A code of laws was framed for his guidance; and it does not appear thenceforward that there was any lack of criminals to keep the machinery in working order. Soon after the country came directly into the hands of the king, M. de Tracy was sent out with a colony far more complete than any that had before been seen there. A large number of settlers accompanied him : they brought with them horses, cattle, and sheep ; none of these animals had before been seen in the colony. The Canadians, aided by the new arrivals, were now able to make head against the Indians. They proceeded to push their discoveries behind the English settlements, and along the course of the Mississippi from the great lakes nearly to the Mexican Gulf.

In 1689 we find Mr. Randolph writing "from the common prison of Boston," whither he had been sent by Governor Andros, to the Lords of the Committee of Trade and Foreign Plantations, an account of the great danger which, in his opinion, menaced

New England. He considered it likely that the French would, if not timely prevented, overrun the whole country. His letter gives an accurate picture of the quarrels which constantly existed between the French and English colonies.

He says that about the year sixteen hundred and eighty-five, the French of Canada encroached upon the lands of the subjects of the crown of England, building forts upon the heads of their great rivers, extending their bounds, disturbing the inhabitants, and laying claim to those lands which for many years had belonged to the English. That under pretence of a right to the sole fishery between the degrees of forty-three and forty-six north latitude, they had seized eight New England ketches loaden with fish off the coast of Nova Scotia, taken away all their fish, treated the masters most barbarously, and afterwards carried them and the ketches to Rochelle, where they were a long time imprisoned. The masters came afterwards from thence to New England. " I then " writes Randolph, " assisted them in their applicacion to the Earl of Sunderland and to the Lord Preston, then Embassador in France ; but his Lordship, though he pressed the matter, could obtaine noe redresse. Whereupon it was advised and ordered in Council that the three small Colonyes of Connecticott, New Plymouth, and Rhode Island, not able to make any defence against the French, together with the Provinces of New Hampshire and Maine, should be united and made one entire Government, the better to defend themselves against invasion." Accordingly a Commission was directed to Sir Edmund Andros with instructions to take them all under his care. Randolph proceeds to say, that "The French about Canada intending to engrosse the whole beaver trade to themselves, did in the time of peace surprize about twenty-seven of the chiefe captains belonging to the five nations of the Indians (traders with the towne of Albany in the government of New Yorke), who had subjected themselves to the crowne of England many years agoe, and have bin accounted subjects and protected both by the Dutch and English government att New Yorke." "They very much court the five nations of Indians to submitt to the government of Canada, and by their Jesuits strangely allure them with their beades, crucifixes, and little painted images, gaining many new converts." Before the end of the century the French had obtained a settlement at the mouth of the Mississippi. The immense political importance of this proceeding will be immediately seen. The English declared that their colonies had no western boundaries but the ocean; the French pointed to the discoveries of Joliet and La Salle, and in right of their explorations in Louisiana and the Valley of the Great River, claimed the right to hem the English settlements into the narrow strip of ground between the Mississippi and the Atlantic. One Monsieur Town-to, says Randolph, in the letter already quoted, a French officer from Canada, has enlarged their pretentions, and settled a fort and garrison upon the Lakes on the back side of Carolina. During this cessation upon the treaty of peace and commerce, they are not idle, but attempting upon the English in these parts of the world."

The Monsieur Town-to referred to by Randolph is Henry de Tonti, son of a Spanish governor of Naples, who, after the revolution in that kingdom, removed with his family to France. Henri, who was afterwords well known in Canadian frontier warfare, entered the army as a cadet, in which capacity he was employed in the years 1668 and 1669; he afterwards served on board ships of war and in galleys. When the enemy attacked the port of Libisso, his right hand was shot away by a grenade. The troops being discharged at the peace, he repaired to court, where he was fortunate in gaining the protection of the Prince de Conti, who recommended him to La Salle, with whom he went to Canada in 1678. He exercised a commanding influence in the western country, where he was known by the soubriquet of "Bras de Fer," or the "Iron Hand," from a knob of metal which he carried, covered with leather, as a substitute for the hand he had lost. With this weapon he would dash into the centre of an Indian melée, and at a blow break the head that came in contact with it. The settlement which Randolph mentions was one among the Illinois Indians. Next to La Salle, de Tonti contributed the most to the exploration and knowledge of the Mississippi Valley.

When D'Iberville, in 1698, obtained permission to

embark at Quebec for the Mississippi, de Tonti joined him. The armament consisted of two frigates and smaller vessels; and D'Iberville had on board a company of marines and about two hundred settlers, including women and children, most of the men being disbanded Canadian soldiers. The Mississippi had never been as yet entered from the sea, though La Salle and various others had descended the stream.

Spaniards from Vera Cruz had already established a post at Pensacola: from this point was drawn the dividing line between the Spanish possessions in Florida and the French in Louisiana. In obedience to the Spanish policy of the day, the governor of Pensacola would allow no foreigners to enter his harbour: the French, therefore, sailed a little to the westward, and cast anchor opposite what is now the port of Mobile. The view that met their gaze was flat and dreary beyond imagination to conceive; still it was not without variety and interest. Bayous, or natural canals, crept slowly among the marshes to the sea, which occupied about a third of the horizon to the south. On the east and west, marshes, bristling with roots, trunks, and branches of trees, extended as far as the eye could reach. The bars which stretch across the mouth of the river are formed of the mud brought down at all times, but more particularly in the wet season. Similar deposits are taking place on all sides, so that the bottom is gradually raised to the surface of the water.* When the river is low, immense tracts are laid bare. In spring, or

* Captain Basil Hall's Travels.

rather winter, when the freshes or floods come down, they bring with them millions of trunks of trees. In February and the beginning of March the quantity of these logs is so great that not only the river itself, but also the sea for several miles, is so coated with them, that it requires some skill to get through. The whole ground—if the loose, muddy soil can be so called—appears to be formed of layers of logs matted together into a gigantic raft of rough timbers, many fathoms in depth, and extending over hundreds of square leagues. These rafts settle on the mud as the waters subside, and are cemented by fresh deposits. In a short time a rank growth of cane and reed springs up, which helps to keep them together. This is called a cane brake—a wild, dreary, impassable marsh. The reeds, by retarding the flow of the river, collect the mud at the next season, and by the process of their own decay, help to form the alluvial soil of the delta. " Fresh logs, and fresh mud, and new crops of cane go on forming for years. At length a poor kind of shrub takes root in these slushy territories; the empire of the alligators, who delight to flounder about in the creeks or bayous which cross the delta in every direction."*

On his return from his successful search, D'Iberville erected a fort at the head of the Bay of Biloxi. It was built upon a sandy shore, and under a burning sun. Tonti came down from the Illinois, and, in company with D'Iberville and his brother Bienville,

* Bancroft, History of America.

ascended the Mississippi. A bluff, where Natchez now stands, was selected as the site for a town, and was named Rosalie, after the Countess de Pontchartrain, wife of the Governor of Canada. The settlement of the French did not long remain at Biloxi; it was transferred within a short time to the western shore of the Mobile. The colonists, of whom scarcely thirty families had been left by disease, dispersed in search of pearls, of the wool of the buffalo, and of gold mines; or scattered themselves over the country for hunting and discovery. " On the shelter of the Mississippi, where a fort had been built, Bienville and his few soldiers were at the mercy of the rise of the waters of the river ; and the buzz and sting of mosquitoes, the hissing of snakes, the croaking of frogs, the cries of alligators, seemed to claim that the country should still, for a generation, be the inheritance of reptiles."* Prosperity was impossible. At the best, only a compromise could be made with the far stronger colony of the Spaniards close at hand. To till the sandy desert was impracticble. But the main object was achieved : the settlements of the English were completely hemmed in. The lilies of France cut on forest trees, and crosses erected on bluffs of the Mississippi, at length marked a chain of posts from the Mexican Gulf to Hudson's Bay.

* For a description of the delta of the Mississippi, see Captain Basil Hall's Travels.

CHAPTER XV.

POLITICS IN THE ENGLISH COLONIES UNDER WILLIAM III.

[1685—1702.]

Views of James II.—He confiscates Colonial Charters—Accession of William and Mary—Political Temper of Carolina : of Virginia : of Maryland : of Pennsylvania : of New York—Their position with regard to the French and Indians.

KING JAMES was greatly elated with the easy and complete victory he had obtained over Monmouth: henceforward he counted on complete submission from his subjects. In the blindness of his zeal for the Roman-Catholic religion, he thought that he could overleap every obstacle and bear down every opposition. His brother Charles had by his victory over the Whigs left the way open to the establishment of a merely secular absolutism. But absolute power seems not to have been the object of his ambition, except so far as it would assist him in his plan of entirely extirpating heresy. If James II. had decided to make himself a despotic king, many things would have aided his views. The Episcopal clergy had diffused the doctrine of passive obedience throughout the community. He himself, with the assistance of

CHAPTER
XV.

1685

2 c 2

the infamous Jeffreys, had proved that his temper was unbending, and that he could follow its dictates in bitter earnest. The country had already tried regicide, and still retained the recollection of the sufferings which that crime had entailed. The reaction of feeling which produced the restoration had not yet died away. His personal safety was therefore secure; and a strong disposition existed on the part of the people to submit to anything rather than incur the miseries of a new revolution. There was, however, one condition on which they were resolved to insist. The Protestant religion was established by law—it should not be interfered with. They were determined that on religious matters their consciences should not again be forced. But this was exactly the point upon which the perverse temper of James was bent. He set to work without delay. Churchmen and Dissenters, Tories and Whigs, had no difficulty in perceiving his intention: it was shown in all his public acts. It was avowed without prudence and without disguise. Papists were introduced into the privy council, the magistracy, the bench. They obtained high commands in the army. The king newly modelled the corporations. He interfered with education at the fountain head by attempting to coerce the universities. He sent an embassy to the pope. He established an ecclesiastical commission for the cognizance of spiritual offences. All this was done within the space of three years. The people saw that there was no alternative: immediate and uncompromising resistance, or complete submission.

The oppressive acts of King James were not confined to England. He was informed even by the subservient crown lawyers that the planters of New England continued to possess the rights of English subjects, although their charter had been forfeited. Yet he appointed a governor-general and legislative council who were empowered to make arbitrary laws and execute them, to impose taxes and to compel payment. The New Englanders declared that "the whole unquestioned right of the subject was taken away."

It appears to have been the deliberate policy of James to vacate, whenever it was possible, the colonial patents.* Formal articles were exhibited before the Lords of the Committee for Colonies, accusing the colonial corporations of breaches of their charters and opposition to the acts of navigation. Writs of *quo warranto* were issued. Rhode Island, Connecticut, and New Plymouth resigned their charters, taking care, however, to frame their acts of surrender in such terms of ambiguity as to leave room for future controversy, whether they intended to resign their authority, or only to submit to superior and irresistible force. New York and New Jersey were obliged to follow suit. In all of these colonies the arbitrary government of the king was established. But the policy of King James,

* Chalmers, Hist. of the American Revolt.

however arbitrary in other respects, was sound in one instance. If it had been followed up by his successors, it might have saved much bloodshed in after times. The ambitious designs of France in America were already visible, though it would have been impossible then to foresee to what an extent they would in future times be carried. James commissioned Andros* to unite under one government the various plantations between the Delaware and the St. Lawrence. Andros was appointed captain-general of the whole under the name of New England. But though it was wise to consolidate, as far as possible, the governments of the various colonies, it was neither wise nor right to interfere with their liberties. The governor of the new territory was to be assisted by a legislative council composed of the chief inhabitants of the different colonies, selected by the king. The inhabitants in vain petitioned for the re-establishment of an assembly, elected according to their original custom ; but the concession was denied. Maryland, the Roman Catholic colony, was perhaps the only one that did not incur, for one reason or another, the grave displeasure of King James. Yet even the Marylanders were too liberal to please his despotic temper. The inhabitants of South Carolina incurred his anger with some reason ; they had lately devoted their whole attention to piracy : and to such a pitch did their depredations reach, that it became necessary to send a fleet out to destroy their ships.

† See Randolph's Letter, quoted ante, p. 382.

They soon after engaged in a quarrel with the Spaniards. James confiscated their charter as he had done those of the other colonies. The restless Carolinians were not disposed to be kept long in subjection to any authority. To habitual turbulence succeeded universal anarchy. The administration, already weakened, was overturned, and, to use the words of a contemporary historian, "imprisonment and proscription completed the miseries of a people who learned at length, from adversity, that it is the violent and vicious who alone profit from disorder."*

The English people, on either side of the Atlantic, were not of a temper tamely to submit to oppression such as this. They determined neither to throw away the liberties for which during so many years they and their fathers had fought, nor to repeat the errors by which the lustre of their forefathers' triumph had been dimmed. They resolved, not to kill the king, but to depose him. Never in history was a national defection so sudden and so complete. The change of government was effected without bloodshed or popular commotion. The Prince of Orange was invited to take the throne, and his administration was submitted to as quietly as if he had ascended it in the ordinary course of succession. The fleet received his orders. The army, without murmur or opposition, allowed him to remodel them. The City of London supplied him cheerfully with money. Such is the safety with·

* Chalmers, i. 195.

which a great revolution can be effected when the people are united in their resistance to oppression.

If we except Georgia, which was afterwards planted, and Nova Scotia, the Floridas, and Canada, that were successively conquered in later times, the continental colonies were, in 1689, firmly established. They contained about two hundred thousand inhabitants.*

Massachusetts, with Plymouth and Maine, may have had forty-four thousand. New Hampshire, with Rhode Island and Providence, each six thousand. Connecticut from seventeen to twenty thousand. New York about twenty thousand. New Jersey ten thousand. Pennsylvania and Delaware twelve thousand. Maryland twenty-five thousand. Virginia fifty thousand. The two Carolinas about eight thousand.†

Their commerce was carried on by twenty-five thousand tons of shipping, and two thousand six hundred seamen. The commissioners of customs informed the ministers of William, that the duties derived from the products of Maryland and Virginia, amounted to about two hundred thousand pounds a year.‡

The constitutions of all the colonies, though extremely liberal and free, were remarkably unlike in their detail. They were divided into charter, proprietary, and royal governments. The forms under

---

* Chalmers estimates their number, at the time of the accession of William III., at 250,000 men.—*Hist. of the Revolt*, i. 217.
† Bancroft, Hist. Am. Rev. ii. 682.   ‡ Chalmers, i. 217.

which their laws were administered may be found in charters and commissions given under the great seal of England. Massachusetts, Rhode Island, and Connecticut had been, till the aggression of King James, chartered colonies enjoying systems altogether democratic, and hardly yielding to England the appearance of obedience. New Jersey, Pennsylvania, Maryland, and Carolina were proprietary plantations, in which the lords of the soil acquired from the king the rights enjoyed by counts palatine. The proprietors stood in the place of the sovereign, who possessed within their limits no power to enforce the decrees of the supreme legislature, and hardly even a right of superintendence. Virginia, New York, and New Hampshire were royal governments. In them the governor, the council, and the delegates formed a miniature of the king, the lords, and the commons.

The local legislature, whether of the charter, the proprietary, or the royal governments, enjoyed within its jurisdiction the supremacy which is incident to legislation, owning a distinct allegiance and obedience to the superior authority of the Imperial Parliament. This account of the political institutions of the colonies is an epitome of the description given at great length by Chalmers. The English people are now completely familiarized with the method of governing colonies thus presented to our view; and it is unnecessary to dwell upon details which were quite proper when addressed to

CHAPTER readers at the time of the American war of independence; nevertheless it is not generally known how very liberal were the forms of government under which English colonists lived at the end of the seventeenth century. "We search history in vain," writes Chalmers, "for models of provincial systems so favourable to freedom and prosperity as those which England, without design, gave to her transatlantic territories. It is curious to trace the cause why forms thus liberal in their spirit, though not always so in their details, should have given rise to contest, refractoriness, and civil war."

While this was the machinery of government on the American side, the administration of the affairs
1660 of the colonies in England was intrusted to "a Committee for Trade and Plantations," which was composed of lords of the privy council, and incorporated
1696 by royal commission. This committee subsequently gave place to a Board of Commissioners for Trade and Plantations. The board continued in operation
1782 till 1782, when the business of the plantations was transferred to one of the secretaries of state.

1689 Such was the position of the colonies when the flight of James placed William III. upon the throne. It will not be pretended that at this early time they had suffered much from the operations of the navigation law, or from English encroachments on their privileges or their trade. It is, therefore, not uninstructive to see what their conduct was on the occasion of the accession of William III. A careful examination of the history of the colonies will show that they, with few exceptions, formed, soon after this time, the resolution of becoming independent of the mother-country.

In 1689 war broke out with France : it was not till after the formation of the grand alliance that the colonies became engaged in the struggle, but from the time of that alliance not a quarrel took place in Europe but it was re-enacted in America. There was a characteristic difference in the temper with which the French and English colonies joined the fight. The religion, the roving enterprise, the peculiar feudal organization of the Canadians, secured the hearty support of their leaders to Louis XIV., and the rank and file followed with unquestioning submission. William was popular in the English colonies ; he was looked upon by them as the representative of national and religious freedom; of the right of the nation to choose whom it would as king; to banish a tyrant who had violated the laws and attacked the liberties of his country. The Canadian settlers obeyed the summons to arms with the well-drilled obedience of feudal times, the English, at least those of the northern colonies, obeyed because they happened to approve the cause for which they were called on to fight. Even among those who were loudest in lip-loyalty to the new king, there was a riot when the governor, in 1689, undertook, in the king's name, to call the militia under arms for the war.

The tyranny of James had fallen upon his English

and his transatlantic subjects alike. Both were therefore delighted to welcome the advent of William and Mary. The flight of James was so sudden, and the distance which separated the colonies from home so great, that the news of the accession of William was not in every instance believed. Various and contradictory rumours were spread among the people : some said that since there was no king in England there was no government in the plantations; but on the whole it was considered prudent in most of the colonies to acknowledge the title of King William. The Stadtholder and his wife were at once proclaimed " Lord and Lady of Virginia." The Carolinas were not so prompt in their acquiescence.

The constitution of Shaftesbury and Locke, with its grotesque caricature of nobility, its landgraves and caciques, was still in force in Carolina: some of the emigrants, cavaliers of the Restoration, had brought with them the feelings and the vices of Charles's court: these formed the nobility, who, together with the rest of the high churchmen, endeavoured to set up a colonial oligarchy against the Calvinists, Huguenots, Cameronians, and other dissenters who formed the other and more numerous part of the population. The opposition seized the opportunity of King James's flight to resist the pretensions of the royalists by force of arms. The governor appointed by the proprietary was deposed, and one chosen by the people from among the dissenting party. Military stores were provided; a revenue, or rather the machinery for collecting a revenue, was established, and a militia formed for the protection of the province.

The acts of the insurgent legislature were not devoid of wisdom, but a long and desultory quarrel ensued, which ended with the destruction of Locke's model constitution. The proprietaries favoured the small oligarchical faction with protection and advice, but they could not afford, at their own expense, to quell their mutinous subjects by force; and the opposition were able, after the abrogation of the constitution, to carry their own reforms, and to remodel the political institutions of the colony at their will. They virtually chose their own governor; they elected their assembly every two years; they obtained a preponderating influence in the council. Land disputes which agitated the colony were settled in the manner dictated by the majority. Quakers and Huguenots were enfranchised, and liberty of conscience granted to all denominations of Christians, with the exception of the Roman Catholics. The proprietaries attempted from time to time some legislative interference: they asserted the abstract proposition that "all power and dominion are most naturally founded in property:" the Provincial Assembly debated the assertion, and rejected it on a division. An attempt of the proprietaries to establish the Church of England and to disfranchise the dissenters met the same fate.

Meanwhile the colony grew in wealth and in population. Rice had been introduced from Madagascar and cultivated with success. The country swarmed with negro slaves. Indian traders penetrated into the interior, and a brisk fur trade was established.

The southern part only of the province was fully organized: the northern part was a kind of political Alsatia: fugitives, whether from persecution or justice, found there a safe asylum. " Quakers, Atheists, Deists, and other ill-disposed persons " dwelt there. But though there was a governor, there were no laws and no form of government. Every one did that which was right in his own eyes. An ill-advised effort to establish the Church of England amidst such a population, had no other effect than to produce a miniature civil war, in which the governor, assisted by his friend the governor of New York and a couple of score soldiers, marched and countermarched among the streams and morasses, till weariness put an end to their bloodless military promenade. Meanwhile German emigrants from the deserted Palatinate, flying from the tyranny of Louis, found here a refuge; and a few emigrants from Switzerland formed a settlement, which they named New Berne.

It was fortunate for Carolina that, in the war of 1689, England and Spain were allies. Friendly relations had sprung up between the colonists and the neighbouring Spanish settlement of St. Augustine; reciprocal courtesies were interchanged. Indian converts of the Spaniards, who had been captured by a hostile tribe and exposed for sale, were ransomed by Governor Archdale, and sent to the Governor of

St. Augustine. An English vessel was wrecked on the Florida shore; the Spaniards treated them well, and forwarded them to Charleston.

A powerful aristocracy had gradually arisen in Virginia at the time of the Restoration, and the party thus formed became a strong ally of the royal government and its officers. The first assembly after the Restoration had consisted of landholders and cavaliers. Its acts had shown a jealousy of popular power, and respect for English precedents, which were little in accordance with the feelings of the large body of the people. The power acquired by the crown, injudiciously used by its officers in the colony, reacted unfavourably on the conduct and views of the Virginians. Antagonism sprang up as it did in Carolina between the colonial aristocracy and the democratic party. Constant struggles for power terminated, as it did in that colony, in the victory of the popular party. I said that the antagonism was between the colonial aristocracy and the people. The expression is hardly correct. There were, in truth, three parties—the royalists, the landed aristocracy, and the dissenters. The quarrel was mainly between the royalists and the dissenters. The landed aristocracy formed a body which inclined now to one side now to another, and invariably turned the scale for the time. By its dislike of democratic influences it was attracted to the royalists. By its jealousy of royal interference with the details of trade it was constantly compelled to reconcile itself to the people and make common cause against the common oppressor. In cases where sentiment pulls one way and self-interest another, it may be confidently predicted that sentiment will yield. The Virginian aristocracy offered no exception to the rule.

For a considerable time after the Restoration the aristocracy held the ascendancy in the legislature. Under their directions the laws were codified; the committee to whom the duty was intrusted performed their task rather in the interest of the government than of the governed. Enactments which had been passed while Virginia governed herself were replaced by laws copied from the English statute book. The Church of England was established as the religion of the State. Nonconformity was punished with impolitic severity. The penal laws were re-enacted and enforced against the Quakers. Baptists were fined. Non-attendance at church became a misdemeanour. In all the Puritan colonies the governor was paid by salary annually voted by the assembly. In Virginia, while the chief magistrate was elected by the people, the same rule had been observed; now the royalist legislature established a permanent revenue by an export duty on tobacco. In the judiciary, the same temper was shown: the governor and council, who were crown nominees, were the highest ordinary tribunal; the justices of the peace were appointed by the governor and held office at his pleasure. The franchise was curtailed; the authorities professing to discover that the way of choosing burgesses by the votes of all freemen was productive of disorder, they enacted that none but freeholders and householders should have a voice in elections.

These abuses of power naturally corrected themselves. The county commissioners, who were empowered to raise money for the support of the government, were resisted by the people. Nothing was wanting to bring rebellion to a head, but an excuse for assembling in arms. Such an excuse could not long be wanting. The Virginian farmers lived a solitary life in the woods. Roads were merely marked out by notches or "blazes" on the trees. There was not a bridge in the colony. There was no other town than the capital, few churches, few opportunities except in James Town of gatherings for any purpose, social or political. The planters visited each other on horseback, or paddled their canoes along the creeks. Their isolated position and defenceless state invited attacks from the Indians; in every farmhouse atrocities were committed by the savages: the colonists demanded leave to assemble and protect themselves; the governor was imprudent enough to refuse. A rebellion broke out which was quelled with the greatest difficulty : but though defeated the insurgents were still partially successful. The landed aristocracy, though they obeyed the governor's mandate to lay down their arms, threw their influence into the scale of the malcontents, and demanded the dissolution of the assembly.

The temper of the new assembly was far different

from the last. The act for the disfranchisement of freemen was "little regarded," and every freeholder took part in the election. The members seemed fully inclined to make large reforms in the administration of the colony, but Sir William Berkeley obtaining reinforcements from home, definitively crushed the rebellion, which afforded an excuse for refusing the full amount of concession which they demanded. Although the royalists were thus far successful, the dissenters by no means lost heart: men of Anglo-Saxon race cannot long be governed without their own consent. Abuse of the royal prerogative alienated the warmest supporters of royalty in Virginia as it had alienated the supporters of royalty in England: the colonial aristocracy, always sufficient to turn the scale in favour of any side it might embrace, was unanimous against the court. An assembly met shortly before the revolution, composed mainly of the old opposition: its temper was such that the governor was compelled to give way, nor did the royalists ever regain their former ascendency.

With the accession of William and Mary all cause of complaint ceased in Virginia. It cannot be denied that before that time they had been much misgoverned. But they shared in this respect the fortunes of England herself. During the evil times of the Stuarts, England groaned under oppression of various kinds. She was herself more grievously oppressed than ever were her colonies. When she emerged out of darkness into light, she gave the colonies the benefit of the change. As her own government became milder, their burdens were relaxed. It has been too much the fashion to look upon the smallest restriction placed upon the colonies as one grievance out of many, which accumulated during long years, at last became intolerable, and drove them to revolt. American history has been written by Americans who glorify republicanism as essentially beautiful in itself; they quote as their authorities the impassioned declamations of English opposition orators at the time of the war of independence—orators who were fully as anxious to confute political antagonists as to stop the war : their conclusions have been received without either examination or denial: but before English dealings with the colonies are condemned, the maxims of government which obtained in England at the time, ought to be investigated, and allowance made in each case for time and circumstance.

The Virginians had lost one check upon the governor, inasmuch as a permanent revenue had been voted ; but the amount of the revenue was small. It was always exhausted long before the necessities of the government were provided for. The granting of additional supplies was in the hands of the assembly, which dealt them out with a very sparing hand. A treasurer appointed by the burgesses looked eagerly after the interests of the colony, and effectually prevented any misappropriation of funds. Virginia refused in

CHAPTER XV.

1691 to contribute her quota towards the defence of the colonies against the French. She disregarded the injunction for assisting Albany. Bancroft admits that from 1707 to 1718, "Eighty-three pounds of tobacco* for each poll was the total sum levied by all the special acts of the assembly of Virginia."† When we remember that the wages of each burgess in the assembly of Virginia at the time of the Stuarts was two hundred and fifty pounds of tobacco per day,‡ the amount of taxation thus raised in ten years—years, moreover, of war in which the American colonies were largely interested—cannot be considered excessive.

By the act of the provincial legislature which established the Church of England as the religion of the colony, the governor might recommend a parish clergyman, and the Bishop of London issue his licence ; but the right of presentation was reserved to the parish. The habit of the colonists was to receive a minister and pay him a yearly stipend during their good pleasure ; but by withholding the presentation, to prevent him from obtaining a freehold of his benefice. In these and a thousand similar instances, the Virginians, casting the expense of their defence upon the mother-country, and not alleging

---

* Lord Baltimore for his quit-rents received tobacco at twopence a pound.
† Bancroft, Hist. United States, ii. 712.
‡ "The taxes for this purpose were paid with great reluctance ; and as they amounted to about two hundred and fifty pounds of tobacco for the daily emoluments of each member, became for a new country an intolerable grievance."—Banc. *Hist. U.S.*, i. 501.

any distinct cause of grievance, yet opposed a passive resistance to English authority, and retained in every instance the substance of power.

In Maryland, the proprietary, but not the people, had reason to complain. In 1689 Lord Baltimore was absent from his government. When the news arrived of the flight of James, Baltimore's deputies hesitated to proclaim King William: the dissenters, who by this time had become more numerous than the original Roman Catholic settlers, drove them to a small stronghold on the Pantuxent, and obtained from them their assent to an act incapacitating Papists from holding provincial offices. They then proceeded to address King William, denouncing " the influence of Jesuits, the prevalence of popish idolatry, the connivance by the government at murders of Protestants, and the danger of plots with the French and Indians." The proprietor, who was in England, on receiving the orders of the Privy Council to proclaim King William, had at once agreed to obey : his subordinates in America brought down upon him threats of parliamentary inquiry and the loss of his charter; he sent renewed orders, by a special messenger, who, however, arrived too late to preserve the peace or to save his employer's authority. Before he landed in America, a man named Coode, who, in the reign of Charles II., had been prosecuted for seditious practices, and who was afterwards convicted of blasphemy and treason, put himself at the head of seven hundred men, and seized St. Mary, the capital, which the militia refused to defend. Joseph, the president, and his principal officers were forced to capitulate. A committee of safety was organized, of which the insurgent leader took the command. Baltimore was formally deposed, and a long act of accusation was drawn out, in which he was accused of every crime. The rioters then proceeded to declare William and Mary as their sovereigns, and to assert that they were henceforth a royal and not a proprietary colony: the Church of England was established as the religion of the state, and the capital which was too intimately associated with recollections of the proprietary, and too full of Roman Catholics to please the persons who had now seized power, was removed to Annapolis. Every form of religion was tolerated, with one exception. The Roman Catholics were disfranchised on the very soil which they had themselves selected as a place of refuge from persecution, and which with rare liberality they had opened to all denominations of Christians. Maryland consented in 1695 to pay its quota towards the defence of New York.

Pennsylvania, at the revolution, became for a short time a royal colony. Penn was in England, and was two or three times imprisoned: during that time a royal governor was appointed: the assembly refused, on the ground of dislike to the shedding of blood, to vote any money for the defence of the colony, but a small supply was with difficulty obtained by the governor, who suggested that if they would not vote money for the prosecution of the war, they might at least aid those who suffered by it. If they refused to assist in the purchase of arms or the outfit of soldiers, they might not refuse to feed the hungry and clothe the naked whom the war left destitute. A year or two later the assembly framed a democratic constitution. They degraded the governor to a mere chairman of the council, which, as well as the assembly, were to be chosen by the people. The time of election, the time of assembling, the period of office, were placed beyond the power of the executive: the judiciary were made dependent on the legislature: "the people constituted themselves the fountain of honour and of power."* Penn, on his return, was obliged to acquiesce in this arbitrary act of his people, and eventually returned to England, leaving his government, a pure democracy, to look after itself. The assembly seized the occasion of his departure to vote that the proprietary had no property in the unoccupied lands (which he had bought and paid for), and to decide that such lands belonged of right to the people.

Bancroft thus sums up their condition: "An executive dependent for its support on the people; all subordinate officers elected by the people; the judiciary dependent for its existence on the people; all legislation originating exclusively with the people; no forts, no armed police, no militia; perfect freedom of opinion; no established church; no

* Bancroft, Hist. U.S. ii. 732.

difference of rank; and a harbour opened for the reception of all mankind, of children of every language and every creed; could it be that the invisible power of reason would be able to order and to restrain, to punish crime and to protect property? Would not confusion, discord, and rapid ruin successively follow such a government? Or was it a conceivable thing, that in a country without army, without militia, without forts, and with no sheriffs but those elected by the rabble, with their liberty shouts, wealth and population should increase, and the spectacle be given of the happiest and most prosperous land?"

A similar spirit actuated New York. At the time of William's accession the colony had been newly acquired from the Dutch: one of the governors who was first sent out was foolish enough to assert, in a style which reminds us of James I., that the province was a conquered country, and depended for its liberties on the goodwill of the sovereign: the legislature at once passed an act, declaring that " no tax whatever shall be levied on his Majestie's subjects in the province or on their estates on any pretence whatsoever, but by the act and consent of the people in general assembly convened." On William's accession an address was sent to the king, praying that all the colonies might be ordered to bear their quota of the defence of Albany: in this is to be observed almost the first indication of a recognition of the principle of federation. Sometimes the colonists desired to submit themselves to the central authority of the crown; sometimes they acknowledged the supreme authority of parliament; and sometimes the idea of a legislative union occurred to them. But in one form or another the idea of a federation, for mutual defence or for aggression, was constantly before them.

The injunction to all the colonies to assist in the defence of Albany was very badly responded to. Virginia and the Carolinas flatly refused; Pennsylvania declared itself unwilling to encourage war: most of the colonies, on one pretext or another, excused themselves from the payment, and the rest, except Maryland and one or two of the New England states, acknowledged the justice of the demand, and evaded it.

Connecticut, as might be expected, saw the accession of William with delight: the people sent him an address, comparing him to their favourite Old Testament heroes, and compared the disunion which existed among his enemies to the division of the waters of Jordan when Joshua passed over: they then proceeded to announce that they reserved the supreme power to themselves: they elected their own governor, council, and assembly men, as well as their magistrates: they proclaimed the people as the source of all power. In fact, they utterly and completely set aside the authority of the prince they were complimenting, and virtually declared themselves independent. Nor were they long in finding an opportunity for justifying their assertion. Fletcher, governor of New York, was invested with the command of the militia of the northern provinces, in view of the war then pending with Canada. The people of Connecticut refused to acknowledge his authority. Fletcher hastened to Hartford, where he found the train-bands paraded, under the command of William Wadsworth, the senior captain, who was putting them through their drill. Fletcher advanced to assume the command, ordering his aide-de-camp to read his commission. Wadsworth ordered the drums to beat and the aide-de-camp's voice was drowned. Fletcher commanded silence; Wadsworth ordered the drummers to redouble their exertions. The rival commanders each reiterated their behests, and while the drums beat out their loudest point of war, and the unfortunate aide-de-camp in vain attempted to be heard amid the din, Wadsworth drew his sword, and advanced on Fletcher with a threat to "make daylight shine through him in a moment." The governor glanced his eyes around: he saw the sturdy yeomen of Connecticut approaching with ominous gestures; Wadsworth, *en garde*, with drawn sword and wicked eye; the train-bands, as one may suppose, grinning in the ranks, in despite of discipline; poor Bayard, the aide-de-camp, hoarse with shouting, and making no impression on the crowd. Fletcher was human; his courage yielded. The Hartford train-bands finished their drill under their valiant captain, and the Connecticut men were so pleased with him that they made him governor of the colony.

It is not necessary to examine the action of each settlement in detail. No demand was made which really called their self-government in question; if any interference was suspected, it was at once fiercely resented. Orders were constantly sent from England that the colonies should contribute to the common defence against the French and Indians; but the demand was entertained or rejected by the colonial assemblies as their own policy prompted. Every one of the colonies passed declaratory acts asserting their right to the privileges of Magna Charta, and to freedom from taxation without their own consent.* These acts were generally disallowed by the crown, but no attempt was made to establish any right upon such disallowance. The right of the mother-country to tax the colonies was at any rate adjourned. The colonial legislatures had their own budgets. They settled for themselves the questions whether the amounts they granted should be appropriated to certain specified purposes, or whether the appropriation should be left to the crown. They decided whether the salaries of royal judges and governors should be voted annually, or be made chargeable on a permanent revenue. The colonial press was free, or at least as free as in England. Massachusetts, by an act of the legislature, claimed the benefit of the writ of habeas corpus. The act was disallowed. Lord Somers

* Bancroft, Hist. U. S. ii. 763.

declared that the privilege had not yet been granted to the plantations; it was, however, conceded to Virginia by Queen Anne.

By this sketch of the colonies at the opening of the eighteenth century, it will be seen that England did not even attempt to thrust on the colonies any oppressive legislation: that, on the other hand, they refused to acknowledge any interference whatever, and claimed rights which amounted to absolute independence. The desire of the colonies for independence existed from their very first foundation: it is therefore quite clear that they would have asserted their right so soon as they were in a condition to do so, whether the course pursued by the home government had been tyrannical or not. Separation might have been postponed, if the government had consented to continue to defray all expenses connected with the defence of the colonies—to give up all right whatever to interfere in their concerns, and to ask, in return for its concessions, no advantages whatever, of trade, or of any other kind. But even this would not have satisfied them permanently: the experiment has been tried with British America from 1846 to 1855, and Canada was with difficulty prevented from establishing differential duties as against the mother-country.*

The protection afforded to the American colonies by the mother-country was quite indispensable to

* See Circular of Lord John Russell to the Governors of her Majesty's Colonies, 12th July, 1855.

their existence : they were threatened on the north and west by the French and Indians, and on the south by the Spaniards. They only desired to retain their connection with England as long as that standing menace continued. French statesmen perceived this : one of them confidently predicted that the fall of Canada would be followed by the downfall of English power in America. Englishmen could not be brought to believe that colonies which enjoyed unquestioned what their own country had so long struggled for, and had so hardly won—freedom of speech, of action, and of religion—would resent taxation imposed solely for the purpose of defending that liberty ; more especially since taxation fell far more heavily on other parts of the empire than it ever did on them : nor could the English people see why colonies should grumble at commercial restrictions to which the metropolitan and commercial cities of Great Britain submitted without a murmur.

CHAPTER XVI.

PARTITION TREATY.

HOW BULL THE CLOTHIER, FROG THE DRAPER, AND BABOON THE BARBER, DIVIDED LORD STRUTT'S ESTATE.

[1689—1702.]

The Partition Treaty—Pamphleteers of the reign of Queen Anne—Grand Alliance—Death of William III.

THE accession of William III. to the English throne introduced a new and most important element into European affairs. Haughty, taciturn, and ambitious, he was the only man in Europe who had at once the power and the will to crush the power of Louis. The revocation of the Edict of Nantes, and the cruelties inflicted during the dragonnades, had not faded from men's minds, when Europe was horrified with the still more stupid and cruel devastation of the Palatinate.

Louis sustained single-handed the assault of all Europe. During eight years, the attack of so many enemies told severely on his rapidly waning resources. He had to encounter, at the same time, the Spanish, the English, the Austrians, and the Dutch. One army under Marshal Catinat operated in Italy: another under Luxembourg attacked Holland. Tourville engaged the Dutch and English fleets in the Channel, and drove the merchant marine of the allies from the sea. The Dauphin was sent into Germany; de Noailles into Catalonia.

It was impossible to keep up such exertions for any considerable time. The position of Louis was made more untenable by a dreadful famine in France; the allies began to recover lost ground, and it became evident that they would soon conquer a peace. But another and stronger reason decided Louis at once to suspend hostilities. He had never given up the hope of uniting under the sceptre of a prince of his own line the crowns of Spain and France. His son was nearest in blood to the childless king of Spain, and that king was near his end. Louis wished for leisure that he might devote his whole attention to the Spanish succession. The first step was to make peace, and he thought no sacrifice too great to obtain it. All the conquests made during eight years of war were resigned to their respective owners, and William III. was recognized by Louis as the legitimate king of England. This latter concession, which was granted with apparent reluctance, was, in truth, an advantage to the French king. It was impossible, as he well knew, for him to succeed in his designs on the throne of Spain, while the wariest and ablest politician in Europe watched him sword in hand. His only chance was to detach William from his allies, and make with him the best terms he could.

For the first time since the revolution an English

ambassador went to Versailles. Bentinck, King William's nearest friend and most trusted councillor, was selected for the important trust, and made his appearance in France with a degree of magnificence which attracted attention even at that extravagant court. We are told that the Parisians were never tired of admiring his horses, his coaches, and his plate. The young English noblemen who accompanied him squandered large sums in the pleasures of the gayest city in the world. In short, Bentinck and his embassy made great efforts to please, and were greatly courted in return. It was long before Louis could induce the ambassador to express any opinion on the Spanish succession. Even when the subject was fairly opened, and the main point, William's readiness to enter into negotiations, ascertained, it was long before the negotiators could come to any understanding.

A treaty was concluded, of which John Arbuthnot, one of the cleverest of the political pamphleteers, who waged a paper war during the latter days of Queen Anne, gives a most amusing version in his "History of John Bull." At the time when this satire was written, party warfare was at its greatest height in England. Pamphlets, rejoinders, reflections, letters to a noble lord, and such like compositions, issued in quick succession from the presses of Grub Street. Each champion hit hard and without much regard to the feelings of his rival. An opposition scribbler knew well that if discovered, he stood a chance of standing in the pillory, or enjoying the forced seclusion of the Tower. A ministerial champion was aware that a change of fortune might consign him at a moment's notice to a similar fate.

Steele and Addison led the literary hosts of the Whigs : Swift maddened with hatred and disappointment, and Arbuthnot overflowing with animal spirits, wrote for the Tories. Of all these men—three of them literary giants—Arbuthnot, as a writer of political squibs, was perhaps the most witty. There was something saturnine, something ferocious in the mighty intellect of Swift, which made his lightest pleasantry seem grim. Addison, who wrote the purest and most graceful English which our literature can boast, was of too kindly a nature to hit hard. His weapons were too highly polished, too keen, too pliable for rough cut-and-thrust work. Steele was no match for either of the others. The best known of the squibs attributed to him, "The Crisis,"— which was stigmatized by the House of Commons as a false and seditious libel, and for which he was expelled the house,—was not his own. Arbuthnot was the very man for a battle of pamphlets. Overflowing with pleasantry, full of ingenuity, endowed with a sense of humour which at once caught the ridiculous side of an argument, and presented it in a guise the most provocative of laughter. Every electioneering candidate knows what it is to have the laugh on his side. Arguments rarely turn party men—ridicule sometimes wins a cause.

Of all Arbuthnot's political works, the most ingenious in construction, the most elaborate in workmanship, is the "History of John Bull." In the form of a history of John Bull, an honest English clothier, who went to law with his neighbours and was half ruined thereby, Arbuthnot gives a truthful though comic account of the actual events of Europe. The work was written before the peace of Utrecht, when the dearest object of the Tories was to dim the lustre of Marlborough's victories, and to make him appear the meanest of men. Marlborough therefore figures under the guise of a low attorney, who persuades his client to go to law, and makes every advantage gained over the defendant a reason for protracting law procedure, and enhancing, for his own profit, the expenses of his client. This view of the war swayed the public mind from the consideration of its brilliant success. The people began to regard it as a mere matter of profit and loss, in which the general and the Dutch were the winners, while the British bore the expense. The King of Spain, in this history, figures as Lord Strutt,—the Emperor as Squire South—Louis and his grandson as Lewis and Philip Baboon. The Dutch were represented by Nic Frog, the linen-draper; Marlborough was Humphry Hocus, the attorney; the English Parliament was John Bull's wife.

The extract at the foot of next page is from the chapter in which John Bull gives an account of the Partition Treaty at the desire of his wife, who wishes to know what fate or chance brought such disorder into his once flourishing business.* It gives a tolerably true account of the transactions which actually occurred. Charles II., the reigning king of Spain,

* JOHN BULL.—" Who could help it ? There lives not such a fellow by bread as that old Lewis Baboon! He is the most cheating, contentious rogue upon the face of the earth. You must know as Nic Frog and I were over a bottle, making up an old quarrel, the old fellow must needs have us drink a bottle of his champagne; and so one after another, till my friend Nic and I, not being used to such heady stuff, got drunk; Lewis all the while, either by the strength of his brain or by flinching his glass, kept himself as sober as a judge. 'My worthy friends,' quoth Lewis, 'henceforth let us live neighbourly. I am as peaceable and quiet as a lamb, of my own temper; but it has been my misfortune to live among quarrelsome neighbours. There is but one thing can make us fall out, and that is, the inheritance of Lord Strutt's estate. I am content, for peace' sake, to waive my right, and submit to any expedient to prevent a lawsuit; I think an equal division will be the fairest way.' 'Well moved, old Lewis,' quoth Frog; 'and I hope my friend John here will not be refractory.' At the same time he clapped me on the back and slabbered me all over, from cheek to cheek, with his great tongue. 'Do as you please, gentlemen,' quoth I; ' 'tis all one to John Bull.' We agreed to part that night, and to meet the next morning, at the corner of Lord Strutt's park wall, with our surveying instruments; which accordingly we did. Old Lewis carried a chain and a semicircle; Nic, paper, rulers and a lead pencil; and I followed, at some distance, with a long pole. We first began by surveying the corn-fields, close by close; then we proceeded to the woodlands,—the copper and tin mines. All this time Nic laid down everything upon paper, and calculated the acres and roods to a great nicety. When we had finished the land, we were going to break into the house and gardens, to take an inventory of his plate, pictures, and other furniture."

MRS. BULL.—" What said Lord Strutt to all this?"

JOHN BULL.—" As we had almost finished our concern, we were accosted by some of Lord Strutt's servants. 'Heyday! what's here? What the devil is the meaning of all these tramgrams and gimcracks, gentlemen? What in the name of wonder are you going about, jumping over my master's hedges and running your lines across his grounds? If you are at any field pastime, you might as well have asked leave; my master is a civil well-bred person as any is.'"

MRS. BULL.—" What could you answer to this?"

JOHN BULL.—" Why, truly, my neighbour Frog and I were still hot-

CHAPTER XVI.

was suffering from a complication of mental and bodily ailments, any one of which was sufficient to kill him. It was certain that he could not last long. His kingdom, the shrunken, but still exten-

headed. We told him his master was an old doating puppy, that minded nothing of his own business; that we were surveying his estate, and settling it for him, since he would not do it himself. Upon which there happened a quarrel; but we being stronger than they, sent them home with a flea in their ear. They went home and told their master : 'My lord,' said they, 'there are three odd sort of fellows going about your grounds with the strangest machines that ever we beheld in our life. I suppose they are going to rob your orchard, fell your trees, or drive away your cattle. They told us strange things of settling your estate. One is a lusty old fellow in a black wig, with a black beard, without teeth; there's another thick squat fellow, in trunk hose; the third is a little long-nosed thin man. (I was then lean, being just come out of a fit of sickness.) I suppose it is fit to send after them, lest they carry something away."

MRS. BULL.—"I fancy this put the old fellow in a rare tweague."

JOHN BULL.—"Weak as he was he called for his long toledo; swore and bounced about the room, ''Sdeath! what am I come to, to be affronted so by my tradesmen? I know the rascals; my barber, clothier, and linendraper dispose of my estate! Bring hither my blunderbuss. I'll warrant ye, you shall see daylight through them. Scoundrels! dogs! the scum of the earth! Frog, that was my father's kitchen boy, he pretend to meddle with my estate! with my will! Ah! poor Strutt, what art thou come to at last? Thou hast lived too long in the world to see thy age and infirmity so despised; how will the ghosts of my noble ancestors receive these tidings? they cannot, they must not sleep quietly in their graves.' In short, the old gentleman was carried off in a fainting fit, and after bleeding in both arms, hardly recovered."

MRS. BULL.—"Really this was a very extraordinary way of proceeding. I long to hear the rest of it."

JOHN BULL.—"After we had come home from the tavern, and taken t'other bottle of champagne, we quarrelled a little about the division of the estate. Lewis hauled and pulled the map on one side, and Frog and I on the other, till we had like to have torn the parchment to pieces. At length Lewis pulled out a pair of great tailor's shears, and clipped a corner for himself, which he said was a manor that lay convenient for him, and left Frog and me to dispose of the rest as we pleased. We were overjoyed to think Lewis was contented with so little, not smelling what was at the

sive remnant of the conquests of the early Austrian princes, suffered from disasters apparently as incurable as those of the king. There was no direct heir. Louis XV. could not hope that the king of England would willingly permit the Dauphin to succeed. He could and did hope for an advantageous compromise. Failing the royal house of France, the succession would go to the family of Hapsburg. But the union of the crowns of Germany and Spain would be looked upon with as deep dismay in Europe as the union of the crowns of France and Spain. Statesmen remembered that it was not so very long ago since leagues against the overweening power of Austria were made, under a sense of danger as keen as that which had dictated the Augsburg League of 1689. There were two alternatives —a compromise or a partition.

The Spanish treasury was exhausted. The nobles

---

bottom of the plot. Then happened, indeed, an incident that gave us some disturbance. A cunning fellow, one of my servants, two days afterwards, peeping through the keyhole, observed that old Lewis had stole away our part of the map, and saw him fiddling and turning the map from one corner to the other, trying to join the two pieces together again. He was muttering something to himself which he did not well hear, only these words, ''Tis a great pity : 'tis a great pity.' My servant added he believed this had some ill meaning. I told him he was a coxcomb, always pretending to be wiser than his companions: Lewis and I are great friends; he's an honest fellow, and I dare say will stand to his bargain. The sequel of the story proved this fellow's suspicion to be too well grounded, for Lewis revealed our whole secret to the deceased Lord Strutt, who, in reward for his treachery, and revenge to Frog and me, settled his whole estate upon the present Philip Baboon. Then we understood what he meant by piecing the map."

divided by intrigue. Energies which should have been put forth for the good of the state were devoted to tripping each other up in their pursuit of objects of most puerile ambition. A long train of misfortune and misgovernment had brought Spain financially down to the verge of bankruptcy, morally to the verge of ruin. The causes of that wide-spread misery, which must have struck even the apathy of Philip with dismay, lay deep in the national character, and had been the growth of ages : the oppression and misgovernment which hurried Spain from the height of prosperity to the verge of ruin have been already described; the last and greatest cause of her decay was the expulsion of the Moorish Christians. The crime was promptly followed by retribution : the victory of the Church gave the last blow to Spanish prosperity. In other parts of Europe, even where Catholicism was triumphant, some rays of light had pierced into the darkness : sometimes the Church submitted her high pretensions to discussion ; or at least had recourse more sparingly than before to the secular arm. But in Spain, every trial made her more secure; every victory more intolerant and more unyielding : if she was powerful before she was absolute now ; the minds of men lay prostrate before her, and the result was that the population diminished, the industry of Seville dwindled away, the vines and the olives were uncultivated, and the army, which held half Europe for Philip II., was sent to certain defeat by his son. Rocroi was fatal to the once invincible infantry; they were not only defeated, but cut to pieces bv Condé; the troops became mutinous; many deserted;* all were in rags. Some died of hunger. A few years later it was found impossible to raise even a small force for the service of the state.

Bacallar† describes the fortifications as tumbling to pieces. He mentions many which had neither munitions of war nor provisions. So completely was the art of shipbuilding forgotten, that the king had but a few galleons engaged in the American trade, and a few which rotted at their anchorages in Carthagena harbour.‡ The woollen factories of Toledo were carried away by the Moriscoes to Tunis. The glove-trade disappeared. The tax-gatherer plied his calling in vain in a poverty-stricken land, and was unable even to collect a revenue to keep the government from going to pieces.§ The Spaniards, accustomed to rely for direction and control upon the personal exertions and talent of the king alone, were lost when a succession of incapable princes left them without a head. Accustomed to obey the king, and no one else, the grandees formed a knot of mere helpless intriguers when the king did not govern as well as reign. When the accustomed

* Le peu des soldats qui résistaient à la désertion étaient vêtus de haillons, sans solde, sans pain.—*Mémoires de Louville*, vol. i. p. 72.
† Commentarios de la Guerra de España, vol. i. p. 43.
‡ Se habia olvidato el arte de construir naves y no tenia el Rey mas que las destinadas al commercio de Indias, y algunos galeones; seis galeras consumidas del tiempo, y del ocio, se ancoraban en Cartagena.—*Commentarios de la Guerra de España*.
§ Buckle, vol. ii. p. 71.

head failed, there was no one to assume the command. Mutual jealousies prevented the nobles from intrusting power to one of their own number. The elevation of one was the signal for all the others to unite to trip him up. It was natural that almost all power should centre in the church. Philip IV. was for two-and-twenty years a contemporary of Louis XIII.; for two-and-twenty more he was the contemporary of Louis XIV. During his reign lived Bacon in England, Descartes in France. He might have watched, if he had eyes to see and a head to understand, the whole progress of the masterly policy of Richelieu, and of his pupil and successor Mazarin. During the forty-four years of his reign the persecution of religion was deliberately and systematically abolished in France. Complete effect was given to the Edict of Nantes. Huguenot leaders were admitted to their share of the administration of the state. So far was this toleration carried, that when the Protestants tried to revive the civil war, Richelieu put down their rebellion, but refused to persecute their heresy. During his reign the laymen of France emancipated themselves from the leading-strings of the church. Original and bold speculations, such as a few years before would have infallibly drawn down upon their authors the thunders of the church, were published without even the slight veil of a dead language, and without risk. Yet during that very time the church was allowed to obtain such unrestrained dominion in Spain that even the broken Cortes plucked up spirit to remonstrate. They said that there were no less than nine thousand and eighty convents in Spain. They complained that the laity were daily despoiled to enrich the clergy. Davila says that there were at that time thirty-two thousand Franciscan and Dominican monks in Spain. According to Dunham,* there were a like number of chaplains in the bishoprics of Calahorra and Seville alone.

While the clergy were thus increasing in number, industrious inhabitants were dying out of the land. Large tracts of country, formerly the abode of an industrious and ingenious population, were given up to the wild cat and the snipe; vegetation became rank; dense undergrowth overspread what had once been cultivated ground; pools and marshes spread round the ruins of Moorish aqueducts; deadly miasmata arose from the morasses; the country became a waste, without other inhabitants than the bands of brigands who took refuge in the mountains. By 1625 the last Moriscos had been tortured and executed by the Inquisition, had fled the country, or had been made Christians by the mopst† of Spanish soldiers. A few years later, Madrid lost half her population. The looms, the vines, the olives of Seville became neglected. The woollen manufactories of Toledo were removed to

* Hist. of Spain, v. 274.
† " L'un d'eux prit un balai et aspergea la foule de Musulmans en répétant les paroles sacramentelles," &c.—Circourt, *Hist. des Arabes d'Espagne*, vol. ii. 175.

Tunis. The glove trade was destroyed. The distress among the poor was so great that the common hangman used to go out into the villages round Madrid to compel the inhabitants to send their goods into the market.

1701　When Charles II. became king, the decay of the Spanish power was complete. For thirty-five years a deadly lethargy was upon Spain; her navy had decayed: a hundred and forty galleys, in the days of Charles V., used to attend upon the Dorias and Mendozas who then commanded the royal fleets. Now the ships lay rotting in the ports, with rigging and hulls decaying, without men enough to work them out of harbour. The Spanish army presented but a caricature of the splendid battalions who were wont to crush every foe that came before them. The new levies were so unwilling to serve, that they were marched to the rendezvous in chains.* Many enlisted on condition that they should be allowed to desert when they got outside Madrid, in order that their officers might pocket the head-money. There were no native Spaniards fit for military command. Berwick and Vendome successively led the forces of Spain. The royal guards were in rags; their pay was in arrear; famine stalked gaunt and ghastly in the royal palace itself, it was therefore no wonder if the soldiers were so ill-fed that they lived chiefly on the alms of the charitable, or else disbanded and took to the hill-sides.

* Clarendon, State Papers, vol. i. 275.

Education was neglected; the schools and colleges were shut up. On one occasion the police, unable to obtain their arrears of pay, mutinied and pillaged the capital.

When William III. came to the English throne, the Hon. Alexander Stanhope was sent as ambassador to Spain. He stayed there nine years. Lord Stanhope, the historian of the Spanish succession war, has given to the world a selection of his ancestor's letters, which give the most vivid contemporary picture which we possess of the state of Spain at the time of his residence. The ambassador, Stanhope, in the course of a few years' residence, acquired very naturally an extremely low estimate of the people. When we remember the extraordinary levies of the emperor and those of Philip his son, we hear with surprise of the extraordinary exertions which were required to fit out a very small force in the latter days of Charles II. When the king, in 1697, announced his intention of marching to the relief of Saragoza, more parade was made about the expedition than Philip made about the Armada. "Five hundred horse are raising here," writes Stanhope, "and all the saddlers and tailors in town are set to work in all haste. 1,500 foot are also ordered to be raised, for which and other charges of that expedition, many more men being to be raised in other parts, the queen offers to pawn her jewels, the Archbishop of Toledo to rob several churches in Madrid, and also to make bold with another treasure deposited in Toledo by a saint, a former archbishop, for some extraordinary exigency either of church or state." The king himself is described as "so weak he can scarcely lift up his head to feed himself, and so extremely melancholy that neither his buffoons, dwarfs, nor puppet-shows— all which have showed their abilities before him— can in the least divert him from fancying everything that is said or done to be a temptation of the devil, and never thinking himself safe but with his confessor and two friars by his side, whom he makes lie in his chamber every night."* Yet this account was written two whole years before his death, which did not occur till 1700.

We have many glimpses of the extraordinary shifts to which the court was put from want of money. In 1693 the government bills sent to Flanders were returned. The remedy adopted on that occasion was seizure of all the effects of the famous Genoese banker, Grillo. The ill-gotten supply did not last long. A month or two later the king reduced all salaries by a third, and confiscated all life pensions. In 1698, the superintendent of the royal revenue formally announced that all branches of the royal revenue were anticipated for many years, and that he was unable to provide the king with food! The Marquise de Villars, in her 'Mémoires,' gives a similar account of the condition of the royal household in 1681, seventeen years before. The servants declared to her that they had not received for some

* Stanhope to Earl of Portland. 11th Mar. 1698.

time past their accustomed rations either of bread or meat. "La faim," she writes, "est jusques dans le palais." So the royal household appear to have been in a chronic state of starvation.

In 1699 there was a bread riot in Madrid, in which many people were killed. The ambassador himself, as he writes a few days later, was obliged to apply to the corregidor for a daily allowance, and to send for it a distance of two leagues, with a strong armed guard to prevent its being seized by the famishing populace.

"My secretary, Don Francisco," he says, "saw yesterday five poor women stifled to death by the crowd before a bakehouse. In the midst of all these horrors the prisoners in the Carcel de la Villa went mad with hunger and broke open their prison, got into the Alcalde's armoury, knocked off their fetters, and then took refuge in the convents."

Then, too, came in flocks of beggars from the country — 20,000 at the least. The most frantic measures were adopted; the coinage was debased and the public creditors were ruined. Yet even amidst all this misery, ambassadors had time to fight for precedence, and the people crowded to the bullfights, where even grandees of Spain condescended to risk their lives—not without the approbation of the king.

"The sixth instant," writes Stanhope, in Nov. 1697, "being his Catholic Majesty's birthday, we had our Fiesta de Toros. It was very unfortunate by many fatal accidents, four or five being killed upon the place. What is most lamented is the death of Don Juan de Velasco, one of the Toriadores, whose leg and thigh were ripped up by the bull's horn as far as the groin, of which he died three days after. He had newly had the government of Buenos Ayres given him. The king has made his son a *titulo de Castilla*, and the queen has sent for his daughter from Seville to be one of her *damas*."

The nobles, always disposed to turbulence, were now more so than ever. Scenes resembling the Irish faction fights, but with more deadly weapons, were of constant occurrence. A certain Conde de Cifuentes having quarrelled with the admiral of Castile, was banished by the king. Cifuentes challenged the admiral, who refused the invitation. Such was the state of the law that this nobleman, attended by an armed party of his friends and retainers, appeared for weeks publicly in the streets of Madrid, and defied all attempts to arrest him. Two thousand doubloons were offered for him dead or alive. He was declared a "bandito," and proclamation made by the common hangman against any one who should harbour him.

The king was at that time well enough to enjoy the only sport he ever pursued—that of hunting. He, as well as all the rest of Madrid, was exceedingly amused at the terror which Cifuentes inspired in the breast of the pusillanimous admiral. "One day last week," writes the ambassador, "hunting the wild boar, the boar pursued by a rabble made towards the king; and the king called out to the almirante to have a care as Cifuentes was coming!"

In October, 1691, the ambassador's chaplain died of dysentery. There being no place assigned for the burial of heretics, Stanhope applied to the corregidor to know how he should dispose of the body. The corregidor consulted with the President of Castile, and finally assigned a retired field some distance from the city, and appointed an officer to attend the funeral on behalf of the authorities, lest it might be supposed that a murdered man was being interred by assassins. The burial took place as authorized: the body was sent out in the ambassador's coach, with a party of armed servants and a Spanish alguazil.

No sooner had the English left, than by order of one of the alcaldés, the body was dug up, the coffin broken, the shroud torn off, and a jury of surgeons summoned to view the corpse, on pretence that the man had been murdered. The body was ultimately returned to the ambassador's secretary. " He might have considered," writes Stanhope, " that I was in the same difficulties how to proceed as at first, and that a body which has been buried a day and a night, and taken up again, will not admit of the Spanish phlegm in resolving what is to be done with it. To conclude, the body was again brought to my house, and I was forced to bury it in my cellar. They had cut and mangled it in several parts, and some not decent to be named, and tore off most of the hair from his head."

CHAPTER XVI.

Amidst such sights and sounds Charles II. lay dying, while the emissaries of foreign princes quarrelled almost in his presence for the succession to his throne. The principal claimants were three: the Emperor of Austria, the Dauphin, and the Elector of Bavaria. The aunt of Charles II.* had married the father of the reigning Emperor of Austria. The eldest sister of Charles† had married Louis XIV., and was mother of the Dauphin: his youngest sister‡ had been the first wife of the reigning Emperor of Austria: her only daughter had married the Elector of Bavaria. The nearest in blood of the three claimants was the Dauphin. To him, in the common course of succession, would descend the monarchy of Spain, its dukedoms, countships, and lordships. But it was not to be supposed for a moment that European princes, who had established league after league for the purpose of limiting the power of France, would stand tamely by and see the Spanish and French monarchies united. Such a union would raise a storm from one end of Europe to the other. Even at the time of the marriage of the infanta with Louis this had been distinctly foreseen. Marie Antoinette, at her marriage, had renounced all claims to the Spanish succession. Her husband had accepted her renunciation. He had sworn by his honour, by his kingly faith and word, by the cross,

---

* Mary Anne, daughter of Philip III.
† Mary Antoinette, daughter of Philip IV.
‡ Margaret, daughter of Philip IV.

by the holy gospels, by the mass, that he would keep the renunciation sacred. The Cortes of Spain had accepted the act. It was considered impossible that the king could break the word so solemnly plighted. Politicians were therefore at liberty to examine claims less direct, but unbarred.

Margaret, on her marriage, had renounced her right of succession; but her renunciation had never been accepted by the Cortes, and Philip IV. had mentioned her in his will as his successor, failing male heirs. Her claim was therefore considered as open at least to discussion. Though the emperor was but distantly related to the Catholic king, his claims, such as they were, had never been renounced. To allow the Emperor of Austria to succeed would as surely light up an European war as the succession of Louis himself. The Electoral Prince of Bavaria excited no jealousy, and his chance of the coveted succession seemed best of all.

It was not in the nature of things that the dominions which had been collected by Charles V. and Philip II. should long remain together. They were brought together by the strong hand; the strong hand alone could keep them together. While able princes remained upon the throne, the want of coherence in the monarchy was not perceived. But when power was wielded at once with extravagance and incapacity, the monarchy went to pieces. The intense loyalty to the person of the sovereign, which was one of the most marked characteristics of the

Spanish character, still maintained its ground, and induced the Castilians to excuse signs of weakness and imbecility which in any other country would have caused the downfall of the royal power. Every Castilian was deeply concerned in the maintenance and integrity of the monarchy. For Castile was the very *omphalos* of the monarchy. Castilians enjoyed viceregal power in the palaces of Peru and Mexico; the chief commands in the army and navy were theirs; they ruled in Naples, in the Milanese, in the Netherlands. It was to Castile that Spaniards came to spend, in splendid hospitality, the wealth they had amassed in other quarters of the empire. Dismemberment of the monarchy, or even decrease in its importance, was a thought bitter to the Castilian soul. It was evident that the claimant for the succession most popular with the Spaniards would be he who had the best chance of keeping the monarchy intact. To such an one their loyalty would be transferred entire.

Louis was anxious if he could not enjoy the whole, to obtain a share. William, too, was of opinion that a partition was the safest, and, indeed, the only feasible plan. But it was foreseen that the Spaniards would be furious when they heard that the dismemberment of their monarchy had been agreed upon. It was resolved that the negotiations should be secret. Holland, France, and England agreed to a treaty: the young Prince of Bavaria was to succeed to the throne of Spain, the American possessions, and the

Netherlands; the emperor was to have the Milanese; the dauphin the two Sicilies. Secretly as the negotiations were carried on, they were known in Madrid almost as soon as they were signed. Charles for a moment exhibited the spirit of his race, and expressed his anger at the humiliating position in which Spain was placed. He determined to make a will, leaving the monarchy entire to the Prince of Bavaria. Within a few months the question became more complicated than ever; for the Prince of Bavaria, whose succession might have commanded the consent of all the claimants, died at Brussels. A second time the politicians of Paris and London framed a treaty of partition. This was too much even for the phlegmatic blood of Charles. He dismissed the representatives of Holland and Spain with every mark of displeasure.

The prize now seemed to lie between the houses of Bourbon and of Austria. The king was in a state of mental and bodily prostration. His digestion was shattered, his constitution ruined, his mind a wreck. He was kept alive on a diet of hens fed on vipers;* even that extraordinary dish disagreed with him, for the peculiar formation of his teeth and jaws obliged him to bolt each morsel whole. He resorted to witches and exorcisms, when he ought rather to have tried a discontinuance of ollas and sweetmeats. In a word, the king was a fatuous idiot under the absolute control of those who happened to surround

* Stanhope's Correspondence.

him. A battle took place for the possession of his person and the direction of his mind. The queen sided with her own royal house: so likewise did the confessor of the king and many of the ministers. On the other side were the French ambassador, the Marquis of Harcourt, and Cardinal Porto Carero, Archbishop of Toledo. There was no representative of other European powers to interfere with the exercise of Harcourt's diplomacy; Louis had managed to divert resentment from himself, and to fasten it on England and Holland, whose representatives had in consequence been dismissed from Spain. The queen and her party worked strenuously; but the German envoy, Count Harrach, made himself so unpopular that he ruined all their plans. The marquis and the cardinal were more than a match for the queen and her German allies. Charles died in 1700, and left the whole Spanish monarchy to the Duke of Anjou.

As soon as the contents of the King of Spain's will were known, all was activity at Versailles. Louis made no pretence of hesitation : he accepted the will in favour of his grandson. His kingly word, his oath on the cross, the renunciation of his wife's claims at the time of his marriage, were all forgotten. Philip V. hurried to take possession of his new dominions. Hardly a month elapsed before he was on his way to the frontier. His brothers and the great nobles of France escorted him. The Pyrenees, Louis said, were barriers no longer. But Philip had neither the energy nor the talent which the crisis required. Like all who had lived much with Louis, he had become so accustomed to obey that he was neither capable nor desirous of commanding.

As if this rupture of the Partition Treaty were not sufficient cause of quarrel with England, Louis added another still more complete. James, the dethroned king, was on his death-bed: Louis visited him, and in presence of his courtiers promised to recognize his son as King of England. Such a declaration might have been wrung from a young and generous prince, overcome at the sad spectacle of a monarch dying in exile. Louis was not young. His generosity, on this occasion at least, was rather quixotic than laudable. Indeed it is not easy to understand how such a master of diplomacy could have committed so strange a blunder. Louis did not for a moment seriously think of replacing the Pretender on the throne whence his father had been driven; but he must have perceived that to proclaim his sympathy so loudly was an insult to England which would rouse the whole nation. William was unpopular: his foreign policy was hardly understood. At the best it was rather acquiesced in than approved. He might have found it difficult to arouse the warlike spirit of the nation on the subject of the Duke of Anjou's inheritance. The acknowledgment of the Pretender by Louis at once gave the game into his opponent's hands. No need now to search for a pretext, to explain a policy, to reason, to persuade. A pretext was ready to

William's hand at which every English heart would throb and every ear tingle. The intelligence reached him at the Loo. He instantly despatched two couriers, one desiring the Duke of Manchester to leave Versailles without delay, the other ordering that Poussin, the French ambassador, should be sent out of England. William was by this time near his grave; his health was such that he could hardly speak above a whisper; his body was emaciated. But his spirit was as strong as ever. From his palace at St. Loo he made a new coalition—one which once and for ever destroyed the fear of the overbalancing power of France. Holland, Germany, and England signed the Grand Alliance in 1701. William hastened to London, where he exerted the last of his strength in preparing for war. He despatched the Earl of Albemarle to hasten matters at the Hague. Scarcely had the envoy returned, when the king, who a few days before had fallen from his horse, died. Anne quietly succeeded him on the throne, and within a few months war with France was declared by concert at London, Vienna, and the Hague.

CHAPTER XVII.

SPANISH COLONIES.

[1713.]

Council of the Indies—Character of Spanish Settlement—Mode of life among the Creole nobles—The Indians—The American Church—A Spanish Mission—Inquisition—Revenue.

WHILE the colonies of the English and French were slowly extending their limits, the Spanish rule spread rapidly from California to Patagonia. On the whole continent of America, west and south of Louisiana, no European nation, except Portugal, pretended to dispute the exclusive title of Spain. Brazil was a territory as large as the whole of Western Europe put together; but even that large deduction was trifling compared with the enormous extent of territory that belonged to the Spanish crown.

There were no more conquests after the first half of the sixteenth century. Cortez was master of Mexico by the year 1521; Peru, Quito, and Chili were overrun by Pizarro by 1535; Terra Firma in 1532; New Granada in 1536. But it was long before the Spaniards spread their settlements over the vast country of which they had taken possession.

CHAPTER XVII.

The internal provinces, as the countries north of Mexico were called, and the territories which are now known as Patagonia and Rio de la Plata, did not, till many years afterwards, form part of the Spanish dominions. Spain founded her right to the American continent on the bull of Alexander VI., which granted all lands discovered, or to be discovered within certain limits, to Ferdinand and Isabella. The king was in his American dominions the sole source of honour or of power; all authority, ecclesiastical as well as temporal, was centred exclusively in him. The leaders who conducted the various expeditions, the governors who presided over the different colonies, the judges who administered the laws, even the ministers of religion, were all appointed directly by him, and were removable at his discretion. Pope Alexander VI. was naturally unaware of the importance which the discovery of America was destined to assume. He was ready to oblige a dutiful son of the Church, even at the risk of some small loss to her revenues; he was therefore not unwilling to grant the tithes of all the newly-discovered countries to the crown of Castile. Julius II. completed the sacrifice, which his predecessor had partly made, by conferring on Ferdinand and his successors the rights of patronage, and the absolute disposal of all benefices in America : thus all authority, ecclesiastical as well as temporal, centred exclusively in the kings of Spain. The machinery of government was arranged upon the fundamental maxim that everything was done by the power of the king alone, and under his immediate orders. The supreme government of Spanish America was vested in a body of which the king himself was the head, and which held its meetings in whatever place the sovereign happened for the time to reside: it was called the Council of the Indies. This celebrated Council was established within a very few years of the first conquest, and, indeed, before the conquest was yet complete: its jurisdiction extended to every department, ecclesiastical, civil, military, and commercial. All laws and ordinances relative to the government and police of the colonies were originated by it, and must be approved by two-thirds of its members before they were issued in the name of the king; the appointment to all offices of which the nomination was reserved to the crown was decided by it; to it the viceroys made their reports, and consigned their gold; it dealt with the schemes and plans of Castilian adventurers, who dreamed of some new kingdom to be brought under the sway of Spain; it deliberated over the dark plans of Ximenes and Quevedo, and loosed the familiars of the Inquisition on their prey. The king was supposed always to preside at the sittings of the Council; a chair was kept vacant for him when he was not present. The Spanish monarchs exerted all their power to decorate it with every splendour which could strike the imagination, or render it formidable to their subjects on both sides of the

CHAPTER XVII.

Atlantic. It would be unjust not to acknowledge that, in spite of many absurd and some wicked regulations, such measure of public virtue as existed in America was owing to the influence exercised by this august tribunal. As soon as the conquest was completed, the Spanish monarchs divided their new dominions into two vast kingdoms—the viceroyalty of Mexico, and the viceroyalty of Peru. It was not till the increasing number of the Spanish settlers rendered it impossible to govern such extensive districts from the two centres of Mexico and Lima, that it was found necessary to subdivide the country into other subordinate governments. A Spanish settlement extended itself in a different manner from that of any other nation. English colonies were agricultural: the planters aspired to raise up farms and homesteads in the wilderness; they dispersed over the face of the land, and settled wherever wood and stream, valley and pasture, gave promise of future markets and means of communication. French emigrants congregated in feudal seigniories, where the exigencies of military science required the establishment of a post to defend the frontier, or to afford a base for aggressive operations on the English or the Indians. The Spaniards were attracted by the precious metals alone. Partly to be near the scene of their labours, and partly for defence, they acquired the habit of congregating in towns built in the immediate neighbourhood of the mines: their society assumed the character of an oligarchy, while the

Europeans formed a dominant class in the midst of a subject pōpulation. The Creoles fared little better, and were little more considered, than the native races. American Spaniards were deprived, by reason of their Creole birth, of the best part of those privileges which alone made life in America worth having: though their blood might be as pure Castilian as that of any hidalgo of Madrid, every avenue of distinction was shut against them; they were subjected by the government to numerous and petty restrictions. So systematically were they excluded from public life, that the very clerks in the government offices were brought over from Spain.

The settlements of the Spaniards at the beginning of the eighteenth century rarely extended far inland. There was a thin fringe of inhabited country along the sea-coast and on the banks of gold-bearing streams. A few cities were scattered among the high table-lands of the Sierra Madre and the great Cordillera. Peru and Chili were both enclosed between the mountains and the sea: throughout their whole extent, impassable deserts, ravines, and snow-clad mountains stretched in long succession between one settlement and another. The population of Mexico was rather more equally distributed. Even here the cities were few and far between, with wide intervening tracts of desert, in which the Spaniards were chiefly represented by priests who lived among and lorded it over an obsequious population of Indians. Only traders of Spanish birth, who by dint of heavy

CHAPTER XVII. payments had bought permission to wander, and religious persons belonging to the Indian missions, could give any account of the interior of the country. A traveller, journeying for pleasure or instruction, was a being unknown in a land where foreigners were forbidden to set foot on pain of death. The account given by these privileged pilgrims, who occasionally gave the world the benefit of their observations, described scenes and adventures unlike any that could be encountered elsewhere. After leaving a Spanish settlement, the wayfarer might ride many hundred miles through forests and over deserts, ravines, and ice-covered mountains, without seeing a trace of the presence or habitation of man: at length, when he had half persuaded himself that the furthest outpost of civilization was leagues behind him, he would come upon an *estancia,* or grazing farm, tended by a solitary shepherd; within the next few miles he would find stations nearer together, and would discover that he was penetrating into an isolated centre of busy life. Anon he would reach a stockaded town, surrounded by the dwellings of native Spaniards and Creole grandees—dukes, counts, and marquises—the owners of many a square league of territory; " encomenderos" of many thousand slaves, who pursued their toil amid hideous mortality and suffering in the neighbouring mines.

Enormous as was the nominal wealth of these Creole lords, their riches could procure few of the comforts and none of the luxuries of life. Spanish America had no manufactures. A dozen ships, twice a year, carried all the European goods that the Americans were allowed to enjoy. The prices demanded for these coveted articles were excessive: to the original cost was added an exorbitant charge for freight; it was still further augmented by the profits of the monopolist exporting merchant at Seville, by the monopolist importing merchant at Carthagena, and, finally, by land transport of many hundred miles, on the backs of mules or the heads of Indian slaves. Except to the richest nobles, and to those in the immediate vicinity of the trading ports, these successive enhancements of price amounted to prohibition.

The Creole grandees lived in rude magnificence, and valued themselves much on their hospitality, which they considered as a proof of the purity of their Spanish blood. Frezier says, rather satirically, "The most beggarly and meanest of the Europeans become gentlemen as soon as they find themselves transplanted among the Indians, blacks, mulattoes, mestizos, and others of mixed blood. That imaginary nobility causes them to perform most of their good actions." It was, in truth, the main secret of their mode of life, which exhibited a mixture of simplicity and patriarchal hospitality with barbarous magnificence. The house of every Spanish American was open to all comers, who were welcome to remain as long as their convenience or their avocations allowed. The licensed merchants of Biscay, who held most of the inland trade in their hands, were thus enabled to travel much at small expense to themselves. The Creoles revenged themselves for their exclusion from the offices of trust and emolument, which the European Spaniards entirely monopolized, by affecting a supreme contempt for the intellectual powers of their rivals. "Cavallos"—horses, was the uncomplimentary name by which they distinguished a Spaniard from home.* But we are assured that they did not consider it safe to give prominent expression to their estimate of the mental capacity of their countrymen in mixed society. Travelling and hunting were the only laborious pursuits in which the Creoles took delight. The latter is said by Ulloa to have been so dangerous, that the sport could only be followed by the most dexterous riders, the consequences of a fall being generally fatal. The meet was ordinarily at daybreak; and the horsemen, each accompanied by his hounds, stationed themselves on the highest passes of the mountains, while the Indian beaters and the footmen ranged the slopes, shouting to raise the deer. The company extended sometimes, according to their numbers, over four or five leagues. Ulloa declares that the most celebrated horses of Europe must yield the palm to those of America, compared with whose fleetness their boasted activity was but dull. Although the awe with which he describes the incidents of the chase, perhaps points to the conclusion that Ulloa was not a good horseman, the animated description which he gives of the rough country over which

* Voyage en Amerique.

American sportsmen rode, showed that their hunting must have been a manly and exciting pastime:—
"On the starting of any game, the horse which first perceives it sets off, and the rider being unable to guide or stop him, pursues the chase sometimes down such a steep slope that a man on foot, with the greatest care, could hardly keep his legs; from thence up a dangerous ascent, or along the side of a mountain, that a person not used to this exercise would think it much safer to throw himself out of the saddle, than commit his life to the precipitate ardour of the horse."* It is probable that the Spanish Americans, living in the saddle almost from their cradle, and pursuing no other occupation than the chase, may have had sufficient control over the movements of their steeds, and have been in a position keenly to enjoy the excitement of the sport.

So quickly did the climate tell upon the constitutions of Europeans, that even those who were bred to labour in Spain, within a short time grew idle in America. The siesta after dinner wasted a considerable part of the day, and, in the towns, contributed not a little to raise the price of workmanship.

The Creoles enjoyed the reputation of being fully a match in making bargains with the Europeans; but their constitutional indolence, and, still more, their extreme vanity, which did not permit them to engage in any transaction where the profit was not large and the labour small, threw most of the trade

* Voyage en Amerique.

into the hands of the Biscayan pedlers, who travelled up and down the country, living free of cost at the various *haciendas*, and buying up the produce of the country, to be retailed at the semi-annual fairs of Portobello and Vera Cruz. Cattle from his vast estates supplied a Mexican or Peruvian grandee with most of the necessaries of life. His Indians, armed with their lassoes, brought him in as many wild bulls or horses as he cared to have; Indian women spun and wove the llama hair that made his cloak, and twisted the prairie grass into a broad-leafed sombrero: the enormous rowels of his spurs were rudely fashioned with silver from his mines; his saddle was a double sheepskin, which served him for a bed at the camping-ground; his stirrups were great square boxes of wood, or on grand occasions of silver; his horse furniture generally was made after the patterns brought to America many years before by the conquerors. In the towns, the breast-plate and other parts of the harness were covered with scales of solid silver, sometimes even with gold and jewels: in the country districts, those parts which the European Spaniards made of iron and silver, were copied by the natives in horn and wood. The Indians soon after the conquest learnt the use of horses, and became extraordinarily expert. Frezier, who was in Chili in 1712, says that the horses brought from Spain had multiplied to such an extent that the Indians used them for food, " preferring them to beef, which they said gave them the stomach-ache!"

A horse which was not of extraordinary beauty would fetch but two or three crowns at La Conception. If the grandee was too lazy to ride, troops of slaves were ready to carry him in a "serpentino,"—a hammock of fine cotton, with mosquito nets and awnings, hung on bamboo poles; behind him ran negroes, carrying his sword, and huge extinguisher-shaped umbrellas: you may see a picture of one in Monsieur Frezier's "Voyages." In the mountains the Creoles sometimes travelled on chairs slung on the back of a single Indian, many of whom, if report be true, were "expended" in a toilsome march. Field hands cultivated just so much land as would supply him and his household with food; there was no market for the surplus produce, so there was no inducement to extended cultivation. At meals, the whole establishment ate together, the masters handing over their shoulders each dish well seasoned with burning "axe," or "pimiento," to the expectant servants behind.

Learning was entirely uncultivated; few households could boast of the possession of books or the ability to read them; even the few who possessed the requisite knowledge had few opportunities of gratifying their tastes; there were no printing-presses in the American dominions of Spain, and the energetic surveillance of the Inquisition prevented the admission of any works which might excite discussion or inquiry. The sole occupation of a Creole grandee was the chase; his relaxations were his cigar, his chocolate, and his siesta; thus he dawdled away his time in the midst of a harem of dusky ladies and a crowd of "Mestizo"* children.

In the towns were usually quartered a guard of soldiers; but the inglorious heroes who dreamed away their time in remote American posts, were but indifferent representatives of the famous battalions who in old days had fought successfully against almost any odds. The men were no more who had vanquished the famous pikemen of Switzerland and the cavalry of France; who had rushed with Cortez against Aztec and Indian warriors, that outnumbered them by three hundred to one; the yellow jerkin was now worn by men who adapted themselves completely to the indolent security in which they lived. Waited upon by crowds of Indians, dreaming away life with endless "chica" cigars, and dice, their business was no longer to hunt down Indians, but to watch their own countrymen, on behalf of the government to collect taxes, to prevent smuggling, and bring to instant punishment any who should attempt to establish any kind of manufacture. The European Spaniards formed an exclusive caste among themselves, and were connected by no ties of affection with the country of their temporary sojourn. Each man was eager to get back to Spain, and enjoy the riches he had amassed in the full sunshine of court favour, under the eye of the king in Old Castile. For it was the Castilian and the Castilian alone, for whom the full enjoyment of

* Persons of mixed Spanish and Indian blood were so called.

Spanish nationality was reserved. From among the Castilians were selected the great nobles who ruled in the Netherlands, in Naples, in the Sicilies, in Franche Comté, in the golden viceroyalties of Peru and Mexico. All the offices of state, even in America, were filled by Spaniards of Old Spain. The very clerks in the government offices were selected from the favoured class. All, from the highest to the lowest in the great hierarchy of oppression, made haste to be rich at the expense of the unhappy natives, in order to get back to the goal of every true Spaniard's ambition.

It was obvious that when settlement began at so many distinct centres simultaneously, it was not possible that the boundaries should be very accurately marked. Each new settlement, or village, was made with the sanction of the government, by whom a corregidor was appointed : the corregidory was attached to a district under the command of an intendant; the intendant, in his turn, reported to the viceroy, generally a grandee of Spain. It was in this way, as the country became settled, that new governments were formed : intendencies swelled into viceroyalties, and were removed, one by one, from the central jurisdiction; corregidories became subject to captain-generals or intendants : small villages increased into great cities, with municipal institutions. The municipalities alone, of all the governmental machinery of Spain, showed some recognition of the principle of self-government and the ordinary administration of justice; the minutiæ of internal government in the cities were intrusted to "cabildos," assemblies consisting of the alcaldés and other officers of justice, together with a certain number of regidors selected from among the principal inhabitants: the regidors were not selected by the people, but by the king, from whom nominations were obtained by purchase: a large portion of the royal revenues depended upon such-like ignominious vails.

The cities of Spain were represented in the council of Castile; and in like manner the cities of America, which did not possess cabilaos, were represented in the council of the Indies. The old cabildos themselves were borrowed from the old municipal institutions of Spain. They were originally established in that country for the same reasons that impelled Louis le Gros to introduce communes into France, or Henry VII. to enlarge the power of the Commons in England—namely, to curtail and counterbalance the power of the nobility: these bodies, when they had served their turn, were allowed in France and Spain to fall into disuse: it is fortunate for England that the example was not followed in our country in the way that has just been described.

Isolated patches of population spread themselves over Mexico and Peru. The boundaries were not noted, but farms and grazing stations spread out from the centre of each separate community, till the wilderness was reclaimed. In by far the greater number of instances the intervening country was never sufficiently recovered from the waste to make it worth while formally to run the boundaries. But as each village was established with the sanction of the government, farms belonging to persons living in that village were held to be within its limits; and, as it was always possible to ascertain to whom a frontier farm had been granted, there was no difficulty in deciding to what corregidory the land belonged.

The whole central country, which belonged formally neither to Mexico nor Peru, was called Terra Firma: Mexico was divided into New Spain and Guatemala; the first under a viceroy, the second under a captain-general. A few years after the Treaty of Utrecht, the old limits of Peru contained the viceroyalty of Granada, the captain-generalship of Caraccas (now the Republic of Venezuela), the captain-generalship of Chili, and, towards the end of the century, the viceroyalty of La Plata, or Buenos Ayres.

It seemed, during the first few years after the conquest, that the aborigines of the mainland would hardly fare better than the Indians of the Mexican and Caribbean Seas; but it was soon found that unless economy of life was exercised in some small degree, the inhabitants and the mines would soon come to an end together; for neither white man nor negro could stand the labour that was required. Regulations, framed in a spirit of apparent mercy to the natives, were sent out from Europe; and even in the early days after the conquest, Spain could turn with pride to laws respecting the treatment of natives infinitely more humane than any that had ever been dreamed of either by the French or English.

"To do all men right," says Peter Cieza, in his travels, " I must declare that all the Spaniards were not 'guilty of thus misusing the Indians, for I have often seen, and can affirm of my own knowledge, that they were kindly treated by good and moderate men, who, when they happened to be sick, would bleed and serve them with their own hands." Cieza is a somewhat partial witness; he further states that "now no Spaniard, though ever so great, dares offer them (the Indians) the least injury; that the sovereign courts never fail to punish those who wrong the Indians; that they are on a level with the Spaniards; as free of their persons, and as absolute masters of their estates, as they; and every township is appointed what moderate taxes they have to pay," with much more in the same strain.

The mass of the Spanish population was concentrated on the small table-lands and elevated valleys of the great mountain chain which runs north and south through the whole continent of America. The first adventurers found in these plateaux, both in Mexico and Peru, tribes of agricultural Indians, who exhibited very advanced civilization. In after years, the richest settlements of the Spaniards were formed in the same districts which had been the principal centres of native population. Throughout its whole extent, the great backbone of America bears gold: in the elevated valleys of the Aztecs and Peruvians the Spaniards came upon stores of wealth, such as their forefathers had dreamed of in vain: compared with the rich profusion now before them, the mines of Hispaniola sank into insignificance. The first thought of the discoverers was to divide the native population among the Conquistadores, and hurry them off by troops to labour in the mines, replacing them with others as soon as, in the barbarous slang of the time, they were "gastados"— used up. But waste of life so tremendous could not long be maintained; epidemic diseases raged among the slaves. The government of Castile had not yet lost the head to will and the power to execute; it stepped in with well-meant though necessarily experimental legislation. The Indians were first divided among masters, who had a property in their labour, but not in their persons. This plan was not successful: they were then distributed in "encomiendas," or districts, each *encomendero* taking the Indians of his district under his protection, and exacting from them a tribute or produce rent: this succeeded little better than the other. For many years the native population were subject to the extremest brutality: no laws and no restrictions availed to protect the natives from the fiendish excesses of the Conquistadores and their immediate descendants: a wise and moderate system was at length adopted, which restored the Indians to a state of comparative comfort. But not even in after times, when their lives became comparatively safe, did the government ever contemplate making them free.

The policy of Spain was to keep the Indians in a condition of perpetual minority.* Men of pure Indian blood were incapable of making legal contracts; they could not be pursued for debt: they were placed under the immediate protection of the king, to whom they paid a capitation tax, and of the clergy, to whom they paid the dues of the church. A mixed race soon arose, who shared their disabilities in a minor degree: the number of female emigrants from Old Spain, compared with the number of men, was always so small that large numbers of intermarriages took place between the Spaniards and the natives: the descendants of the mixed marriages lost rank: every man's social position varied in proportion as he approached pure white. The standard of purity was fixed, not only by the customs of society, which were rigid, but by the law itself: it required two generations of pure white marriages to efface the stain of one mixture with the Indian race: the American Spaniards who had ever so slight an admixture of Indian blood were excluded from all offices of trust under the state. There was a numerous titled aristocracy among the Creoles: they were possessors of large estates, transmitted by "mayorazgos," or entails from father to son; but all

* Merivale, p. 6.

this did not suffice to wipe off the stain of Indian blood.

Protection such as that under which the Indians lived, though it prevented the race from rising in the social scale, or acquiring the character of free men, still it was perhaps the best plan that could be adopted to protect a timid and cringing people from a masterful class dominant among them. To assign the aborigines as wards to the crown, and, as far as possible, to deal out equal justice to both, was the only way to prevent the Gothic settlers from destroying them.

As is now the case in British India, it was found that the European race, in a few generations, dwindled and died. It required admixture with the native blood to keep it alive at all: the second or third generation from the Conquistadores altogether lost the spirit of their forefathers, and sunk with inconceivable rapidity to a position lower than that of the aborigines themselves: it thus necessarily came to pass that a succession of adventurers from Old Spain formed a social aristocracy in the midst of a degraded population, of which Mulattos, Quarterons, and Quinteros were looked upon as little, if at all better than the full-blooded Indians. The "Criolios," according to Gage, an English traveller who visited Spanish America as a missionary friar, in the time of Cromwell, hated the Spaniard of the old country more than in Europe the Spaniard hated the Frenchman, or the Hollander, or the Portuguese. He declares that he had often heard them say "that they would rather be subject to any other prince than to the Spaniard." On the occasion of a tumult in Mexico, when the archbishop, Don Alonzo de Zerna, caused the viceroy to fly for his life, the Creoles at once took part with the archbishop, and very nearly succeeded in overturning the Spanish power. No Creole was ever appointed viceroy, or, indeed, to any office of trust: this would not be noteworthy, if the society in New Spain had been, as in the English plantations, purely democratic : it would be unwise to select one person to hold an exalted station and enormous power from among a society where all were theoretically equal; but in the Spanish colonies were men possessing enormous hereditary wealth, and holding the highest titles of nobility by direct descent from the purest blood of Spain, yet excluded by arbitrary laws from even so much as a clerkship in a government office. Had not the deleterious effect of climate, aided with almost magical rapidity the systematic policy of the Spaniards, the insults that were heaped upon the Creole race would have produced frequent scenes of revolt and bloodshed.

The natives of Mexico and Peru represented a civilization as advanced, though less vigorous than that of their invaders: there was consequently not the same distaste as might otherwise have existed to intermarriages: many of the largest estates were acquired by adventurers who contracted alliances with the families of great native chiefs, and were confirmed in their possession by the authorities of Spain. Many of the conquered race gave evidence of very considerable abilities. Garcillaso and Torquemada were two of the best historians of the New World; one was a descendant of the Meas; the other a citizen of Tlascala: the preceptor of Velasquez the astronomer was an Indian. Nevertheless, Spain offered very little encouragement to learning on the part of her American subjects; letters led neither to distinction nor to wealth; there was but one exception: a constant supply of priests was required, and though large numbers were constantly brought over from Spain, it was found necessary to supplement them by ecclesiastics of native birth. There was little disposition to allow Americans to visit Spain, it was therefore decided to establish colleges where the students of divinity might pursue their preparatory labours: a university was established in Mexico, and one at Lima; but for a long time the students at both those seats of learning consisted only of those who intended to take orders; it was not till a late period that they began to influence the taste or the intellectual calibre of the Spanish Americans. The Spaniards were men of business. Their fondest wish was to wring from their intendancy or corregidory sufficient money to enable them to go home and dazzle their relatives in Old Castile with a sight of their magnificence. They had no time to attend to learning, even if the familiars of the Inquisition had been less unpleasantly curious about

CHAPTER XVII.

[1713.

the orthodoxy of such books as might find their way into the Catholic king's American dominions. A time arrived when, as Humboldt tells us, prohibition stirred up curiosity, and induced such numbers of Spanish Americans to devote themselves to learning, that they learned to look down with contempt on the intellectual position of Spain: when that time came, the day of independence for the Spanish colonies was not far off.

It has been already mentioned that the church of Spanish America was completely emancipated from the control of the pope. It is curious that men so entirely devoted to the interests of the Catholic faith, as the kings of the Austrian line, should have held their exemption for so many generations, and have pertinaciously refused to give up the concession which he had made to them. Robertson, in his history, speaks with great admiration of this limitation of the papal jurisdiction: to it he attributes "the uniform tranquillity which has reigned in her (Spain's) American dominions." It is much more likely that the exemption deprived the unfortunate Indians of an efficient protector: the sole object of the temporal rulers, was to make the church an engine of their political system: those who remember how nobly, during the middle ages, the ecclesiastics stood up against the power of the nobles in favour of the oppressed feudal serfs, may reasonably feel that the entire subjection of the Spanish American church to the civil power was a great misfortune.

The hierarchy was established in the same form as in Spain, with its full train of archbishops, bishops, and deans. There were three inferior grades: "curas," "doctrineros," and "missioneros." The first, were parish priests in those parts of the country which were settled by the Spaniards; doctrineros had charge of the Indians who were subject to the Spanish government; missioneros were sent forth to instruct and convert the rude frontier tribes, who, secure in their mountain fastnesses, defied the power of the conquerors. The revenues of the church were enormous: churches, convents, monasteries, were to be seen in great numbers in every city:—stately piles endowed with the offerings of many pious generations, with rich stores of plate and jewels, carved screens and elaborate altarpieces.

Hardly had the Spaniards overrun the country, than crowds of monks and nuns poured in. While yet the settlers were almost without the comfort of female European society, convents were crowded with Spanish ladies: even the Spanish monarchs were at times alarmed for the result of that extreme infatuation for monastic life that took possession of the Spaniards in America. At first, no one but a Spaniard of Old Spain could be admitted into a convent, so that every person in every convent may be looked upon as one withdrawn from the duties of active life, just at the period when the demands of colonization were most imperative. For example, in the two capital cities alone of New Spain and Peru, there were sixty-five religious houses, besides a crowd of hospitals, colleges, and parish churches: when Frezier was at Lima, the friars had taken up the finest and greatest part of the city: the Dominicans had four monasteries; the Franciscans four; the Augustines four; the Mercenarians three; the Jesuits five; the Benedictines, Minims, and Brothers of St. John, one each; the Bethlehemites two. There were also twelve convents of nuns.* In the city of Mexico there were eighteen convents, of which the Franciscans had four, the Augustines four, the Dominicans two, &c., and fourteen nunneries.

Torquemada, in his "Monarquia Indiana," estimates the number of monasteries in New Spain at four hundred; and Robertson mentions in a note that Philip III., in a letter to the viceroy of Peru, written in 1620, declares that the monasteries of Lima cover more ground than all the rest of the city put together.

The clergy held such enormous power for good or evil, that any one who would understand the national life of the Spanish Americans must closely observe their character as a body: the secular priests were mostly of Spanish birth; it is a moot point whether Indians were ever ordained at all. The rank and file of those who volunteered to serve in the New World were for the most part men who had small prospect of advancement in their own country: a land as full as Spain was of priests sending out the least promising members of such a very numerous fold, was

* Frezier's Voyage. Herman Mons Atlas.

likely to furnish a considerable percentage of men of whom no country could be proud. In truth, the priests of the American church soon acquired an unenviable notoriety: scandal was given more particularly by the monks, who really appear to have cast off all sense of decency in the New World: but the secular clergy, at least in the lower ranks, were by no means clear. If we had received our picture only from men like Gage,* who describes his adventures with the glee of a schoolboy let loose, and comments on the morals of his former brethren with the proverbial acrimony of a deserter, we might hesitate to accept it; but grave historians of the Roman Catholic religion speak of the morals of the Spanish American clergy in terms quite as severe as Gage. Frezier, a man particularly zealous for his own religion, Benzoni, Gentil, Correal, all follow in the same strain. The Jesuit historian, Acosta, considers the state of morals which he deplores a natural consequence of permitting crowds of monks to leave the retirement and discipline of the cloister, and mingle again with the world.

All the authors who are strongest in their strictures on the regular clergy, except the Jesuits from their censure; all admit that the members of that wonderful society, bound by a discipline much more perfect than that of any other, maintained an irreproachable demeanour in the midst of corruption, and were ever ready as missionaries to venture,

* New Survey of the West Indies.

with their lives in their hands, among the most untameable and warlike tribes. It is right, in these days, when among a particular class of Protestants the name of Jesuit is but another and stronger name for a liar, a synonym for everything that is sly, underhand, deceitful, to call to mind that although they were often used by unscrupulous superiors as tools in the commission of many wicked acts, they were also the boldest missionaries, the most eloquent preachers, the most frequent martyrs among the heathen. It is hardly possible to point to an Indian massacre, either in the French or Spanish settlements, where the earliest victim was not a Jesuit. It is by no means necessary to defend the Jesuit code of ethics, or the adaptability of their marvellous organization to political intrigue ; but if it was true of any men that "they counted not their lives dear unto themselves," it was true of the Jesuits. The manners of the regular were even worse in general than those of the secular clergy. The first missionaries were monks, and the popes, as soon as the conquest of each province had been completed, and its ecclesiastical establishment began to get into shape, allowed the monks of the four mendicant orders to assume the care of parishes as a reward for their zeal. These men were exempted from all interference with their proceedings on the part of the bishops of their diocese ; they were subject only to the censures of the superiors of their own orders : a great career was thus opened to members of the regular monasteries of

Spain. Two classes of monks hastened to avail themselves of the privileges offered to them: restless minds, who, conscious of great views and great talents, pined under the monotony of cloister life, eagerly seized the permission to make their escape. The highest ecclesiastical honours of the New World were open to them: they filled the pulpits of the great cathedrals of Mexico, Panama, Lima: three archbishoprics, thirty-two bishoprics, three hundred and forty-six prebendaries, abbacies, chaplaincies, headships of more than eight hundred convents, were open to their ambition. It is not pretended by their worst foe that these men did not well support the dignity of their offices. But there was another class—unhappy men who, either from ennui, or from deliberate wickedness, or from disgust at a mistaken vocation, or hating the restraint of monastic life, eagerly seized the opportunity of escape; they were numbered by thousands: life beyond the limits of the law, a benefice among mountains and streams, far away from superior or prior, an exemption from censure even from the wearer of a mitre, unless he were also a dignitary of their own order—these things offered an attraction which the worst class of Spanish monks accepted as willingly, as the best accepted their chance of a new and honourable career. Thus it came to pass that while the seculars dozed away existence, and the superior clergy were for the most part men of blameless life, thousands of unworthy priests, far away in the provinces, lived a life that was the scorn and scandal of all good men. The Dominican monks and the Jesuits elected the general of their order for life; the generals of other orders remained in office for six years. The subjects of these generals were dispersed in provinces both in the Old and New World: each province under the charge of a provincial, elected by the provincial chapters every three years. Early in the seventeenth century, Spanish America was divided into many provinces, each of which was in the habit of electing, at the triennial meeting of its chapter, a procurator to proceed to Europe, and express, at the general chapter of the order, the wants and requirements of his province. The procurators were usually provided, by way of adding emphasis to their requests, with very considerable presents to the general, the pope, the cardinals, and the nobles of Spain. Lucky was the buccaneer who came across the procurator of a province on his way to the general chapter; for, as Gage pithily expresses it, " they are commonly the best prizes met with." Amongst the business of a procurator, one principal item always was, to make arrangements for a fresh mission of his own order: armed by the newly-elected general with a patent as vicar-general for his province, the procurator— generally an Indian friar*—presented himself and

---

* Gage, New Survey of the West Indies, p. 16. " Then the tauny Indian fryer being well set out with high commendations, and fairly painted with flattering elogies, presents these his patents," &c., &c. Rohis patent to the pope, from whom he received a bull, authorizing him to search the cloisters of his order, and take out such of the brethren as might volunteer for the work: the arrival of a pope's commissary is described as a joyful day for such among the young monks as were weary of their cloisters, or for those who, lying under censure for some breach of monastic rule, saw an opportunity of escape.

We have an account from the pen of one such restless friar of the coming of a pope's commissary, and the commotion that it excited in the Dominican cloister at Xeres in Andalusia. The monk himself was an Englishman of Roman Catholic family, who had been sent abroad by his relations, to be trained up as a Jesuit in Spain. The young man entertaining an invincible repugnance to the four-cornered cap and black habit of the Jesuits, took refuge with Dominicans, and thereby incurred the severe displeasure of his father, who angrily told him that he would rather see him scullion in a college of the Jesuits than general of the Dominicans, and peremptorily ordered him at once to take the vows of the order of St. Loyola. The

---

bertson, Hist. of Amer. B. vii., says that Indians were never ordained. M. Clavigero controverts this statement. Whereupon Robertson in a note rejoined, and apparently had the best of the argument. The statement of Gage appears as evidence on the other side. Gage ought to know, as he was himself, before becoming a Protestant, a missionary friar. His statements in general are highly coloured by the proverbial zeal of a convert; but in this instance the information is given incidentally, and is apparently trustworthy. In another place he expressly states that they had been kept down and suppressed as much as possible, lest by their numerical superiority they should " prevail against those brought from Spain.".

CHAPTER XVII.
[1713.
arrival of a pope's commissary offered an opportunity of escape : the lad listened eagerly to the tale of one Melendez, who had been deputed by the commissary, Mattheo de la Villa, to beat up for recruits in the Dominican convents of Andalusia. He was invited to " a stately supper," at which the good Xeres sack was not spared. " Bacchus metamorphosed Melendez from a divine into an orator, and made a Cicero in parts of rhetorical eloquence ;"—and so on, according to the style of that time, till the young novice was fairly enlisted, and sent off to Cales to await the departure of the Indian fleet. The Dominicans, who preferred to remain under rigid discipline at home, frowned on the youthful missionaries who had made a different choice. But the pope's bull was incontrovertible, and the Andalusian cloister definitively left behind. The monk regaled his recruits by the way with reading a memorandum of the fish and flesh, the sheep, the gammons of bacon, the fat hens, the hogs, the white biscuit, the jars of Casalla wine, the rice, figs, olives, capers, raisins, lemons, sweet and sour oranges, comfits, preserves, conserves, and Portugal sweetmeats, which he had provided for the voyage. He told them likewise that they should be made Masters of Arts and Divinity on their arrival at Manilla.

Leaving their chests and books for the superior of their convent to send after them, they set out for Puerto de Santa Maria, travelling " like Spanish dons on their little boricoes " (donkeys), and sleeping at night in stately convents. On arriving at the

Puerto, Don Frederique de Toledo, the governor, hearing of the arrival of four Indian apostles, entertained them royally at supper. The people turned out into the streets to gaze upon men possibly destined to martyrdom, and the galley-slaves in the port " strove who should sound their waits and trumpets most joyfully." Thus they proceeded on their way to Cales.

One July evening, the admiral of the galleons ordered a gun to be fired to recall stragglers, passengers, and mariners to their ships. A " crab-faced English fryer," one Pablo de Londres, excited the extreme wrath of our pilgrim by obtaining an order for his arrest, on the ground that no English monk ought to pass to the Indies, Englishmen having a country of their own to convert. An empty biscuit barrel and some friendly connivance on the part of the sailors enabled the young missionary safely to elude pursuit. The gallant ships went out one by one with shouts and salutes, and good wishes waved to the outward bound from balcony and pier-head. The fleet consisted of forty-one sail, eight of them royal galleons which were to convoy the merchant ships on their way till all danger from Holland cruisers should be safely passed. Of the rest, some were bound for various ports of the isles of the ocean ; but the main part for Vera Cruz, the legal distination of the semi-annual fleet. It may serve to show the scale on which Spain carried out her missions to say that in one of the ships was a mission of thirty Jesuits for the Philippine Islands. In another, the Dominican mission of twenty-four friars; in a third, a Mercenarian mission of twenty-four friars bound for Mexico. That there was no lack of friars even then in Mexico is shown by the fact that these very twenty-four Spaniards, were, on their arrival, set upon and maltreated by the Creole Mercenarians of Mexico, on the express ground there were enough Creole friars without the admission of Spanish interlopers. At a certain period of the voyage, the admiral of the galleons withdrew his command and returned to Spain. "The departure was most solemnly performed on each side, saluting each other with their ordnance, visiting each other with their cock-boats, the admiral of the fleet feasting with a stately dinner the admiral of the galleons," and so farewell with salute of artillery and ceremonious rowing to and fro of cockboats. Gallantly the fleet slipped down the trades. Wearily the friars sought relief from the monotony of their voyage by catching dorado and flying fish, "and such feasts and sports as are used on shipboard." On the last day of July, the day dedicated to Saint Ignatius, the Jesuits performed a masque or pageant on board their ship. The vessel was trimmed about with white linen, the flags and topgallants were decorated with the Jesuit arms and with pictures of St. Ignatius. All the morning the fathers marched in solemn procession, singing anthems and psalms. "All this seconded by roaring ordnance, no powder being spared for completing that day's joy and triumph. All that night the waits ceased not from sounding, the rigging was illuminated with lanterns, squibs and other fireworks were let off, and the cannon saluted as before."

On the 4th of August came the feast of St. Dominic. It was now the turn of the Dominicans. Powder, squibs, waits, lights, and music enlivened the night. The whole mission of the Jesuits, with the captain and passengers of their ship, were invited to "a stately dinner both of flesh and fish;" after which a comedy of the famous Lope de Vega was as stately acted and set forth in shows and good apparel as might have been upon the best stage in the court of Madrid. Then a banquet of sweetmeats, ere the cockboats carried back the guests under the invariable salute of " waits and chiefest ordnance."

One other incident of the voyage appears characteristic of the time. Towards the end of August, "the admiral of our fleet, wondering much at the slowness of our sailing, called to council the pilots of all the ships, to know their opinion concerning our present being and the nearness of land. The ships therefore drew near to the admiral one by one that every pilot might deliver his opinion."

Landing with much pomp at Vera Cruz, they assisted in the gorgeous reception which was given to the new viceroy of Mexico, who had been a passenger in the fleet. The only remarkable thing in this reception besides banners, waits, canopies of state, and such-like court millinery, was a comedy which was acted by the townspeople in the cathedral church. The "apostles," as they are called, after two days' sojourn at St. Juan, started off on mules for Mexico. At all the villages on the way the chief inhabitants came forth on horseback to meet them, bringing with them nosegays of flowers, and escorting them in with trumpets and waits, singing men and choristers, " who leisurely walked before us, singing Te Deum Laudamus." In the market places, booths of boughs were made and stores of refreshment, boxes of conserves, diet bread, and chocolate, after which speeches delivered by the chief Indians kneeling, and kissing of hands, and so to the saddle again and away, leaving blessings to a kneeling crowd that filled the market place. Sometimes the company passed the nights in Indian huts: more frequently they reached the hospitable shelter of some cloister, where the more sedate members of the party were scandalized at the sight of cards and dice with which the friars passed away their evenings, and the rich dresses and plate owned by men who were sworn to poverty. At one convent of their own order the new missionaries were still further shocked by troops of dancing girls, whom the fathers boasted they had trained themselves.

Numerous as were the Creole monks, it was long before they could succeed in making any persons of American birth priors of the monasteries in Mexico and Peru; the provincials of the orders and superiors of the convents were all from Old Spain. But a great change took place at last in some of the provinces: "Now lately," writes Gage in 1625, "some provinces have got the upper hand, and have so filled their cloisters with Criolios that they have utterly refused to admit the supplies of Spanish missions which were formerly sent unto them. In the province of Mexico there are Dominicans, Franciscans, Augustines, Carmelites, Mercenarians, and Jesuits, whereof the Jesuits and Carmelites only prevail against Criolios, bringing every two or three years missions from Spain." In Guaxaca the Creole party was predominant; but in Guatemala no Creole had ever been provincial or prior. Peru was fully supplied with monks principally of the Dominican order—all Creoles: in Granadà, in Carthagena, in Santa Fé, and in Popayan, parties were pretty equally divided. In Yucatan the Spanish faction prevailed. But in no part of the Spanish dominions were the quarrels so violent as in Mexico: in 1625 a mission was sent to the Mercenarians, and so violent was the disagreement between the Creole and Spanish members of the brotherhood, that at the next election of a provincial the friars drew their knives, and were only prevented from cutting one another's throats by the personal intervention of the viceroy, who arrived in haste at the cloister and stopped the tumult.

From the earliest times the temper of the Spaniards had been intolerant; the establishment of the Inquisition was therefore but feebly opposed. It was introduced in the city of Seville in 1481; six Jews were burned within four days from the time of its establishment. Mariana, the Spanish historian, records with thankfulness the blessings which he supposes to have arisen from it: he declares it to be the greatest possible terror to the bad, and the greatest advantage to Christianity: he combats the idea that the secresy of the tribunal militates against its justice: many calumnies and frauds are thus, he says, avoided; as to the departure which it involves from the ancient laws of the Church, the laws must conform to the necessities of altered times: he states that seventeen thousand men and women, of all ages and conditions, hastened to reconcile themselves to the Church in the first year of its establishment: two thousand were slain.* Ferdinand the Fifth resolved on establishing the Inquisition in the New World; the Cardinal Ximenez de Cisneros (to whom the king had confided the charge of this matter) nominated D. Juan Quevedo, Archbishop of Cuba, to be Inquisitor-general to the Spanish colonies, then known under the designation of the kingdom of Terra Firma, with the power of selecting all the judges and officers of the tribunal: Charles V. extended it: D. Alphonso Manso, Bishop of Porto Rico, and Fr. Pierre de Cordova, vice-principal of the Dominican friars, were made inquisitors for the Indies and the Isles of the Ocean. The new Inquisition began to pursue the baptized

* Con esta esparanza, dicen se reconçiliaron hasta diez y siete mil personas entre hombres y mugeres de todas edades y estados. Dos mil personas fueron quemadas, sin otro mayor numero de los que se huyeron a las provinçias comarcanas.

Indians who continued to practise some of the ceremonies of their ancient idolatry; the viceroy complained of the evil which such a system was likely to create : he pointed out that the frightened Indians fled into the interior of the country, and joined the savage tribes who had not yet been subjugated by the Spaniards: his representations caused Charles V. to forbid the Inquisition to practise their terrors on the Indians. The Inquisition, however, paid no attention to the prohibition, and continued to treat with the utmost rigour the unfortunates who fell under their hands. "Hélas! la voix du souverain se perdait dans la vaste étendu des provinces américaines, au préjudice des intérêts de la conquête, pendant qu'on y faisait servir la religion de prétexte aux mesures de la plus affreuse intolérance."*

Philip II. resolved on putting the Inquisition of America on the same footing as it was in Spain : in 1569 that prince sent a royal decree, in which it was stated that, as the heretics disseminated pernicious doctrines by means of books, and even by oral communication, the Inquisitor-general had decided, by advice of the supreme council, to name an inquisitor and servants for America; and the viceroys were therefore ordered to give them every assistance, and to assist them in establishing themselves on the same footing in New as in Old Spain. This resolution was put into execution without delay : the inquisitors were received with great pomp, first at

* Llorente. Histoire de l'Inquisition.

Panama and then at Lima. At Lima they were placed in possession of a house where they established their courts, their offices, their prisons, and their abode.*

Philip II., on establishing the Inquisition in Mexico, gave directions that such regulations should be made as would prevent any conflict of jurisdiction between it and the other establishments of the holy office. A new ordinance, at the same time, addressed to the viceroy of Peru, regulated the procedure of the Inquisition in Lima: in the following year these plans were digested into a scheme which divided the whole of America into three districts—one at Lima, one in Mexico, and a third at Carthagena: limits were assigned to each jurisdiction, and all subordinated to the authority of the inquisitor-general and the supreme council of Madrid. It was some years before an auto-da-fé took place in Mexico. It happened in the year of Ferdinand Cortez's death, and was celebrated with such magnificence that eye-witnesses wrote of it that it wanted but the presence of Philip II. and the royal family to equal in splendour the famous auto-da-fé celebrated at Saragossa in 1559. A Frenchman and an Englishman, condemned as relapsed and impenitent Lutherans, were burned, and eighty persons were "reconciled" who had been condemned to penance, some as Jewish heretics, some as followers of Luther and Calvin, some as bigamists

* Recopilaçion de Indios, in which the laws on this subject are given, especially Book i.

or magicians. Among the victims was a woman who declared that she, living in Mexico, could, within two hours, by the use of magic, bring her husband, who lived in Guatemala, to her side.

Philip II. did not consider it sufficient to establish the Inquisition on land: the great fleet of the Catholic League, which, under Don John of Austria, conquered the Turks at Lepanto, gave him the idea of establishing a peripatetic Court of Inquisition, which should take cognizance of cases of heresy on board captured vessels. It was at first objected to this plan, that the jurisdiction of the Spanish king did not extend beyond the limits of the Spanish monarchy; but the zeal of Philip was not to be baulked by such an obstacle: a bull was obtained from the pope authorizing the Grand Inquisition of Spain to establish the new court, and to name its judges and officers. It was first designated the Inquisition of the Galleys: the title was afterwards changed to the more comprehensive designation, Inquisition of the Fleets and Armies. As one of the principal objects of the Inquisition was to prevent the introduction of heretical books into the Spanish dominions, a new order was sent to the officers of the holy office at those ports whence foreign trade was carried on : the commissioner was to visit every ship, to receive the declaration of its captain, to register at the custom-house the chests and bales of merchandise which were on board. At Cadiz, the place of visiting commissioner became exceedingly lucrative : he was ordinarily accompanied by officers and familiars whose services he might at any moment require : he was received with a salute of guns : he was regaled with refreshments, and, as it is hinted, with compliments of a more substantial nature, to secure his report that nothing had been found contrary to the export laws.

The colonial government, in no very long time, became a machine of singular complexity : the king had a right to the fifth of all gold and silver, but the king's fifth became attenuated in proportion to the number of hands it passed through. One of the principal items of revenue was the sale of places ; when an officer was appointed, a dozen others were required to watch him : the taxes hardly produced more than the expenses of collection. The whole body of officials, from the highest to the lowest, were in a constant state of quarrelling, greediness, and misery. In the customs, in the mines, in the revenue department, they united only for one object—to plunder the king and his American subjects : offices were so certain a road to wealth, that they were often solicited without salary : around every clerk sat a dozen human vultures, waiting for him to die or be detected in a defalcation, in order to scramble for his place. There was one and only one instrument of orderly government—the ecclesiastics. The result was that the church acquired a far larger share of power than the civil government : the strong arm of the law was but weakness, in presence of the power wielded by the church and the Inquisition: spiritual and bodily terrors were both in the hands of the hierarchy; if accounts be true, they were most unsparingly wielded: the priesthood was itself dependent on the crown, so that all power, honour, and dominion centred in the crown, less what men in office could plunder by the way. From the lowest officer to the viceroy, from the doorkeeper to the chiefs of justice, from the meanest notary of the administration to the intendant, from the porter of the cathedral to the bishop, all were nominated by the king. Every employ of dignity, honour, or power was given by the monarch, or in his name, for ready money.

The pope had granted to the king the ecclesiastical tithes: these were divided into nine parts: one for the king; two for the bishops; two to the cathedral dignitaries. The remaining four were divided again into nine. One for the king; four for the curates; two for repair of churches; two for the foundation of new benefices and hospitals. The king had also many monopolies: he exacted tribute or protection money from the natives. He had the proceeds of a tax on sales—a tax known and hated in Old Spain under the name of the "alcavala:" he shared in the plunder of conquered tribes: he had a monopoly of quicksilver, without which the mines could not be worked.

The source of revenue next in importance to the fifth of the produce of the mines, and the alcavala, was the customs: the duties on merchandize amounted to thirty-four per cent! Nor was this all: Arispe, an inhabitant of Coaquila, in a memoir on the internal provinces of Spain, states that European merchandize passed and paid duty at thirty different custom-houses on its way from the port of landing to Coaquila: among taxes of minor importance were the shipping and landing dues, and the armada and armadilla, a tax originally levied to raise and equip light vessels for defending the coast against pirates, and retained, as all other taxes were retained in Spain, long after the necessity had passed away. The king had also the monopoly of tobacco, salt, and stamped paper, upon which the law compelled every agreement both public and private to be written.

A government that thus made itself felt at every turn could not fail to be very oppressive: it could only have been kept up in a very ignorant, a very scattered, or a very poor-spirited population: the inhabitants of New Spain were all three. "It did not suit the policy of Spain," said the Buenos Ayrean manifesto of independence, "that sages should rise up among us." The Cabildo of Buenos Ayres was forbidden to establish a mathematical school, on the ground that "learning did not become colonies." Gil de Lemos, the viceroy of Peru, went even further. He told the collegians of Lima that "an American should know no more than how to write, read, and say his prayers." Chemistry was forbidden in the college of Santa Fé de Bogota. Godoy, another viceroy, forbade with whimsical perversity the study of "Derechos de gente" — the law of nations. Thus the deliberate policy of the government was to keep the Americans ignorant in order the more easily to enslave them: for the same reason caste prejudices were encouraged. A partly coloured man looked down upon a wholly coloured man, and a white man looked with the most serene contempt on both. The Spaniard who came over to make his fortune by sitting in the antechamber of a Spanish grandee till the incumbent of some office died and left his place for sale, looked down upon the Spaniard as white as himself, who, having had the misfortune to be born in the colony, had become "criolio."

Amidst all this cruelty, injustice, poverty, misery, murder, ignorance, superstition, there is but one sight upon which the eye can rest with satisfaction. It is not upon great viceroys, living in more than regal splendour, with body-guards, and slaves, and crowds of obedient vassals; not upon the great fathers of the church, honestly as many of them did their duty; not on the ignoble crowd of office-bearers and office-seekers; not on the tyrants over slaves in the far-off mines of the Sierra Madre or Potosi; but on the missionaries, toiling on with brave hearts in daily and deadly peril among the heathen.

APPENDIX.

TABLE showing the Number of LAWS to which the Royal Assent was refused, in each Year from 1836 to 1864 inclusive.

	Upper Canada.	Lower Canada.	Canada.	Nova Scotia.	New Brunswick.	Newfoundland.	Prince Edward Island.	TOTAL.
1836	..	..	..	1	..	..	..	1
1837	—	—	—	—	—	—	—	—
1838	..	..	..	..	2	..	..	2
1839	5	1	..	3	..	..	1	10
1840	6	..	..	..	..	..	..	6
1841	..	..	..	1	..	..	..	1
1842	..	..	..	..	..	..	1	1
1843	..	..	2	..	3	1	1	7
1844	..	..	..	..	..	1	1	2
1845	..	..	1	..	1	..	1	3
1846	..	..	..	..	..	1	..	1
1847	..	..	..	2	..	..	..	2
1848	—	—	—	—	—	—	—	—
1849	—	—	—	—	—	—	—	—
1850	—	—	—	—	—	—	—	—
1851	..	..	..	..	..	..	1	1
1852	..	..	..	..	1	..	..	1
1853	..	..	..	..	..	1	..	1
1854	—	—	—	—	—	—	—	—
1855	..	..	..	..	..	..	2	2
1856	..	..	..	..	1	..	..	1
1857	—	—	—	—	—	—	—	—
1858	..	..	..	..	..	..	1	1
1859	—	—	—	—	—	—	—	—
1860	—	—	—	—	—	—	—	—
1861	—	—	—	—	—	—	—	—
1862	..	..	..	..	..	..	3	3
1863	..	..	..	..	..	..	1	1
1864	—	—	—	—	—	—	—	—
Since the Union of Upper and Lower Canada, 1840	..	..	3	3	6	4	12	28

www.ingramcontent.com/pod-product-compliance
Lightning Source LLC
Chambersburg PA
CBHW021417300426
44114CB00010B/540